only one of these cases which resembles "conventional" psychological work, he helped a vice presidential "bad boss" achieve lasting changes in his supervisory style. The cases demonstrate the remarkable range of different managerial problems to which the special training of the psychologist can be usefully applied.

SAUL W. GELLERMAN is a management Consultant and Professor of Management at the University of Dallas. His long, distinguished career as a consulting industrial psychologist has taken him into corporations and management associations in 35 countries and provided him with material for nine previous books and numerous articles. He holds a doctorate in clinical and industrial psychology from the University of Pennsylvania and is a Diplomate in Industrial and Organizational Psychology from the American Board of Professional Psychology. An earlier book, *Motivation and Productivity* (1963) was awarded the McKinsey Foundation Prize by the Academy of Management. He is also the producer of 29 management training films.

How People Work

How People Work

Psychological Approaches to Management Problems

Saul W. Gellerman

Q

QUORUM BOOKS
Westport, Connecticut • London

Library of Congress Cataloging-in-Publication Data

Gellerman, Saul W.
    How people work : psychological approaches to management problems /
Saul W. Gellerman.
      p. cm.
    Includes bibliographical references and index.
    ISBN 1–56720–146–6 (alk. paper)
    1. Industrial psychology. I. Title.
    HF5548.8.G397 1998
    158.7—dc21   98–10826

British Library Cataloguing in Publication Data is available.

Library of Congress Catalog Card Number: 98–10826
ISBN: 1–56720–146–6

First published in 1998

Quorum Books, 88 Post Road West, Westport, CT 06881
An imprint of Greenwood Publishing Group, Inc.

Printed in the United States of America

The paper used in this book complies with the
Permanent Paper Standard issued by the National
Information Standards Organization (Z39.48–1984).

10 9 8 7 6 5 4 3 2 1

Copyright Acknowledgments

Several of these cases have been reported briefly elsewhere:

The Lederle case was summarized in the May–June 1988 issue of the *Harvard Business Review* ("Cyanamid's New Take on Performance Appraisal," pages 36–41).

The Schering-Plough case was discussed in the spring 1990 issue of *Organizational Dynamics* ("In Organizations, As in Architecture, Form Follows Function," pages 57–68).

The hearings of the Joint Economic Committee regarding the U.S.R.A. case are reported in documents listed in the 1976 Index of the Congressional Information Service (Bethesda, Maryland) as J841-35, J841-35.1, J841-35.2, J841-35.3, and J841-35.4.

The Würth case was discussed in the May–June 1990 issue of the *Harvard Business Review* ("The Tests of a Good Salesperson," pages 64–71).

The "Shop Floor Strategists" case was reviewed in the May–June 1986 issue of the *Harvard Business Review* ("Supervision: Substance and Style," pages 89–99).

The "Bad Boss" case was summarized in the June 1985 issue of *Personnel* ("A Way to Save an Executive: On-Site Counseling," pages 55–60).

All other cases in this book are published here for the first time.

for Pat
who makes it all worthwhile

Contents

Preface   ix

Chapter One   Lederle Laboratories: Appraising
                          Performance Appraisal   1

Chapter Two   How IBM Did It Right   21

Chapter Three   Schering Reorganizes Its World   43

Chapter Four   U.S. Railway Association: Motivation Meets
                          Politics   67

Chapter Five   Würth Fastener: How to Excel at Selling   85

Chapter Six   Baffling Behavior in the Beverage Business   103

Chapter Seven   Caterpillar: The Anatomy of a Strike   121

Chapter Eight   Shop Floor Strategists   141

Chapter Nine   U.S. Home: A Motivational Pressure Cooker   161

Chapter Ten   The Bad Boss Problem   181

Chapter Eleven   Lessons Learned by Listening   199

Recommended Readings   207

Index   211

Preface

It was my good fortune to work for clients who never let me stop learning. They kept offering assignments that forced me to probe deeply into managerial issues that I initially knew little or nothing about. The only way to handle those assignments was to put myself through a series of self-taught crash courses on topics that were quite remote from my early psychological training. To serve my clients' needs properly, I had to learn about organization structure, labor relations, managerial decision making, the finer points of selling, and the art of factory foremanship—to mention only a few of those topics.

Fortunately, I had the best possible mentors: managers who had devoted their careers to grappling with those problems. The most valuable of all the lessons I learned from them is that one can learn a great deal more by listening than by lecturing. Whatever skills I have acquired as a consulting industrial psychologist I owe to the privilege of having worked with them. They not only enriched my understanding of management, but deepened my understanding of psychology.

Ten of those assignments are recounted here. My purpose in presenting them is to demonstrate what my clients understood before I did: that the skills of a psychologist can be usefully applied well beyond their usual scope. In particular: listening in a disciplined way, making sense of clashing comments, paying attention not just to what people say, but to how they say it, and to what they don't say—all these tricks of the psychologist's trade can help bring otherwise baffling managerial problems into sharper focus.

That makes sound decisions easier for managers to reach. That's why good psychologists make good management consultants.

All ten of these cases came to me unsolicited. Managers decided by themselves that their problem called for skills I either had or could acquire. They pushed me beyond what I had thought of as my limits. By doing that, they eventually caused me to question the very existence of psychological limits. Although I will probably spend the rest of my life trying to sort that out, I am deeply grateful for having been pushed into contemplating it. Meanwhile, if this book increases the awareness of both psychologists and managers of the extent to which they can learn from each other, it will have served its main purpose.

I selected these cases because they help to illuminate three important aspects of management. The first four cases concern the process of managerial work itself. The next two deal with two key components of the marketing process: sales and distribution. The final four explore various aspects of motivation—that is, of why people behave as they do at work. It is from those closing chapters that the title of this book, *How People Work*, is derived.

The Lederle case (Chapter 1) explores two important issues. The first is the ubiquitous, endlessly controversial process of performance appraisal— the annual ritual that most companies force on their managers and the people who report to them. The second issue is also ubiquitous: the role of company politics in influencing decisions and policies.

The IBM case (Chapter 2) looks into decision making at the executive level. Although there was no "manual" of how, when, and whether to commit the company to a course of action, it turns out that there was an at least implicit set of rules that the best executives followed. Those who were not guided by those unwritten rules were less likely to rise to IBM's highest ranks. Arguably, those were the rules that propelled IBM to the top of its industry and kept it there for more than thirty years.

The Schering case (Chapter 3) also has two facets. On the one hand, it deals with questions of organization design: how a worldwide enterprise should be staffed and controlled. But it also deals with some very human issues: the tendency of managers to advocate policies that may be self-serving and the reluctance of other managers to make decisions that might harm the interests of their colleagues.

The United States Railway Association case (Chapter 4) addresses the relationship between ownership and productivity. An attempt was made to reorganize then-bankrupt railroads under an Employee Stock Ownership

Plan. The question was whether converting railroad workers to employee–owners would help to solve any of the problems that had caused the bankruptcy, which included high labor costs and union intransigence. The answer is still controversial.

The Würth Fastener case (Chapter 5) looks into the psychological interplay between a seller and a potential customer. The findings were counterintuitive: the most persistent, insistent, dogged salespeople did not do as well as those who astutely read their customers' moods and reacted accordingly. The case also highlights a theme that recurs in several other cases: that there is more to be gained from improving average performers than from seeking to replace them with above-average performers.

The Beverage Business case (Chapter 6) considers the relationship between two key components in the distribution chain: wholesalers and retailers. The findings call into question one of the icons of American folklore: it turns out that the rugged, self-reliant entrepreneur isn't necessarily either. This means, among other things, that market researchers have to treat their data as selectively as election forecasters treat theirs. (This is also the first of three cases in which the client company declined to be identified. More about that later.)

The Caterpillar case (Chapter 7) examines labor relations gone badly awry, and how the recurrence of a catastrophic strike was averted. Prolonged strikes are complex events with many entangled causes, but in this instance we were able to pinpoint some important ones that management was able to control. Getting to that diagnosis was a complex process involving hundreds of interviews and thousands of questionnaires. Translating that diagnosis into an effective action plan required extraordinary psychological growth by managers, who fortunately rose to the occasion.

The Shop Floor Strategists case (Chapter 8) explores the contribution of first-level supervisors to the productivity of factories. As in the IBM case (which dealt with the opposite end of the managerial pyramid), it turned out that there was an implicit set of rules followed by the most consistently productive foremen. Pinpointing them and making them explicit enabled the average performers to more closely approximate the results of their more outstanding colleagues.

The U.S. Home case (Chapter 9) examines the performance of highly motivated individuals under high-risk and high-reward pressure. The result was extraordinarily high performance, but at an extraordinarily high cost. The formula ultimately proved to be unsustainable, but while it lasted it generated both high profits and high drama.

The "Bad Boss" case (Chapter 10) is perhaps the most "psychological" of the cases presented here. It describes how a frequently denied managerial problem was successfully addressed. It also explores the critically important distinction between a boss who is merely resented or disliked (as most bosses are, at one time or another) and one who actually makes subordinates less productive—a problem that most companies are reluctant to deal with at all.

Of course, I had to request the permission of my former clients to reveal their identity. In most cases, the incident described here was highly confidential at the time but has long since been dealt with, and the company has moved on to more current concerns. That is why these companies could only be identified now, after enough years had passed. Still, these companies were under no obligation to let me identify them, so their doing so is a courtesy that I greatly appreciate. I am grateful to American Home Products Corporation (the new parent company of Lederle Laboratories), IBM, Schering-Plough Corporation, Adolf Würth GmbH & Co. KG, Caterpillar, Inc., and U.S. Home Corporation for agreeing to be identified. The United States Railway Association, which engaged me to do the study described in Chapter 4, went out of existence on April 1, 1987, having served the purpose for which Congress created it.

My former clients who decided to remain anonymous are of course entitled to do so. They gave various reasons. The beverage company noted that my chapter portrayed some of its distributors in an unflattering light and saw no reason to risk their displeasure. Fair enough. The company about whom the "shop floor strategists" chapter was written is embroiled in unrelated controversies and prefers to minimize its public exposure. Again, fair enough. "Mac," the protagonist in the "Bad Boss" chapter, understandably wishes to remain anonymous, and for that reason the identity of his company must also be concealed. Again, fair enough.

I am especially grateful to those individuals who agreed to be identified by name. In some cases, we hold essentially the same views on the issues discussed here, but in other instances we continue to hold differing views on issues that are quite important to them. Hence it was generous indeed for them to let me name them here. In particular, I would cite Dr. William Hodgson of Lederle, Rick Swaak of Schering-Plough, Reinhold Würth, and Guy Odom, formerly of U.S. Home, all of whom helped me to correct my sometimes faulty recollection of the events described here. My former boss at IBM and "Stan," my former client at Caterpillar, are both happily retired and have no desire to revisit the issues that we dealt with together. Both

Jim, the marketing manager in the beverage company case, and Bill L., the human resources vice president in the Shop Floor Strategists case, were willing to be identified, but in deference to the companies from which they have retired, I have concealed their surnames. Nevertheless, I want to record my gratitude to them for their help.

Chapter One

Lederle Laboratories:
Appraising Performance Appraisal

Dr. William Hodgson is a chemist who devoted much of his scientific career to product development for Lederle Laboratories. (Lederle was then part of the Medical Research Division of American Cyanamid Company, which, along with its Lederle unit, was acquired by American Home Products Corporation in 1994.) But when the company made him a manager, he found that he had to unravel even more complex problems, such as how to make a corporate bureaucracy more responsive to its various divisions.

Management was, in a sense, Bill Hodgson's second career, but he took it just as seriously as he had taken chemistry. He attended every management seminar he could get to, and he read everything he could get hold of on the subject. By the time I met him, he headed a highly technical hundred-person section that analyzed the many compounds that Lederle was considering for commercial development.

Bill invited me to visit Lederle's sprawling research campus in Pearl River, New York. Several thousand people were employed there, running the tests that would enable Lederle to decide whether to start a compound down the long, expensive road that might, or might not, lead to approval by the Food and Drug Administration. The stakes were huge, and Lederle had assembled a team of highly educated specialists to do the necessary research.

Bill had read one of my books, which included a chapter on performance appraisal. That chapter had helped him to decide that Cyanamid's corporate-wide appraisal system was not only wrong for his department, but probably also wrong for the rest of the Medical Research Division. For that matter, he thought it might even be wrong for other Cyanamid divisions. This was, of course, quite an audacious stance for a manager assigned to take care of mainly technical matters. But Bill Hodgson was no ordinary technical manager.

The problem was what to do about it. Performance appraisal was the province of Cyanamid's powerful Human Resources Department. To them, Bill was just another manager in another division, far removed from corporate headquarters. But he had a plan, and he wanted to enlist my help. I didn't know it then, but Bill, in addition to being a fine scientist and an astute manager, was also the shrewdest company politician I have ever met.

To understand what happened at Lederle, we'll have to look first at the performance appraisal process itself. Then I'll share some of my "subversive" thoughts on the subject, because they led directly to the experiment that Bill asked me to carry out in his department. Next, I'll describe the appraisal system then in use in Cyanamid, against which Bill was plotting what amounted to a palace revolution. Then I'll describe the plot itself, and how it was carried out.

PERFORMANCE APPRAISAL: A PERENNIAL PROBLEM

Virtually every company that is big enough to have even a single human resources manager also has a performance appraisal system. Although most of these systems share a common framework, they differ in the details. The framework is an annual ritual in which managers rate their subordinates' work and then discuss those ratings privately with each employee. The details, however, are almost infinitely varied. These would include the forms that have to be filled out and filed with human resources; menus of euphemistic adjectives designed to make all performance ratings sound favorable, or at least harmless; and prescriptions for keeping both appraiser and appraisee calm and rational throughout their annual ordeal.

An abundance of books and articles have been published on performance appraisal, and more show up every year. Obviously, they respond to a continuing need. In general, this outpouring of literature purports to show that when performance appraisal is *done right*, it can be a painless and even constructive experience for all concerned. That's exactly what human resource departments like to hear, and that's why they buy these books for their management development classes.

The practical problem that most human resource departments face with their performance appraisal programs is a pronounced lack of managerial enthusiasm. That's because when performance appraisal is done as pre-scribed, too many managers and employees find the experience hurtful, or damaging to their relationship, or both. So it is also entirely understandable that they resist it by not using it as prescribed, or by not using it at all if they can get away with that.

The truth is that performance appraisal in its conventional format presents problems that no one has ever really solved, or is ever likely to solve. Human resource departments find themselves continually having to sell it to reluctant managers, so they continually turn to publishers and other purveyors of how-to-do-it wisdom. And the publishers, just as under-standably, concentrate on the latest twists in how performance appraisal can be done more easily or less dangerously and do not question whether it ought to be done at all. Their focus is all on technique, rather than on purpose.

So they put the blame for unimpressive results on awkward managers or on their misinformed subordinates and propose to solve the problem by enlightening them both. Few raise the question of whether the process itself may be internally self-contradictory, and therefore fundamentally flawed. My book did, and when Bill Hodgson read it, he agreed with it. And that, in brief, is why I found myself visiting Pearl River repeatedly over a two-year period to work with Bill and other Lederle managers on their performance appraisal program.

AN ICONOCLASTIC VIEW

Whenever someone's job performance is formally appraised, a three-cor-nered game is being played. In the first corner sits the manager, who often regards the process as both a potential embarrassment and, worse than that, time-consuming. In the second corner sits the employee whose work is being rated, for whom a great deal may be at risk: his ego, his income, and his job security. In the third corner sits the human resources department, whose role is to insist that the other two players play the game and to record the results.

But the game is uncomfortable for the first two players, so they use a variety of stratagems to outwit the third. They might, for example, turn the process into a quickly disposed-of formality. Or the manager might rate the work of most subordinates as "above average," a statistical absurdity that nevertheless keeps most of them happy. Of course, an alert human resources department will detect these gambits and will devise its own strategies to counteract them. These include putting the managers through yet another series of training programs, or insisting on "forced distributions" of ratings (so that some employees' work must be rated "average" or even "below average"), or requiring employees to sign the rating forms to certify that they have actually seen them.

But these countermeasures simply inspire countercountermeasures, and so on, ad infinitum. These intracompany wars have been going on for at least fifty years and will probably continue until performance appraisal itself either goes out of fashion or changes almost beyond recognition.

In the chapter that Bill Hodgson read, I took the position that the fundamental flaw in conventional performance appraisal programs was that they attempted to simultaneously accomplish two sets of goals that for all practical purposes were mutually exclusive. One set was administrative, and the other was motivational. The problem was that if you did the things that would enable you to accomplish one of them well, you would thereby undermine your chances of accomplishing the other one at all—and vice versa.

Motivation, for example, requires that we encourage people to match or exceed their own previous achievements, whereas administration requires that we seek out people whose performance may be unacceptable. Motivation is inherently a positive process; administration, at times, must be negative. Thus quite different tactics are called for, depending on which of the two processes is appropriate in any given case.

I argued, therefore, that although you could hit either "bird" with one stone, you could not hit both. Instead you had to decide which bird to hit, and which one to just let go. By seeking to reach both goals with one process, as conventional performance appraisal programs are designed to do, you all too often fall well short of reaching either of them. And for your pains you get caught up in those intracompany wars.

Although performance appraisal is sometimes billed as a great motivational tool, its impact on effort and enthusiasm is usually minimal. It consists mostly of reassuring the uncertain and recognizing the unsung. Both are worthwhile goals, but in themselves they hardly call for major corporate programs with heavy bureaucratic support. It's true that more powerful motivational techniques, such as goal-setting, can be used with performance appraisal, but they can also be used without it. On balance, one has to conclude that the motivational claims for performance appraisal are window dressing, designed to make it seem less objectionable to already skeptical observers.

But the administrative effects of performance appraisal are an altogether different story. It is a primary tool for enabling human resource departments to handle some of their most important tasks. These include identifying people who may be promoted or otherwise rewarded, identifying others who may have to be chastised or even fired, and making sure that the biggest pay increases are going to the people who have really earned them.

Those are also worthy goals, but actually reaching them collides with an awkward fact: although human resource departments are entirely dependent on managers to provide them with the information they need, managers themselves have other priorities. They are more likely to be focused on achieving the results that their own departments are expected to produce than on accommodating the human resources department. They tend to be very aware that achieving those results depends heavily on whether they can count on the cooperation of all of their subordinates. So managers tend to be protective of those relationships and to resist anything that might endanger them. They construe performance appraisal, with its comparative ratings, its obligatory discussions of "strengths and weaknesses," and its thinly veiled implications that jobs may not be entirely secure, as just such a danger.

When managers resist performance appraisal, it is because they see it as both a nuisance and a menace. And that, as we shall see, was exactly the situation that Bill Hodgson encountered when he became a manager at Lederle.

THE CYANAMID SYSTEM

When I met Bill for the first time, he told me that Cyanamid had a forced distribution system, right down to the department level. (Officially, this distribution of ratings was only "recommended," but in practice that was a euphemism for "required.") Managers were supposed to rate 20 percent of their employees with the letter O, meaning that their work was outstanding; 40 percent with the letter X, meaning that their work exceeded requirements, and the other 40 percent with the letter R, meaning that they had met the requirements of their jobs.

From an administrative standpoint, it was a beautiful system. Cyanamid management actually knew in advance how the performance ratings would be distributed and could allocate exactly as much money to each department's salary increase budget as it required. But the effect on employee morale, Bill told me, was devastating. The people with the R rating felt that they were being "damned with faint praise." Those with the X rating felt that even if their work was exceptional, they could still be excluded from the top rating if that category was already full.

Another demoralizing aspect of the system was its "zero-sum" implications: That is, for every employee whose work justified a higher rating than before, another had to be downgraded to make room for the newly upgraded employee in the higher rating category. Many of Bill's fellow managers objected that the system could not recognize that a department had improved its overall performance. They were, in other words, locked into a game that none of them could win.

The rationale for this rigid, exclusionary system was that the company had to hold on to its few exceptional people: the ones who made irreplaceable scientific and technical contributions that kept the company ahead of its competitors. The system was designed to identify an elite few and guarantee that they would be so handsomely compensated that they would be unlikely to leave.

The problem with that rationale, Bill told me, was that whereas it sounded hardheaded and realistic, it was in fact naive. Whoever devised it, he said, could not have known much about real scientists. But he had known hundreds of them, and he knew that most had chosen their profession chiefly because they loved it. They were more interested in maximizing their professional satisfaction than in maximizing their income.

He granted that most were paid well and lived comfortably. But that was due to the market's demand for their skills, and not to their pursuit of ever higher salaries. Scientists knew that they could take competitive salaries for granted, so it was not necessary to lock them into their current employment with even higher salaries. They would stay wherever they could do the most scientifically rewarding work.

But Bill's main complaint with the system was not that it misread the motivation of scientists, but that it undermined the motivation of the technical staff that supported their work. Managers were directed to reserve those top-level O ratings for those who were responsible for their department's most important accomplishments. Inevitably, this meant that those who were given the most important assignments would also get the highest performance ratings.

The effect, unfortunately, was to reward education more than effort. The assignments with the greatest consequences went to the Ph.D.'s, who thereby garnered a disproportionate number of the O ratings, and the big raises that went with them. Many of the people who assisted them, most of whom had bachelor's or master's degrees, were either locked into the mediocre X ratings or consigned by the forced distribution system to the barely acceptable R ratings—and therefore to the lowest salary raises— even when their work had been entirely satisfactory. To its credit, the

Medical Research Division required that some of the higher ratings go to the lower-level staff. But despite this "correction," the system still favored the division's elite at the expense of its ordinary members.

The result, Bill told me, was a motivational mess. The technicians saw hardly any relationship between their effort and their rewards, so they came to work with little enthusiasm. The Ph.D.'s were embarrassed, because they felt they were rewarded at the expense of their assistants, some of whom were highly deserving. But the system's most vociferous critics were the supervisors. There were twenty of them in Bill's section (all reporting to one of three middle managers, who in turn reported to Bill). The supervisors complained of having to think of "reasons" why someone whose work was flawless was nevertheless given the lowest performance rating.

Another complaint was that the system required them to to discuss the employee's "weaknesses," even when there were none of any real consequence. The net result was that they had to spend an average of six hours preparing for each interview. That added up to more than half a week of work, just to prepare for a process they felt was seldom useful and often harmful.

"Mind you," said Bill, "I'm not arguing against performance appraisal per se. But this particular form of it does more harm than good, and has to be changed. Unfortunately, our corporate Human Resources Department stands firmly behind it."

"How can I help you?" I asked.

"What I'd like you to do," said Bill, "is to conduct an experiment for us. A nice, controlled, scientific experiment."

THE PLOT

Bill Hodgson knew that Cyanamid's chairman had recently ordered some surveys of the company's own managers to determine what they thought of their company. Most had rated it high on scientific rigor and ethical integrity, but low on innovation and openness to new ideas: in other words, respectable but stodgy. The chairman then gave the managers an opportunity to remake their own culture, by creating a fund for financing projects aimed at making the company a more exciting place to work. Managers could submit proposals for such projects to the chairman's office, and if they could demonstrate that potential, they'd be given the money to see whether their ideas could actually work.

One of the secrets of becoming a master corporate politician is to recognize the potential effect of factors that everyone is aware of on things that only you may know about. Bill saw the chairman's fund as a godsend. It could help him to circumvent the corporate Human Resources Department, whose prestige and power were heavily invested in the existing performance appraisal system. All he needed was a convincing project design to submit to the chairman's office.

He told me that the committee that evaluated proposals for the chairman was scientifically sophisticated. They'd look askance at half-baked ideas but would welcome a carefully thought-out approach that held some promise for making the company a more exciting, and less frustrating, place in which to work. The beauty of it, from a political point of view, was that the chairman's fund could enable him to do an end-run around the Human Resources Department, which still seemed unreponsive to complaints about the problems that its performance appraisal system was causing in the field.

Bill did not want the battle over performance appraisal to be fought by pitting one expert's opinion against another's. Each side could find an expert to support its view, as he had already proved with me. It would be much better, he argued, to gather some relevant facts under controlled conditions and let those facts speak for themselves. "If I can get a decent budget from the chairman's fund," he said, "we'll be able to do this the right way. So see if you can design an experiment that's as defensible as possible, because Human Resources are going to be unhappy, and may even attack it when they hear about it."

Field research, in which we attempt to apply the methods of science under normal working conditions, could never withstand the scrutiny of a doctoral dissertation committee. There are too many variables that can't be controlled, and the number of cases is never large enough to permit sound statistical inferences. The problem with reality, from a scientific point of view, is that it's always complex and sometimes chaotic.

Nevertheless, organizational reality is the proper study of the consulting industrial psychologist. So you simply do your pragmatic best and make no apologies for the deficiencies of the data that you obtain. The real question is whether it is safe to draw conclusions from them, and that boils down to one's tolerance for risk. Academics get edgy when their risk of drawing a wrong conclusion is more than one in twenty, or even one in a hundred. Managers would consider those odds an incredible luxury and regularly commit many dollars to decisions when their risk of being wrong is considerably greater.

But I didn't have to burden Bill with all of those caveats. Having worked, so to speak, on both sides of the ideological "fence" that separates scientists and managers, he already knew all about them.

We decided to adhere to the classical scientific method as closely as possible. We were going to compare the effects of Cyanamid's existing performance appraisal system with those of a system in which motivation was given more importance than administrative considerations. To do that, we needed an experimental group, in which the new method would be used. Bill volunteered his own department, the Scientific Services Section, for this purpose. We also needed a control group, which was at least reasonably similar to Bill's department in terms of demographics and work assignments, but would continue under the Cyanamid performance appraisal system during the experiment. We found such a group in the Toxicology Section, whose manager agreed to cooperate.

Then we established some measurements we would take of both groups before, during, and after the experiment. We decided to run the experiment for two years, in order to rule out the "Hawthorne effect"—the tendency of people who have suffered under an old system to be initially enthused about *any* new one, only to grow disenchanted later if it doesn't address their real problems.

That, in brief, was the outline of the project that Bill successfully sold to the committee that managed the chairman's fund. It was already well launched by the time the corporate Human Resources Department woke up to it.

MEASURING REACTIONS

I devised a twenty-one-item questionnaire that probed such issues as the perceived fairness of the system, the relationship between performance ratings and one's salary increase, and whether the information provided by the system was helpful, superfluous, or damaging. Both groups responded to the same questionnaire three times: first, just before the experimental system was announced; second, after it had been in effect for one year (i.e., midway into the experiment); and third, two years after it began.

Our first use of the questionnaire was designed to give us a baseline to which our later follow-up measurements could be compared. We also had to make sure that the attitudes in the two groups were at least reasonably comparable at the outset. They were, so we knew that both groups were on essentially the same starting line with respect to the issues that interested us.

Both were quite outspoken in their dislike of the forced distribution feature of the system under which their work was evaluated. This was more or less uniformly true at all levels in each department, from the technicians who set up the equipment and read the instruments to the scientists who designed the studies and interpreted the data. And Bill's observation about the managers proved to be correct: they were more vociferous than any of the others in denouncing the system.

Then we held a meeting with Bill's supervisors, and later with his entire department, to explain what we were going to do. We made no attempt to keep the experiment secret, since that would have been futile. On the other hand, we did nothing to publicize it either, because we did not want external attention to influence our results. Also, we did not want to arouse expectations elsewhere in the company, nor had we any desire to antago-nize the corporate Human Resources Department. To the extent that one can gauge these things, it appeared that during the two years of this experiment it remained, if not exactly a hermetically sealed secret, at least not well known to most people at Lederle.

We told the people in Bill's department that we were going to use them as administrative guinea pigs for two years, by trying out a performance appraisal system that would be quite different from the one they were accustomed to. With respect to the new system, we'd keep them in quarantine during that period: no one else in Lederle would be exposed to it. There was no way of knowing whether it would lead to permanent changes later on, or simply disappear when the experiment was finished.

Throughout this period, we told them, if they had any questions about the experimental system, they were free to talk about them with Bill or me. We encouraged them to discuss the system among themselves as much as they liked, but asked them not to raise the subject with people outside the department. If anyone asked them about it, they were free to answer, but we asked them to minimize what they revealed. These people were all quite sophisticated about research methodology, so none of these requests aroused much comment.

The new system would have *no* required distribution of ratings. Each employee's results would be measured against his or her job description, rather than against the work of colleagues. Whatever distribution resulted from this system would be determined by performance itself, rather than by a predetermined formula. No one would be excluded from a rating category simply because someone else had already qualified for that category.

The new system, like the old one, had three possible rating categories. For rating purposes, we would assume that most people, most of the time, did their work well enough for it to be deemed acceptable, and that the range of acceptable results was in fact quite broad. It ran all the way from outcomes that were barely satisfactory to outcomes that might be unusually good, but were not unprecedented. We designated this broad range of expected performance with the letter G, for "good." Although we recognized that distinctions within this range were possible (for example, above or below average), we considered such distinctions neither administratively necessary nor motivationally desirable. We proposed, in other words, to do without the central, defining feature of the Cyanamid system.

But the new system also recognized that job performance could sometimes fall outside the broad parameters of the G range. While unexpected performance is rare by definition, it does occur, so we had to anticipate it. There would be two other rating categories. One would be designated E, for "exceptional," and the other U, for "unacceptable."

Occasionally, we told them, someone's results could so greatly exceed expectations that no reasonable observer could say that it was within the "normal" range. The key point here was that the results did not merely exceed those of others in the same group, but went beyond the demands of the job itself. Merely to be the best in an ordinary lot was not exceptional, and usually it had more to do with luck than with excellence. (For example, the best player on the weakest team in the league might be no match for an average player on an average team in the same league.) To merit an E rating, one would have to achieve seldom-seen results. To guard against the tendency of some supervisors to give superlative ratings mainly out of a desire to be magnanimous, that rating would require an affirmative vote by all three of Bill's direct reports and would then require the approval of Bill Hodgson himself.

But it was also possible that someone's performance could fall short of minimum expectations. That was unacceptable, and something would have to be done promptly to correct the deficiency, or reassign the individual, or begin the process that led to dismissal. The issue here was not whether one's work lagged that of all of one's peers. Someone, after all, has to be the least effective performer in a group, but that person's work might still be well within the bounds of acceptable performance. (For example, the least virtuosic violinist in a major symphony orchestra can usually out-fiddle the average violinist in a less distinguished orchestra.)

We decided, in other words, that under our experimental system, what mattered was not whether someone's performance exceeded someone else's, but whether it satisfied the requirements of that person's job description. If it did not, a rating of U would be given. It was inherently a *temporary* rating, leading either to prompt improvement or to equally prompt reassignment or, if it came to that, firing.

During the experiment, Bill's people would be rated solely on the results of their work, not ranked against each other. I used an analogy that dated all the way back to my experiences on a high school track team: Each of them would be running against the stopwatch, trying to beat his own previous record. They would not be trying to beat each other. The result, I hoped, would be a more optimistic attitude toward their chances of being recognized for having done well, and a corresponding increase in performance.

There was one other refinement in the experimental system. Managers were no longer required to discuss the weaknesses in an employee's performance. There were two exceptions: if the problem could be corrected by simply calling attention to it, the supervisor would do so; also, if the deficiency was part of the reason for a U rating, the supervisor would discuss it in detail. Otherwise, supervisors would comment only on things the worker did well. I hoped this would make them feel both more appreciated and less harassed, and that this in turn would lead them to feel that sustained effort would be worthwhile.

With these new rules for performance appraisal in place, we launched the experiment. We knew that it was only a matter of time before the corporate Human Resources Department caught on to what we were up to. But we were under the umbrella of the chairman's fund, so Bill Hodgson had two years in which to prove his point. Corporate Human Resources, for its part, had two years in which to think of what to do about it.

FIRST-YEAR RESULTS

One of the reasons for using forced distributions is to counteract the tendency of supervisors to classify most or even all of their subordinates in the upper end of the performance range. This is similar to the "grade inflation" that takes place in college classrooms, where professors give their students lots of A's, some B's, hardly any C's, and no D's or F's. Both forms of inflation have the same underlying cause and are explained away with the same rationalization: a mixture of generosity and a desire to avoid conflicts with the employees or students being rated. The rationalization is that this particular department or class "just happens" to contain an unusual concentration of top performers.

But this application of forced distributions is a classical case of using a shotgun to swat a fly. It does far more harm than good. It fails its administrative mission by keeping top performers out of the top rating brackets. Worse than that, it sabotages motivation by creating feelings of futility and impotence, as the following remarks (taken from my early interviews of employees in both departments) show:

"My work could be outstanding year in and year out, but if one other person in my group was also outstanding, my supervisor would have to make an arbitrary choice between us. I could wind up in the second ranking category ("exceeded requirements"), despite my exceptional results."

"Until it's my turn, I can't get a better rating no matter what I do."

"These reviews do give me some information on how my superior rates my work, but I know damned well that they are also influenced by quotas."

"Evidently they want to fit the people within a given section to a bell curve, so they can dole out raises without going over the budget. But as a scientist, I know that a bell curve only applies to a large population. To apply it to a small population, like a department, can be very misleading."

"I don't take it seriously. It's just a Mickey Mouse numbers game. My superior and I just laugh at it, and we get through it as quickly as we can."

Comments like these confirmed the negative effects of the forced distribution system on morale. It remained to be seen, however, whether the new system would have equally negative effects in other areas. For example, would the Ph.D.'s, accustomed to what amounted to "preferred access" to top ratings and the highest salary increases, rebel at losing that preference? Would managers find it more difficult to stimulate the weaker performers? In brief, would the gains from getting rid of forced distributions be canceled out by a new set of problems?

I kept my finger on the pulse of both groups by dropping in at Pearl River every few weeks to speak to the supervisors and a sample of employees and to hear out anyone who wanted to speak to me. So I had a general idea of how the experimental system was being received. My best guess, before the questionnaires were given out, was that the reaction to the new system would be cautiously favorable. However, the economy had suffered a recession during this period, and Cyanamid (like most other companies) had been obliged to tighten its budget, including the portion set aside for salary increases. I anticipated that this would have at least some negative effect on the morale of both groups.

But when we gave them questionnaires at the one-year mark, the results suggested that the experimental group had, in effect, been "inoculated" against the effects of the budget cuts. (Although the control group continued to receive a questionnaire that specified Cyanamid's existing performance appraisal system, the one given to the experimental group now referred only to their new system.)

For example, while the percentage in the experimental group who said they had received a fair appraisal held steady, that figure had dropped in the control group by about a third. The drop in the control group was even greater (about one half) with regard to the relationship between the performance appraisal and one's salary increase, but once again the figures for the experimental group held steady. On the other hand, the percentage of those in the experimental group who said that the factors considered in evaluating their work were clear and relevant more than doubled: from 16 percent under the old system to 37 percent under the new system. There was no significant year-to-year change on this question for the control group. The percentage of those in the experimental group who said the evaluation helped them to do their jobs better jumped from 33 percent to 58 percent, while the corresponding figure for the control group actually declined by about one-sixth.

To this point, I could detect no sign that the senior scientists were upset by the new system, even though they no longer had an advantage in obtaining the higher ratings. (Only 10 percent of the department's employees qualified for the new E level awards, and they went to employees at all levels. The corresponding figure under the old system was 20 percent.) Also, the supervisors in Bill's department reported no slackening of effort, even among those formerly rated in the lowest 40 percent who were included in the broad new G rating (which now included 87 percent of the department). Using the new criteria, the supervisors had identified two employees whose work did not match the department's requirements. They would have to be dealt with, one way or another, long before the next set of questionnaires went out.

This was a promising beginning, although the results were not yet conclusive. Recessions are, of course, one of the many powerful but uncontrollable variables that you have to put up with in field research. In the meantime, continued interview sampling suggested growing disgruntlement in the control group, which was probably part of a companywide reaction to the budgetary strictures. In the experimental group, which was subject to the same strictures, I detected no such dissatisfaction. Of course, the two-year follow-up would be the acid test. If the new system had any lasting effects, they should be evident by then. Besides, the recession was beginning to lift, so the next set of questionnaires would be given under more normal conditions.

Corporate Human Resources was now aware of what we were doing. We had exchanged some polite visits and telephone calls. Their official attitude was that this was an isolated, one-time experiment in one small department of a huge company, and that when it came to its scheduled end it would be over. Bill thought otherwise. He was not the only Cyanamid manager who was dissatisfied with the current system, and he knew it.

SECOND-YEAR RESULTS

As the second year continued, I kept hearing clues that suggested increasing satisfaction with the new appraisal system in Bill's department. Perhaps most notable was the reaction of the previously advantaged group, consisting mostly of senior scientists. Although some of them qualified again for the highest performance rating, most were lumped together with the vast majority who received the broadly defined "good" rating. Virtually all of them preferred the new system. They had considered the old one an embarrassment, because it discriminated against their colleagues, and were glad to be rid of it. As one of them put it:

Some of these people do indispensable work, but until now it has been a thankless task, because the old system simply did not recognize their value. I am delighted that some of them can now receive the recognition they deserve. As for myself, I am quite content. I have said all along that the best thing about this job is that we get to do scientific work all day. It is like being paid to work at your hobby. Of course I enjoy being well paid, but what keeps me here is the work.

Many of the technicians and professionals who supported the scientists had previously been rated in one of the two lower categories. Some now earned the highest ratings, and nearly all of the rest were in the "good" range. Although they had muttered and complained about the old system, they did not celebrate the new system. Instead, they just took it for granted. Their reaction had changed from negative to neutral. From their perspective, they had not gained an advantage, but they had been relieved of a disadvantage. That was all to the good, but for them it was nothing to get excited about.

These people were no longer nursing grievances, because they had none to nurse. They were more concerned with getting on with their work than with dwelling on complaints about things that had previously bothered them, like unfairness and lack of recognition. And that, of course, was all that a realistic manager would want. Your reward for removing an irritant from the lives of your employees is not gratitude or dancing in the streets.

Instead, it is more time and attention focused on getting the job done right, and less of your own time diverted into responding to their complaints. The change wasn't miraculous, but it wasn't a bad deal, either.

If the technicians and professionals were undemonstrative, the supervisors were openly enthused. As far as they were concerned, the change had made the Scientific Services Section much more manageable. Since they no longer had to think of ways to justify classifying 40 percent of their subordinates in the lowest performance group, their preparation time was cut from six hours per employee to three hours. The effect was to restore a full week of work time to their schedules, enabling them to concentrate on the details of their jobs rather than fretting over performance appraisals.

The supervisors reported no detectable slackening of effort by those whose work had previously been classified in the lowest group, but who were now included in the broadly defined "good" category. Nor did they see such an effect among the Ph.D.'s who had previously had a greater likelihood of a top rating, but now were classified (along with nearly everyone else) as performing somewhere in the "good" range. They reported less tension in their relationships with the people who reported to them. All told, they reported gains in working relationships at *no* cost in effort or productivity.

About the only negative feature they reported was concern about what would happen when the experiment reached its scheduled end. They knew full well that the system they liked so well was part of a two-year experiment and that the second year was rapidly drawing to a close. Would they be required to revert to the old system, with all of its well-known problems? As we headed into the final months, no one knew.

Then, with less than three months to go before we were to hand out our final set of questionnaires, the corporate Human Resources Department made an unexpected move. In effect, it was a preemptive strike.

THE BUREAUCRACY MAKES ITS MOVE

Corporate Human Resources announced a new performance appraisal program that would apply not only to the two Lederle departments where our experiment was under way, but to all eleven thousand five hundred salaried employees in every division of the company. Except for some changes in terminology, it looked very much like the experimental system that had been used in Bill's department. The defining feature of the old system, the forced distribution of ratings into categories of prescribed dimensions, was gone.

Individuals would now be rated against the requirements of their jobs, not against each other. There would be three rating categories, none of them with prescribed (or even "recommended") limits: S (for "superior"), Q (for "quality"), and N (for "needs improvement"). The emphasis throughout would be on meeting agreed-upon performance objectives. In other words, the playing field for people with different qualifications would be level. The "attack" that Bill had anticipated from Human Resources had never materialized.

It was clear to me, and a few knowledgeable executives in the Medical Research Division, that the game was not only over, but that Bill Hodgson had played a key role in bringing it to an end. Corporate Human Resources had read the handwriting on the wall and wisely decided to champion the inevitable. Instead of fighting the system being tested in Bill's department, they co-opted it.

My best guess as to what happened is that someone at the executive level in Human Resources had looked at the company's performance appraisal system in the light of the chairman's survey (in which, as you recall, Cyanamid managers had rated their own company as rigid and old-fashioned) and had decided that this particular battle was not worth fighting. No doubt there were those on the staff who were wedded to the old forced distribution system and urged that it be saved. But in the end, they were overruled.

Of course, it's a moot question as to whether the performance-based appraisals used in Bill's department were really the wave of the future, or whether the distribution-based appraisals used throughout Cyanamid until then could have been preserved. But the people who made the decision must have known that although the experiment in Bill's department had not been widely publicized, the system it was designed to replace was strongly disliked throughout the company. In effect, that gave Bill a "secret weapon."

All he had to do was talk about a controlled experiment to his scientifically oriented colleagues in other departments and divisions and quote a few statistics, and the already simmering discontent among them might have reached a feverish level. In any case, corporate Human Resources decided that it had more important things to do than fight a firestorm that could be prevented with the stroke of a pen. In my opinion, that was a wise decision.

Bill Hodgson had expected to win his crusade eventually, but even he was surprised at how quickly it had ended. But he never gloated. Instead, he sent a laudatory memo to corporate Human Resources, praising their judgment and creativity. He also sent copies of his memo to executives in his division who were aware of his experiment. Having accomplished what he had set out to accomplish, he could afford to be magnanimous.

FINAL RESULTS

Although he had already accomplished his purpose, Bill was still a scientist who wanted a complete research protocol on every project, including the one I was running for him in the Medical Research Division. And he was still a manager who wanted his company to get its money's worth for the fees it had paid me. So he insisted, rightly, that we distribute the last set of questionnaires and tally up the results.

These showed emphatically that the new system worked far better than the old one. Over the two-year period of the study, the percentage of those in the experimental group who agreed that the factors on which their appraisal was based were "clear and relevant" more than *tripled* (from 16 to 55 percent), whereas the corresponding figure in the control group declined by almost half (from 34 to 18 percent). Those in the experimental group who agreed that they had received a fair appraisal increased by half (from 41 to 63 percent), while the corresponding figure for the control group fell (from 31 to 24 percent). In the experimental group, those who saw a clear relationship between their performance rating and their salary increase rose by about a quarter, from 29 to 36 percent; the same figure in the control group dropped by half (from 34 to 17 percent).

Another question probed reactions to the promotions that had occurred in the department. The issue here is whether people are perceived to have earned the promotion or to have benefited from favoritism. The question can serve as a kind of morale barometer, since high positive percentages suggest a "halo effect" in which satisfaction in other areas spills over into this one. In the experimental group, the percentage who felt promotions had been fair doubled (from 26 to 51 percent); the corresponding figure in the control group remained static at 32 percent. During the second year, the distribution of performance ratings in the experimental group remained essentially unchanged. About 87 percent were still rated "good," 13 percent received the highest ratings, and the two individuals who had previously received unsatisfactory ratings were no longer in the department.

Although these results were, in a sense, anticlimactic, they documented what Bill had said all along: that a performance appraisal system designed to support egos would yield better results in all respects, and at no greater cost, than one designed to discriminate among them.

IMPLICATIONS

Somehow, the concept of a symmetrical, "bell-shaped" performance distribution has acquired too strong a grip on the imagination of too many corporate planners. But the truth is that it seldom describes reality, unless you are working with populations that are both huge and unselected. The bell-shaped curve describes what you would probably get if you took in thousands of people and, making no attempt to determine their capabilities, put them all to work at some task that most of them could learn to perform reasonably well by themselves. Some would excel, some would fail, and most, to varying degrees, would perform more or less adequately.

But that is precisely what would *not* happen in a well-run organization. You would hire selectively, not indiscriminately. You would invest in training those whom you did hire, and you would weed out the ineffective ones as quickly as possible. You would possibly hire people by the dozens to do the same job, but you would seldom if ever hire the hundreds that would be needed to produce that nice symmetrical performance curve. So what you would get would be a skewed curve, based on a smallish number of people, with few if any of them falling below the midpoint of the general population and most lumped together above it.

That skewed, asymmetrical, aesthetically unpleasing curve is precisely what you'd get if your human resources department had been doing its job properly. Ironically, to assume that the job performance distribution will follow a classical bell-shaped curve is to indict your human resources department for incompetence. Bell curves show what happens when the factors that determine performance are left entirely to chance, and no human resources department worth its salt is *that* negligent.

Another lesson learned from the Lederle case concerns management's chronic overestimation of the effects of money on behavior. There is only one valid generalization one could make about this effect, and that is that money is by far the most complicated of all human motivators. Anything else you could say on the subject would be true only some of the time, with certain people, and under certain conditions. The trick to using money wisely is to use it *selectively*—that is, when it is likely to have a powerful effect on job performance—and otherwise to let market forces determine how much of it is needed to attract and hold the people you need.

In retrospect, Cyanamid spent more than was necessary to prevent its top scientists from defecting to other employers, and not as much as was needed to prevent their support staff from becoming dispirited and indifferent. Better overall performance could have been had by redistributing the same sums more realistically, in keeping with the varying needs of those involved. That is precisely what Bill's department achieved, once it was liberated from the rigidities of the forced distribution system.

The basic issue that has to be addressed with regard to performance appraisal is its purpose. Only rarely is it necessary to single anyone out for special treatment. Most people, most of the time, are performing at or near their sustainable limits and don't need to be bribed or threatened to do more. Most of the time, therefore, the purpose of appraising performance is to maintain it at its present levels, or to move it marginally higher, and perhaps to fine tune it in some respects. The best way to do that is to recognize accomplishments, reset goals for the coming period, and reassure all whose work is acceptable that their value is appreciated.

To those who would object that this would be settling for too little, and that everyone not only can improve but should be made to improve, I can only suggest that they underestimate the effort already going into ordinary job performance. It is true that when a great deal is at stake, most of us can temporarily achieve better-than-ordinary results. But that kind of effort is not sustainable and usually occurs only in a crisis. Most people know how to pace themselves, and in the absence of negative motivation (such as disinterest or outright antagonism) they will usually set that pace close to their own maximum *sustainable* level.

Finally, a word about company politics. It is an ever-present reality, not because cunning and manipulative people inevitably get into positions of power, but because it's human nature to defend and extend one's turf. Those with power will try to keep it, and those without power will try to encroach on it. As many a folk tale and opera libretto have shown, the best weapon of the powerless is usually the ineptitude of the powerful.

In this case, Bill Hodgson realized that corporate Human Resources was trying to defend an ultimately indefensible position. All he had to do was to prove that. The beneficiaries of his insight were the company itself, which was able to utilize both its people and its payroll more effectively, as well as eleven thousand five hundred of Cyanamid's managers and professionals, who were finally able to compete against their job descriptions instead of against each other.

Chapter Two

How IBM Did It Right

In 1956, when *Fortune* first ranked the top five hundred American companies by their annual revenues, IBM was in forty-eighth place. During the next thirty years, it climbed relentlessly up that list, eventually surpassing forty-four previously larger companies. By the late 1980s, after an unprecedented and still unmatched record of annual gains, IBM had become the fourth largest company in the United States.

Then Big Blue finally blundered, falling back to seventh place. Its stock price suffered, too: ten long years would pass before it could regain its previous peak. But despite its well-publicized troubles, IBM has never relinquished its dominant position in the world's computer industry. Its market leadership still dates all the way back to 1952, when the first IBM computer was delivered.

In retrospect, the remarkable point about IBM is not that its planning finally went awry. Sooner or later, most companies manage to misread the tea leaves and commit themselves to an unrealistic plan. What is astonishing is that IBM managed to avoid a significant strategic setback for nearly forty years. To run up that remarkable record, it had to do an extraordinary number of things right.

IBM is a great company that tripped and hurt itself because it couldn't, or wouldn't, see where it was going. The reputation it once enjoyed for invincibility is probably gone forever. But even that loss will probably work to IBM's advantage, because unending success breeds complacency. As it turned out, not even IBM could afford that.

At the time of the case I'm about to relate, IBM was commonly rated as one of the best-run companies in the world, if not the best. There were many reasons for that, and a few of them are revealed here.

THE NEED FOR BROAD-GAUGE EXECUTIVES

When I worked for IBM, my boss was the director of executive resources, whose primary concern was succession planning. One day he asked me whether we could identify young IBMers who were capable, someday, of rising to its uppermost management.

"This company is getting so complicated," he told me, "that the people at the top need a very broad background. Instead, we've got too many narrow-gauge people, like me, who may know one part of the business well, but know very little about the rest. So when you get to this level, you have to make decisions about a lot of things you really don't know much about."

"Then what's the answer?" I asked.

"The answer," he said, "is that we need a supply of managers who have already done well in at least two parts of the business, or even three, before they are forty years old."

My boss wanted to be able to draw on a pool of candidates for top jobs who were still fairly young, but already seasoned. To do that, he needed a way to single them out as much as ten years in advance, so they could be put on a separate track for broadening in a wide variety of assignments. Not all of them would succeed.

"The trick," he said, "would be to find the ones who can handle that kind of exposure, ideally before they're thirty. Twenty-five would be even better."

"That would be tough," I said. "At twenty-five, what you've usually got are 'incomplete adults.' Things that haven't even happened to them yet could have a major impact on what they'll turn into five or ten years later."

"I know it won't be easy," said my boss, "and maybe it can't be done. But if we could, it would be a great advantage for us. We wouldn't have to choose between smarts and stamina when we picked our top executives, because we could have both. And we just don't have a lot of people like that. Not even in IBM.

"We're short," he continued, "on managers who know their way around different parts of the business. And when we place our bets on them, we have to be sure that we're right. So the question is, can it actually be done? What's your opinion?"

"Let me think about it," I said.

THE PERILS OF PERFORMANCE PREDICTION

In most companies, the basis for promoting people to the executive level is simply other executives' opinions of them. Most executives are smart, articulate, and decisive, and they tend to favor people like them. IBM was no exception.

But my boss's point was that brains and assertiveness, by themselves, weren't enough to run a high-technology company that was already huge and was still growing at an explosive rate. To do that, you also needed sophistication and wisdom. And no one is born worldly or wise. Those qualities are acquired, if at all, from experience. And merely exposing clever young managers to different jobs in different places is no guarantee that they will emerge any the wiser.

So the problem came down to this: Who, among a set of relatively inexperienced managers, can grow furthest and fastest if exposed, early on, to the full breadth of an enormous company?

I had once been in the performance prediction business myself, so I knew that its practitioners had much to be humble about. There were lots of problems. The two major ones were these:

First, the results we were supposed to predict would inevitably be influenced by events we couldn't measure, or even guess at, simply because they hadn't happened yet. Second, we never had a clear fix on the performance we were supposed to predict. For both reasons, we always hedged our forecasts with qualifiers like "other things being equal," knowing full well that the "other things" that really count were never equal.

As for what we can, and can't, measure: Psychologists have ways of testing certain aspects of an individual, like mental ability or personality. But those are only part of a larger set of factors that influence job performance, and they're not necessarily the most important ones. How managers' work will be evaluated also depends on factors we have no way of even guessing at. Some examples: yet-to-occur events in their private lives; or the quality of the assignments, training, mentoring, or supervision they get; or the effects of the peers and subordinates with whom they have to work.

Any of these unknowables could derail the career of someone who tested brilliantly, or favor the chances of someone whose test results were only so-so. For these reasons, predicting someone's performance years in advance with psychological tests is not unlike playing poker. Most of the relevant information is unavailable to you, and even with a sensible strategy you will guess right only part of the time.

As for knowing what we had to predict: We were asked to forecast "executive performance," but the truth is that we had only a vague idea of what that was. Executives are rated by their own superiors, or by boards of directors, but both tend to apply their own yardstick and to use a different yardstick in different situations.

Although that uncertainty frustrates psychologists, it is nevertheless as it should be: Most companies face changing challenges, and therefore the requirements of an executive job are necessarily fluid. That left us unsure of what qualities to look for in candidates for executive jobs. Surely they had to be intelligent and determined, but lots of failed executives had been both.

The embarrassing truth was that we simply didn't know what effective executives actually *did* when they were being effective or how that differed from what ineffective executives did. About all we had to go on were some vague generalities and some glowing adjectives. To make matters worse, most executives didn't appreciate our predicament. It was perfectly obvious to them why some executives did a better job than others, and the fact that they couldn't articulate the reasons didn't bother them one bit!

Those of us in the performance prediction business had a name for this dilemma: We called it the "criterion problem." It left us in a position not unlike having to bet on a horse without knowing which race it would run in, at which track, and under what conditions. Then, as I mulled over the problem, it dawned on me that I was in a uniquely favorable position to crack the criterion problem, at least with regard to executive performance in IBM.

IBM was a very large company, with hundreds of executives running divisions, subsidiaries, and the corporation itself. So I could get a broad cross section of executives at work. More importantly, IBM was open-minded about psychological research. It had cooperated in previous studies when it appeared that they might be useful. If I could find out precisely what kinds of activities constituted "effectiveness" at the executive level, that information could be applied in several promising ways.

So I went back to my boss and told him that before we could even try to identify "effective" executives ten or more years in advance, we first had to know what executives did when they were effective and what they did when they weren't. We would have to get "inside their heads," so to speak, and determine just *how* they thought.

In his usual pragmatic way, he asked, "All right. Suppose you can get at that; what could we do with it?"

I told him there were two possibilities. If we were lucky, similar kinds of decisions might crop up in the work of junior-level managers. In that case, we would simply have to refocus their performance appraisals to zero in on those particular decisions. If that didn't work, we could still try to teach all IBM managers to make those kinds of decisions by using the methods its best executives used.

That satisfied him that the answers would be worth getting, so he turned to the question of whether it could be done. "Tell me how you're going to do this," he said.

"I want to interview every executive in IBM," I said, "starting with the level that reports to vice presidents, and from there on up the organization chart, as high as we can go. I'll need to see each of them for about an hour."

He whistled softly. "You're talking about a few hundred very busy people," he said. "Frankly, you'd be lucky to get to see even half of them. But I'll see what I can arrange for you."

CRITICAL INCIDENTS

I decided to use a research tool developed by John Flanagan, a psychologist at the University of Pittsburgh, called the "critical incident" technique. In this sense, an "incident" was a closed case: an event whose consequences were already known. It could be rated as "critical" if, in the opinion of the best-informed people we could find, those consequences either moved the company forward toward its goals or pushed it back from them. Also included were decisions that helped steer the company clear of potentially big trouble. Those turned out to be more important than I expected.

The beauty of this technique for the researcher is that you are working with real life, not theories. Your raw material is a large set of events that have actually occurred. If you gather enough of them, and find some patterns there, those patterns define the reality you are trying to understand.

It is the use of such time-consuming methods that distinguishes research psychologists from their armchair colleagues. Researchers draw a sample of real-world events that is large enough to be reliable and then build a theory on what they find. Armchair psychologists spin theories in their heads and seize on anecdotes that seem to support them. Research psychologists don't know what they're going to find and make their most valuable discoveries when they're surprised. Armchair psychologists know exactly what they're looking for and would be surprised not to find it. I aimed to enter into this project as a researcher, with my eyes, ears, and mind wide open.

My boss managed to work me into the schedules of nearly two hundred of IBM's top leaders. I met with people who ran divisions, people who managed factories, the heads of corporate staff departments, and the general managers of foreign subsidiaries. I interviewed the president (but not the chairman), strategic planners, publicists, lawyers, accountants, and the heads of research laboratories. Altogether, I got quite an education.

I began each interview by explaining my mission and defining what a critical incident was. Then I said, "I'd like you to cast your memory back over the past few years, and see if you can recall some cases that you witnessed up close, or possibly even took part in yourself. Tell me what happened, and why you think it made a major difference for the company."

When they recalled such a case, I'd say, "OK, now here comes the hard part. I need specifics. I need to know exactly what the problem was, and exactly what the executive did about it. And I need verbs, not adjectives. For example, if someone did a 'terrific' job, I need to know exactly what he or she did that was so terrific."

Recalling the details of events that occurred months or even years ago is hard work. These were all highly intelligent men and women who were well positioned to know what was going on in the company. Still, they recalled an average of only about three usable "incidents" in the course of an hour-long interview. Fortunately, because I saw so many executives, I ended up with about six hundred case histories: enough to be confident that the results were reliable.

My next task was to make some sense of all those stories. I read and then reread them several times. Finally some patterns began to emerge. Most of these cases could be classified into one of six groups, none of which involved the glamorous aspects of executive work, such as intuition or charismatic leadership. Instead, all six were focused on different stages of the decision-making process.

In itself, that discovery brushed aside some of the common mythology about what makes executives effective. It's not just a matter of getting things done energetically. With respect to IBM, at least, the data showed that while the sheer intensity of your efforts might hasten your rise to the top management level, it wouldn't help you much once you got there. From then onward, your effectiveness would depend chiefly on what my boss called your "smarts."

MAKING GOOD DECISIONS

Why were IBM's management decisions nearly always right during its "glory" years? In most cases, it was not because its executives had unusual insights or were exceptionally creative. Instead, they ran the company as well as they did by making very few small mistakes and even fewer big ones.

During one of the longest uninterrupted growth spurts in business history, IBM's best executives used a disciplined, defensive approach to decision making. For them, good management seemed to be above all a matter of avoiding fiascoes. Of course, they finally made some lulus in the late 1980s, but we are concerned here with how they managed to keep the company growing *until* then.

IBM executives didn't actually follow a checklist when they made decisions. There was no prescribed procedure. But the critical incident data indicated that when they made the decisions that mattered most, they were much more likely to be right when they adhered to one or more of these six principles. When they didn't, they were much more likely to commit one of IBM's few unpardonable sins: making a dumb decision when they should have known better.

Here, then, is a synopsis of what IBM's most effective executives did, and didn't do, in the years when they piloted their company to nearly the top of the Fortune 500 list:

First, they didn't make decisions at all if they didn't have to. Second, before making a decision, they first made sure they were dealing with the entire problem, rather than just a part of it. Third, they were skeptical of their information and demanded proof that it was reliable. Fourth, they made sure that their plans did not require more money or manpower than they had. Fifth, they understood that in this imperfect world, the best decision is often the one that is least bad. Finally, they allowed for the possibility—indeed, the probability—that the best-laid plans some-times go awry.

The few cases I will present here are drawn from nearly six hundred similar cases that I collected in the course of this study. Each of them, by itself, proves nothing. But they illustrate a mass of cases that was large enough to be convincing, and probably larger than you would care to wade through, as I had to.

EXECUTIVE RESTRAINT: IS THIS DECISION NECESSARY?

The most important decision any executive ever makes is whether to make a decision at all. Should things be left as they are, or should the company be committed to a new course of action?

This most fundamental of all decisions is often made without reflection. In fact, the current management literature exhorts us to have a bias for action or just do it (regardless of what "it" might be).

In some cases, that sort of audacity may work out well. But if we took, say, a hundred executives and told them to take action *now* on a major matter, without considering whether it might be best to leave well enough alone, we could probably count on at least fifty who would simply make things worse.

Contrary to popular mythology, executives are not paid to make decisions. They are paid to make *smart* decisions and to make them consistently. That is no small distinction.

Consider this case:

An IBM executive took over a department that was responsible for, among other things, annual award meetings for salespeople who achieved outstanding results during the preceding year. This included the "100 Percent Club," for salespeople who reached or exceeded their annual quota. But it also included a more lavish meeting, known as the "Golden Circle," for those who had hit their sales targets for five or more consecutive years.

He decided that this two-tier reward system implied second-class status for younger sales reps who had not yet accumulated five consecutive 100 percent clubs. And he saw an opportunity to use the Golden Circle for motivating younger salespeople to exceptionally high achievements. So he introduced one small change in the rules: High-achieving sales reps who brought in at least 120 percent of their quotas could attend the posh Golden Circle meeting, along with the senior salespeople, even if they had not yet made their quotas for five straight years.

Unfortunately, he never bothered to find out why the two-tier system had been set up in the first place. There were good reasons for it. During IBM's high-growth years, most salesmen who were going to become managers were promoted before they had hit their quota for five consecutive years. Those who stayed in sales that long either didn't want to be managers or for various reasons were considered better qualified for selling. It was precisely to avoid a second-class stigma for *them*, and because they were mature enough to be entrusted with the most important accounts, that the Golden Circle had been created.

By blurring the distinction between current high achievement and consistently high achievement, this executive managed to undo the elegant solution that his predecessor had contrived. His own undoing resulted from an irate letter to the chairman, written by a self-appointed committee of senior salespeople, objecting to the dilution of their hard-earned recognition. The chairman agreed, the original rules were reinstated, and the overzealous executive was assigned to less demanding responsibilities.

In this case, the company would have been much better off if the executive had done nothing at all. The status quo was working just fine.

But he suffered from a common conceit: that one has nothing to learn from one's predecessors or in any case can always improve upon what they did. But that is unlikely to be true in companies that are fussy about whom they appoint to executive positions.

Knowing how not to be seduced by one's own enthusiasms is a learnable skill, if it is learned early enough. Some companies now try to head off blunders like this one by providing their younger decision makers with mentors. Like modern-day Cromwells, they have the job of beseeching their younger clients to consider, before committing themselves and their company, that they just *might* be wrong.

What the executive in this case lacked was not intelligence (he had plenty of that), but wisdom. It never occurred to him to ask questions before plunging ahead. With no effective restraints built into an overly eager decision maker, and no mentor to counsel him, an unfortunate result was inevitable.

One could argue that executive restraint makes a company stodgy and conservative. I can only answer that in the era when IBM routinely set records that no competitor could match and grew faster than every other company on *Fortune*'s list, it did so mainly by exploiting its advantages intelligently. That meant, above all, avoiding thousands of potentially stupid mistakes.

One could also argue that it was an overdose of executive restraint that led IBM to its time of troubles, by inhibiting radical changes that were nevertheless necessary. I was not as close to IBM when it got itself into trouble as I was during its high-growth era, so I can't give a fully informed answer.

But if I had to guess, I'd say that those problems resulted from a variant of the same mistake that was made in this case. That is, instead of failing to ask whether a desired action was really necessary, some later executive didn't consider whether an undesired action was nevertheless mandated by changed circumstances. Although separated by several years, both of the executives involved gave the wrong answer to the same question: Is this decision necessary?

BREADTH OF EXECUTIVE VISION: IS THIS THE ENTIRE PROBLEM?

Partial solutions to complex problems are at best inefficient. At worst, they can create an illusion of control, which allows the unsolved parts to continue doing their damage undisturbed. (An example would be fixing a leaking roof while neglecting the termites in the walls.)

As my boss pointed out, problems at the executive level tend to be multifaceted. Therefore it is important not to mistake a piece of a problem, however important or fascinating it might be, for the entire problem. If your problem is an iceberg, you have to deal with the whole iceberg. Otherwise you could wind up as the executive equivalent to the skipper of the *Titanic*.

To address such a problem effectively, you must first establish its dimensions. Does it have more than one cause, and more than one effect? To control all of the effects, you have to deal with all of the causes. That's why the executives who make these decisions have to see them from a wide-angle perspective.

Consider this case:

IBM had a development laboratory that was too small to accommodate the planned growth of its projects. So it faced a choice between enlarging the lab or constructing a new one somewhere else. Although there was enough space at the existing site for the necessary new facilities, using that space meant that there would be none left afterward for still further expansion, should that ever become necessary.

The executive who would have to make the final decision directed his staff to consider all aspects of all options. IBM's growth rate was such that yet another expansion of the laboratory, although not immediately necessary, was by no means unlikely. So the staff was attracted to the idea of a new laboratory on a new site, where there would be plenty of room for future growth.

The two main criteria the staff set for selecting such a site were ample acreage and attractive nearby communities to house the scientists who would work there. Their search eventually narrowed to a beautiful location quite far from the existing laboratory. When the executive reviewed their work, his first question was "What about costs?"

"No problem, chief," was the reply. "We've looked at land acquisition, construction, taxes, maintenance, everything. At today's prices, it's quite reasonable. Besides, it's a gorgeous spot. Having a laboratory there would be great for prestige, and for employee morale."

"I'm sure it's just lovely," said the executive. "But have you considered this? Wouldn't it be less expensive to just add on to our existing lab? True, we couldn't expand it again after that. But even if we have to build another lab eventually, that need is years away. If we built a new lab now, we'd be paying that cost differential for that many years, before we ever find out if we even had to. Now, tell me: Don't we have better things to do with the money we'd save?"

"But chief," said the senior staff member, "the way this company is growing . . ."

But the executive cut him short.

"Let me tell you how this company is growing," he said. "We're growing as fast as we can grow responsibly. We won't increase our costs faster than our revenues grow. Some companies forgot about that, and 'grew' right into bankruptcy, by spending money they hadn't made yet. Now, go back and crunch those numbers again. I need to know just what that cost differential comes to. If it's not much, I might go along with you. But if it's big, no way."

In this case, the staff was so fascinated by one aspect of the problem (IBM's phenomenal growth) that it ignored an equally important aspect (the need to keep a tight rein on costs). In effect, it solved the wrong problem. Fortunately, the executive understood that solutions to pieces of a problem can be worse than no solutions at all.

One could argue that it was the staff that had a bold vision of the future, and that their boss was too unimaginative to see it. In the long run, the staff might have been right: more space might have been needed, and it could not have been provided at the older facility. But even if that were to happen, the accumulated savings on the cost differential would help to pay for it. And if it didn't, the savings would stay in IBM's pocket.

Seeing a problem in its larger context is one of the most valuable of all executive skills—perhaps the most valuable. For a classical example, let's briefly step outside IBM and go all the way back to 1914:

When employee turnover at the Ford Motor Company hit horrendous levels, Henry Ford proposed to double the company's wage rate. His directors were aghast. But Ford was shrewd enough to realize that the effects of the wage increase would go far beyond merely cutting turnover. It would also force up other employers' wage rates, thus enabling both his workers and theirs to afford his products. And that increase in purchasing power would more than double both his market and his market share.

Unlike the IBM executive's staff, Ford was not fixated on a mere part (albeit a fascinating part) of a larger problem. What both the Ford case and the IBM case illustrate is that the task of upper management is always to manage the forest and leave the management of trees to lower levels.

EXECUTIVE SKEPTICISM: HOW RELIABLE ARE YOUR "FACTS"?

My boss had correctly anticipated this finding when he said, "When you get to this level in the company, you have to make decisions about things you really don't know much about." There is also a corollary danger: that you can become dependent on your staff, who often view things from a narrow perspective and are not, in any case, responsible for the decisions that might be taken.

The problem came down to this: How can you be sure you're getting the best expert advice, without, in effect, abdicating your responsibilities and turning your advisers into de facto decision makers?

Two cases in my critical incident file show how IBM executives evaded this trap. Here's the first:

One executive disliked reading reports more than two pages long. So he turned most lengthy reports over to his staff and demanded that they prepare brief "executive summaries" for him, insisting that they focus narrowly on essential issues. Whenever possible, he asked that they inform him of their findings in oral presentations rather than in written reports.

These presentations usually lasted only five or ten minutes. The presenter stood at one end of the executive's office, next to a flipchart on which a few key phrases, numbers, or diagrams illustrated the key points. The executive sat behind his desk, and the presenter would do his or her best to make a case for whatever was being recommended.

The presentations were usually well rehearsed, succinct, and polished. Everyone wanted to "sell the chief" on a pet proposal, because doing so would probably advance his own career. But the chief had his own way of making sure that the presenters had prepared meticulously.

At some unpredictable point during the presentation, he would leap out of his chair, blustering and waving his arms. "Where did you get that?" he would demand. "That can't be right! I don't believe it! Did you make that up? Where's your proof? It sounds ridiculous to me! Show me your facts, or get out of here!"

Of course, it didn't necessarily sound ridiculous to him at all. This was simply his theatrical way of making sure that no one dared enter his office without having thoroughly researched all aspects of what he was going to discuss, mastered all of the details, and thought through the consequences of what he was going to recommend. Obviously, word of his tactic quickly spread throughout the executive's staff and had its desired effect.

"Sure, they know I'm going to do that," he told me when I interviewed him. "But they don't know *when* I'm going to do it. They don't know which of their points I'm going to attack. I'll admit it's a kind of a game.

"But my message is simple," he continued. "If you're not 100 percent prepared to defend every word you say, don't waste my time. They have to convince me that they've been thorough and professional. If they can stand up to that kind of attack, I'll believe them. If they can't, I won't. Those are the rules of the game. Period."

The particular foible against which this executive had to defend himself was the common human tendency to fall in love with one's own ideas. The best antidote is a mandatory rehearsal with one's peers before staking one's career, or one's company, on premises that may not be as well thought out as they should be. This executive's staff learned quickly to edit each other's proposals before their boss ever saw them. Only rarely did the executive discover flawed reasoning, or an unsupported argument, in their proposals. And that was exactly the way he wanted it.

Of course, there is always the danger that one of the wilder ideas shot down by a group of one's colleagues might actually be as brilliant as Ford's. On the record, however, that risk is vanishingly small.

Here's the second case:

An executive had to decide whether to introduce a product that at the time was unprecedented. His staff was divided. The group that favored the product then enlisted the help of a veteran marketing manager who was known to be well liked by the division's chief. They persuaded him that the new product would be successful, so he sought an appointment with the executive to throw his weight behind it.

The marketing manager was his usual persuasive self, predicting a glowing future for the new product. When he finished, the executive said, "Well, you're still a great salesman. But I need proof. Where are your facts?"

"Boss," said the marketing manager, "I've been in this business for years, and I haven't been wrong yet. I don't need any research to tell me that this is a winner. It's just obviously going to be one hell of a product for us."

The executive raised a skeptical eyebrow. "You haven't researched this?" he asked. "You just have a warm, fuzzy feeling, and on that basis you want me to make a multimillion-dollar decision?"

The marketing manager leaned forward. "Boss," he said, "I know *in my gut* that we've got a winner here!"

The executive stood up. "You may be right, and you may be wrong," he said, "but I'm going to have to ignore your advice. If this division has to be run on viscera, instead of facts, then it will be my viscera and no one else's, because I've got the most to lose if I'm wrong."

Both executives forced their advisers to back away from their passionately held convictions and dig out hard facts instead. True, people who have strong convictions that they cannot explain sometimes turn out to be right. But they are at least as likely to be wrong, and since there is no way (short of committing enormous resources) to find out which is the case, the path of prudence is to ignore advice that can't be verified.

That's not a foolproof formula for decisionmakers, but there is no foolproof formula. And by demanding proof, these executives were a lot more likely to be right than to be wrong. What these two cases demonstrate is that running a big company successfully is not so much a matter of having brilliant insights as of avoiding stupid mistakes. The opportunities for the former are rare anyway, while those for the latter are, alas, as abundant as the leaves on the trees.

Psychologists know how to measure your powers of reasoning. But it is much harder to forecast whether, in a given instance, you will use them. It can't hurt to admonish decision makers to keep a tight grip on those powers at all times. But a company that wants to maximize the number of correct decisions its decision makers make will do more than that. Training, mentoring, peer reviews, and independent consultants all help to minimize the danger that viscera, rather than brainpower, will guide the company toward its future.

EXECUTIVE PRACTICALITY: CAN THIS DECISION BE IMPLEMENTED?

It is easy to become so romanced by the ends we want to pursue that we lose sight of the means we have for pursuing them. (The equivalent on a tennis court is having your eye fixed firmly on where you're going to put the ball instead of on the ball itself.) But sooner or later we have to deal with the question of whether what we want to do can actually be done, given the resources we have for doing it.

The next case shows what happens when an executive takes an indispensable requirement for granted:

In those days, IBM's major competitive advantage was its thousands of field engineers. These were the people who installed computers in customers' offices and then took care of maintenance and repairs. They were an uncommonly committed group who would do whatever had to be done, at all hours of the day and night, to keep customers' computers running. IBM salesmen made sure that customers understood the value of those field engineers. They were a powerful argument for placing your orders with Big Blue.

Paradoxically, those same field engineers were also a potential Achilles' heel. Despite its size, IBM was (and still is) nonunion. But if a union were ever to attempt to organize IBM, the two most logical points to attack would be workers in the factories and field engineers. Both did the kinds of work that unions understood, both were the kinds of workers unions had successfully organized elsewhere.

IBM management was aware of this vulnerability and went to considerable lengths to convince its employees that they had no need for "third-party intervention"—its euphemism for unions. Partly because of that vigilance, the unions never made a serious attempt to organize IBM. But the vulnerability remained. One of the premises that IBM managers neglected at their peril was that the field engineers could be relied on only if their loyalty to the company were undivided.

Although no one questioned the value of the service provided by the field engineers, a debate arose within management about its cost. One executive in particular became identified with the view that it was extravagant, and that customers would be equally satisfied if certain excesses were eliminated. He pointed, for example, to expensive parts that field engineers carried with them, even though they were seldom needed. Eventually, he was put in charge of all field engineering operations and told to reduce costs without harming customer satisfaction.

He undertook a variety of cost-cutting programs, many of which were quite effective. However, the payroll was by far his biggest cost, so that's where he looked for the biggest savings. He decided on two changes:

First, he slowed the rate of hiring so that new computers were installed faster than new field engineers were deployed to service them. The result was a rise in the average work load. Second, he slowed the promotion rate for new supervisors, so their "span of control" (the number of field engineers reporting to a given supervisor) also increased. The result was a gain in productivity. More work was done than before, without a corresponding increase in manpower.

But when grumbling arose about the pace of the change, the executive denounced the complaints as unjustified and ordered his staff to ignore any further griping. He thus managed to cut himself off from information on whether the field engineers were still as loyal as ever.

About a year later, a small notice was inserted in the want ad section of the *New York Times*, stating that IBM field engineers were available for hire and giving a box number for replies. To the discerning eye, it was a subtle but unmistakable hint that the loyalty of the field engineers should not be taken for granted.

The ad was neatly clipped out and taped to a blank sheet of paper, which "mysteriously" showed up on the desk of the division's president. It had its intended effect. The president promptly investigated, discovered an alarming slide in field engineering morale, and immediately replaced the executive who had slowed the hiring and promotion rates.

Viewed separately, all of the hapless executive's economies were quite logical. Viewed in their larger context, they could not be implemented safely, because they had been introduced in a way that made the field engineers feel cut off from their previously benevolent employer. Whether the field engineers would actually have been receptive to a union organizing attempt at that time is a moot point, because the company quickly undertook to restore their loyalty. What is not moot is that once the executive began taking their morale for granted, his plans became impractical, because they exposed the company to a greater danger (as IBM perceived it) than the high cost of keeping its customers happy.

Why did this essential point escape an otherwise astute executive? Probably because so much of his ego was invested in his cost-cutting strategy that he was blind to its limitations. Many high-level executives run the same risk: The more power they have, the less exposure they have to people who dare to point out the flaws in their reasoning. The more astute executives realize that this freedom from criticism is not a fringe benefit. It is their Achilles' heel.

HARD EXECUTIVE CHOICES: WHAT ARE THE TRADE-OFFS?

It's easy to choose between a good outcome and a bad one. It's harder to choose between two good outcomes, and harder still when your choice is between two bad ones. Unfortunately, that's what most executive decision making is like.

My boss called those decisions "trade-offs," because (in their easier version) you have to trade away an advantage to gain what you hope is a better one. In the more difficult trade-off, you elect to swallow something that tastes bad in order to avoid something that tastes even worse.

The problem, of course, is to know the difference: to distinguish what is best from what is merely good, or what is merely bad from what is worse. And that makes for a hard choice, as this case illustrates:

IBM established an executive training academy at the old Guggenheim Estate at Sands Point, New York, on the north shore of Long Island. Promising midlevel managers from all over the country were sent there for specialized courses designed to prepare them for more advanced assignments.

The instructors were expected to rate their students, as well as to teach them. But that led to a debate, because some instructors feared that students would try harder to impress them than to learn. They were bothered by the thought that to play either of their two roles well, they would have to risk sacrificing the other.

It was customary for the final session of each class to be attended by the chairman himself, or by another high-ranking executive, who would give the closing address. He would also mingle with the students, dispensing wisdom and forming his own impressions of the company's future leaders. Afterward he would meet with the instructors to get their ratings of the students.

At one such meeting, the visiting executive expressed himself bluntly. Two of the students had seemed awe-struck and passive, lacking clear-cut opinions of their own. "How did they get here?" he demanded. "Who sent them?"

He was told the names of the managers who had nominated the offending students for the Sands Point program. The executive shook his head in disbelief. "Well, don't take any more recommendations from them. And from now on, send every nominator an evaluation of how well his people did here."

The director of the school took a deep breath and then pointed out that both students had done very well in their classes, and both had compiled excellent performance records back in their home offices. Both of them, he assured the executive, had good minds.

"Maybe," said the executive, "but I don't think you get the point. We have lots of smart people in IBM. But if you're going to run a company this big, just being smart isn't enough. You've got to be able to make tough decisions, and give people the confidence that you know what you're doing. And frankly, I don't think you can teach things like that at Sands Point or anywhere else."

"Are you saying, sir," asked the school director, "that our mission is not to teach these people about management, but just to rate them on these personal qualities?"

"No," replied the executive. "I'm saying that your mission is to teach people with these qualities about management, and not to teach it to people without those qualities. We have lots of training programs elsewhere for smart people who are not as decisive as someone should be to come here."

Today we would say that the executive was an elitist. I think he would have cheerfully admitted that and added that in order to run as complex an enterprise as IBM, he had no choice. But the point of the story is that he concentrated the minds of the instructors on why their jobs had been created in the first place.

They were to be both evaluators and educators, but *in that order*. If that meant that some students learned less, it was a price the company was willing to pay. Besides, the kinds of people IBM was seeking usually learn more from their own experience than from lectures, textbooks, and even classroom discussions.

When a decision presents us with no attractive alternatives, the temptation to ignore that harsh reality can be overwhelming. In such cases, we often "restate" the problem in our minds, treating it as an easy choice (between good and bad) rather than the hard choice (between bad and worse) that it really is. The executive in this case had the tough task of reminding the instructors, who in order to live more comfortably with their job requirements may have mentally restated them, of why their jobs existed in the first place.

THE PRUDENT EXECUTIVE: IS THERE A WAY OUT?

Executive decision making takes place among so many unknowns and unknowables that some mistakes are inevitable. When they occur, the practical problem is to cut your losses and look for an alternative way to reach your goals. Sometimes you even have to abandon a goal that is too costly, or too unlikely to be reached.

One seldom gets a medal for leading a retreat, but there are times when that has to be done. The most elegant way to do it is to have a preplanned strategy for extracting yourself and your company from a plan that has gone badly awry. The alternative is a hastily improvised retreat, which is all too likely to turn into a rout. The next case is a combination of both approaches: an elegantly improvised strategy for keeping unforeseen damage to a minimum.

This case involved an executive who led a task force that introduced a large-scale application of computer technology to savings banks. They had developed a new program for calculating the interest payable to individual savings accounts, posting those amounts to the bank's records, and notifying the customers of the new balance. The executive decided to introduce it at one of the largest savings banks, reasoning that if it worked well there it could easily be sold to hundreds of other banks around the country.

In themselves, calculating and posting interest payments were not particularly difficult. What made this case different, however, was the huge number of accounts involved. The program was to be run for the first time at night, and all of the results were to be available in the morning. The executive personally supervised the final check-out of the new system and then ordered a three-person team—an IBM manager, a field engineer, and a systems analyst—to stay at the bank all night in case anything went wrong.

Not long after he went to bed, he was awakened by a telephone call from the manager. "Sorry to bother you," he said, "but we've got a problem here. We're picking up intermittent errors. Not many, and there's no pattern to them, at least not yet. The bank has a night manager down the hall, but I thought I'd tell you first."

The executive rubbed his eyes and tried to concentrate. "OK," he said. "The best thing to do is let it run for a while so we can pick up more errors, and hope to find a pattern that will tell us what's wrong. But you go down the hall and tell the night manager about this. Keep him calm. Tell him I'm coming down. Explain that it would be a mistake to shut down, because that way we won't know how to fix it. I should be there in thirty minutes. At this hour, there won't be much traffic."

Then he dressed hastily and left his home. As he drove through deserted streets to the bank, he considered his options. If the problem could not be fixed quickly, he would have no choice but to shut the computer down. But the problem had not even been diagnosed yet.

When he arrived, the IBM manager told him, "Still no pattern."

"How's the night manager?" asked the executive.

"Very nervous," answered the IBM manager. "Thinks he should call his boss. I told him it would be better to wait until you got here."

The executive looked at his watch. "Actually," he said, "I'm going to have to go over his boss's head. This is a decision for the president. But call him in. I want him to be here in the room when I make the call."

A few minutes later he placed the call, awakening the bank president. He explained the problem tersely. "We don't know yet if this is really major, or something we can fix in the morning. I can get a few more people in here tonight, but if this is really big it will take a lot more than that. I can have dozens of IBMers in here by 8:00 A.M., but by then it will be too late to put your statements in tomorrow's mail. I want to avoid that for you if I possibly can."

"What do you recommend?" asked the president.

"I'm asking you to let us keep running for another thirty minutes," said the executive. "If we're lucky, we may know by then how bad this really is. But if we don't know by then, we should shut down."

"Ill give you fifteen minutes," said the president. "That's as much of a risk as I can take with something like this. The bank will look pretty bad if we're late with the statements, but it would look even worse if a lot of them were wrong. If you don't know what it is by then, shut it down and get the whole IBM army in there first thing in the morning. Call me in fifteen minutes, either way."

The executive called in his three IBM colleagues. "Our best hope," he told them, "is that this will turn out to be the kind of problem that we can find quickly. There's no point in looking for any problems that take more than fifteen minutes to identify. Let's make a list of possibilities that can be checked out quickly. Then we'll divide them up between us, and get to work."

With about three minutes left to go, the systems analyst cried out, "I've got it!" The executive raced over to him. "Prove it to me," he said. "I've got to be certain that what you've got is the whole problem, and that we can fix it fast enough to let all of the statements go out tomorrow." The systems analyst then demonstrated that a small programming error had caused the problem.

"Fix it now," said the executive. Then he called the president. "We know what it is, and we can fix it," he said. "I recommend that we just keep running. We'll correct all the errors that have already slipped through, and you can have your statements in the mail tomorrow."

It was pure luck that the problem in this case was caused by an error that could be uncovered quickly. But finding it quickly was not luck at all. That was the result of a deliberate strategy, devised on the spot and under pressure. But the executive's game plan also provided for the possibility that the error might not be found within the tight limits imposed by the president. In that case, the damage to the bank's records could have been minimized, simply by shutting down the computer.

The important point was that the client had been notified and was in control, deciding exactly how much of a risk to take. Had the client not known of the problem until the following morning, the damage would have been far greater: not just to the bank, but to its relationship with IBM, and to the IBM executive's credibility.

All of that was finessed by his decision *not* to try to cover up the problem and to put the ultimate decision were it belonged: in the client's hands. If worse had come to worst, he had left himself and his company with a way out of what might otherwise have become, to say the least, a very untidy situation.

The executive in this case was unflappable. He never confused the secondary objective (completing the project without interruption) with the primary one (preserving the client's trust in IBM). He was prepared to capitalize on luck and so was able to accomplish both. Overall, this was a superb demonstration of crisis management.

FACING THE "SO WHAT?" TEST

When I reported these results to my boss, he asked the question that all researchers eventually have to face. "This is all very interesting," he said, "and it makes a lot of sense. But what are we going to do with it?"

I first tried to design a checklist that IBM managers could use to analyze the ways in which their subordinates made decisions. But it quickly became apparent that any such list that worked would also be too time-consuming. "It may be a great idea," said my boss, "but the managers won't buy it. What else can we do with these results?"

"I don't think that anyone is born with these decision-making skills," I said. "I think they are learned. And if that's the case, they can also be taught."

So with my boss's approval, I went out to Sands Point and showed my research data to the instructors. They worked the six principles into the courses they taught to IBM's aspiring executives. Whether that made them into more effective decision makers than they might otherwise have become is one of those questions that always leave educators stumped. It can only be answered in terms of probabilities, not certainties.

But on that basis, I would argue that the six principles probably enhanced some managerial careers and spared IBM some managerial blunders. If such things actually happened, they were IBM's payoff for this research project.

From a psychological standpoint, the project demonstrated that the wisest decisions are made by executives who maintain the clearest focus on what must be done, regardless of the pressures or temptations of the moment. It is this quality of being in command of one's self, more than brilliance or ingenuity, that made the difference. Are some people born with that quality, and can it be taught to others? I am convinced that the answer to both questions is yes.

My own view is that the most important executive skills are learned, not inherited, and that the sooner they are learned, the better. That means that in selecting future executives, there are two key qualities we must either find or inculcate: first, the ability to turn one's own learning process into the habit of a lifetime, rather than a skill to be abandoned when one is no longer compelled by teachers to use it; second, the discipline to follow a methodical decision-making process consistently, time after time.

Knowing what I know now, I would rather try to teach these skills to reasonably bright people than to test them for an inclination (if there is such a thing) to use them instinctively. Beyond a certain point, which we have probably already reached, there is more to be gained from good teaching than from pushing the art of performance prediction much further than it has already been pushed.

Chapter Three

Schering Reorganizes Its World

In the routine process of thrashing out decisions, managers will often disagree. In fact, they're expected to, because their debates clarify the pros and cons of the options facing their companies. Ordinarily, these everyday arguments do more good than harm. Sometimes, however, the infighting can become really damaging, and when it does, it's likely to involve questions of organizational structure.

More is at stake here than in routine operational disputes because changes in organization structure can make or unmake careers. In these reviews, companies periodically have to reconsider such gut-level questions as which jobs still need to be done, which can be eliminated, and who will supervise the jobs that will remain. Organizational questions are intensely political. That's why it often takes a long time to settle them. Nearly everyone knows that there will be winners and losers. Until the decision is finally made, the politicking is likely to be fast and furious, as it was in this case.

Schering's international division made and sold prescription medicines in thirty-nine countries and employed almost eight thousand people. Rick Swaak was its vice president for personnel. He had called me in to see whether I could help with the division's toughest problem: Where should decisions that controlled Schering's international business be made?

"Here's the problem," he explained, pointing to a map of the world. "We run the division from New Jersey, right here. From here the chain of command runs out to three regional headquarters, which in turn run all of our subsidiary companies in their part of the world. We have one region running Europe, another for Latin America, and another for Asia. Altogether, we have about four hundred thirty people in those four headquarters locations, and not one of them, including me, makes even one dollar for Schering."

He explained that all of Schering's profits were actually earned where the products were sold, out in those thirty-nine subsidiaries. So the question he wanted to settle was whether four hundred thirty people were really needed to guide and control the subsidiaries. He noted that everyone in the four headquarters seemed to have an opinion on this question and that unsurprisingly, each favored an organization structure that would in turn favor his own career prospects.

"Nothing unusual there," I said. "But the answer to your question is probably scattered. A lot of people in the division probably know a piece of it. The problem is to pull it all together."

Rick is a man who makes up his mind quickly. "Can you do that for us?" he asked.

"I think so," I said.

"Good," he said. "Now you need to know some other things, as well." He told me that the parent company needed more cash flow and that it looked to each division for its contribution. That's where the urgency came from. The question that had to be answered, and soon, was whether the existing organization structure enabled Schering to get the most profit out of its international subsidiaries.

"Most companies don't look at their organization structures," I told him, "until their accountants make them do it."

Rick smiled knowingly. "I hope your passport is still valid," he said. "Our division president will need your report in five weeks, maximum. You'll have to visit four continents, including North America, between now and then."

In the next five weeks I interviewed one hundred fifty Schering managers in thirteen countries. Only ten of those interviews are summarized here. I selected them because they express views that were shared by many others, and because they trace a chain of ideas that helped me to realize what Schering had to do.

DIVISION HEADQUARTERS—NEW JERSEY

My first meeting at the division's headquarters was with a senior financial officer. He wanted to be sure that I understood how and why the existing organization structure had been formed.

"About eight years ago," he said, "we faced a different problem. But in its own way, it was just as controversial as this one. We had some great products, and they were selling as fast as we could ship them. But our profits were only mediocre. Obviously, something was wrong."

On that earlier occasion, he told me, it hadn't taken long to figure out what was wrong. Many subsidiaries were being run by people whom he called "fast-talking sales types." To them, he said, running a business was simply a matter of signing up customers and collecting the revenue. They knew little or nothing about financial controls. Obviously, he considered that deplorable.

"They didn't seem to understand," he said, "that the way a corporation really makes money is by spending less than it takes in. You could ask them, 'How much money do you have tied up in your inventory?' or 'Which are your most profitable products?' and they couldn't give you an answer."

He paused, looked at me for a moment, and winked. "You understand," he said, "that I have my own point of view on these things. This is not necessarily the company's point of view."

"Everyone has a point of view," I answered. "I came to hear yours."

He nodded. What happened next, he told me, was that the parent company sent in a tough financial expert who had successfully turned the division around. He imposed a rigorous system of controls that was still in effect. The division could now balance its production with demand, for every product in every country.

With evident pride, he told me that the division could measure its inventories "right down to how many doses there are of a particular product on the shelf of a particular drugstore. Now, that's control."

I had to agree.

"And that level of control," he concluded, "is the real reason for those three regional offices."

Each subsidiary filed monthly reports with its regional office, and the regions went through those reports with a fine-tooth comb. They wanted to be sure that each country was following its detailed operating plan to the letter. If there were any discrepancies, the regions demanded explanations and could prescribe corrective actions. Then all of the regions sent all of those country reports to the division's headquarters in New Jersey. There they were combed again, because headquarters wanted to be sure that every dollar, anywhere in the world, was spent where it would do the most good.

I liked interviewing him. He was intelligent, articulate, and not the least bit reluctant to let his biases show. If the rest were like him, I would have plenty of good information to work with. (They were, and I did.)

Next I met a manager in the Treasurer's office who dealt with foreign exchange. Schering would invest in its overseas operations by converting dollars into local currency (yen, for example, in Japan) and would take its profits back to the United States by converting the local currency into dollars. These transactions were his responsibility.

"You've got to understand," he said, "that no matter which way the exchange rates move, somebody wins and somebody loses. If the dollar goes down, for example, American tourists have to pay more for their overseas travel, and foreign companies that export to the U.S. may find that their products have become too expensive for their American customers to afford."

Then he noted that American companies with overseas operations, like Schering, don't really complain about a low dollar. The company's profit in, say, France might be no greater than the previous year's, but because the franc now bought more dollars, Schering took home more dollars home from France than it had the year before. A low dollar actually made it easier for the company to make money overseas.

He held up a copy of the *Wall Street Journal* and pointed to its Foreign Exchange table. "But if you read this every day, as I have to," he said, "you know that we are now on the other side of that cycle. Exchange rates fluctuate, and right now they are pushing the dollar higher. American tourists will love it, and so will foreign manufacturers. But for us, it means that back in France, we will have to run a whole lot faster just to stand still. Even if we earn more francs than we did last year, we can still wind up with fewer dollars coming home, because of the exchange rate."

Eventually, he told me, the dollar would go down again. That was inherent in a system of floating exchange rates. But that might take years, and in the meantime, the timing was very awkward for Schering. The company needed more profit remittances from its overseas subsidiaries, not less, because it had to make huge investments in new products.

"So you can see why we are under such pressure to increase profits," he said. "If we can't do that with profit remittances, we'll have to do it by cutting costs. And those four big, fat headquarters, with their well-paid staffs, make very tempting targets for the cost-cutters."

As I walked to my next appointment, I mulled over what the foreign exchange manager had said. The salaries and benefits for four hundred thirty jobs must surely add up to a lot of dollars. Those jobs were also the current home of four hundred thirty careers, and almost that many families were supported by those salaries. So the human relations implications of

Rick's problem were enormous. Still, he could not ignore the question of whether all of those jobs were necessary.

My next interview was with an executive who was outspokenly in favor of pulling all of the regional functions back to New Jersey.

"One of our most respected competitors," she told me, "has just closed down their regions and centralized everything in New York. They were absolutely right, and we should do the same."

"Why?" I asked.

In her view, the regions, and for that matter, the subsidiaries, too, existed for only one reason, which was to carry out the strategies of the division. She used an analogy to make her point. A region was "just an arm" of the division, and the subsidiaries were the "fingers." The "brain," she explained, was necessarily in the division's headquarters.

I must have raised an eyebrow at that, because she quickly added: "I am not implying that we are any smarter than the regional executives. Some of them are very able indeed. The point is that it is only here, where all of the fragmented information from all over the world finally comes together in one place, that one can see what is really going on, and what needs to be done."

"Then why were the regions created in the first place?" I asked.

She answered that there were various arguments one could make about the regions, both pro and con. Some people argued that if thirty-nine countries reported in to one headquarters, it would be swamped with more information, and more diversity, than it could handle. Also, it couldn't give each country the individualized attention that it needed.

"To all of that, my answer is: nonsense!" she said. "The truth is, all of that information reaches us already, and we are handling it just fine. The only problem is that it reaches us too late, and is often distorted, because it has been delayed and filtered by the regions."

She gestured toward a fax machine on a credenza behind her desk. "With modern telecommunication," she said, "I can be in instantaneous contact with any of our subsidiary managers. So who needs the regions? They actually make our task harder, not easier."

By the time I completed my interviews at the division headquarters, it was clear that sentiment there ran strongly in favor of centralizing its management. Some of the managers even spoke candidly about whether their arguments were not, in the final analysis, self-serving. For example:

It's not a question of whose ox gets gored. There are winners and losers in every reorganization. If I were a regional manager, I wouldn't want my job wiped out, and I'd probably find some good arguments for leaving it alone. But the real question is, what's best for the company? It seems perfectly obvious that under current conditions, three big regions are a luxury we can no longer afford.

LATIN AMERICAN HEADQUARTERS—MIAMI

On my way to three South American countries, I visited the Latin American regional headquarters in Miami. When I entered the office of the regional director, I noticed a document on his desk that was about as thick as a telephone directory. "What's that?" I asked.

"That's the latest monthly report from Brazil," he answered. "They just faxed it in overnight. Would you care to look at it?"

I flipped through it quickly. It consisted of page after page of numbers. I handed it back to him. "You get twelve of these a year?" I asked.

He did, and he also received twelve from each of the other countries in the region. But he pointed out that since Brazil was Schering's biggest operation in Latin America, their report was a bit thicker than the rest.

"It must take a lot of man-hours to put all those numbers together," I said.

He agreed and added that it also took a lot of time and talent for his staff to review those numbers, to figure out what they meant, and to decide whether anything had to be done about them.

"You've probably heard some people in New Jersey say that we tie up a lot of manpower," he said, "both here and in the subsidiaries, just to push numbers. But when you get out to the subsidiaries, you'll see why we have to do it this way."

He explained that Latin America could be very profitable for Schering, but only if the subsidiaries were run properly. Many decisions had to be made every day in each country, more than the general managers could make themselves. To compensate, Schering had installed an "operating plan" in each subsidiary, which prescribed in detail what ought to be done. The monthly reports showed how closely the plan had been followed.

"No general manager can make all of the decisions," I said. "But what about the managers who report to them? What about their staffs? Surely the general managers can delegate some of those decisions?"

"Ah, now you've put your finger on the real problem," said the regional director.

He explained that in many of the countries in the region, the kind of talent needed to run a business like Schering's was scarce. Properly trained accountants, properly trained technical people, let alone properly qualified managers, were all hard to find and very expensive when you could find them.

"And of course," he continued, "every other multinational company in that country faces the same problem. So we all bid against each other for the same people, which pushes the price up. And even if you manage to hire someone, another company will hire him away from you. In fact, in some countries we can't even find a general manager. So we send in a 'third-country national'—perhaps a Cuban refugee, or a Spaniard. It's a tough situation."

"Are you saying," I asked, "that because of the shortage of managerial talent in those countries, you have to make a lot of their decisions for them, here in Miami? And that to make sure they are following them, you make them file these detailed reports?"

"That's part of it," he answered. "The other part is that we can send in specialists on an 'as required' basis, to supplement their needs."

He had just received a call the previous day from a general manager who wanted to enlarge his factory but didn't have anyone locally who knew how to prepare a capital request. So the regional director had told him he'd fly someone in. In effect, the regional office functioned as a management consulting company that charged no fees, supporting the subsidiaries in any way that they needed. "They couldn't operate without our support," he told me.

I decided to play devil's advocate. "Why can't all of this analysis be done in New Jersey?" I asked. "Why can't they send a specialist out from New Jersey to write a capital request? Why do we need a region in Miami to do all of these things for the subsidiaries?"

"First of all," he said, "New Jersey does go through all of these numbers, after we do. So if you're looking for duplication, there it is. More to the point, though, you can't do much good for a subsidiary if you don't speak the language and don't know the culture. Each country has its own market, its own laws, its own politics, its own peculiarities. You could probably station your Latin American specialists in New Jersey, but why put them two and a half hours farther away from where they're needed?"

"And let me tell you something," he said, jabbing his finger for emphasis. "You can't just lump all of these countries together and say, 'Well, they're all Latin American, so they're all alike.' No way! Argentina, for example, is not the same as Mexico. They are just as different from each other as Australia is from Austria. Maybe more so."

The bottom line on why you need a regional headquarters, he empha-sized, is that it takes a lot of specialized knowledge to run all of those diverse businesses as they should be run. And the only way to get that knowledge is to go out to those countries often, to stay in constant touch with them, and, above all, to have a personal relationship with the people who really matter in each country.

I could tell that he had already fought this particular battle many times and was rather exasperated. He stood up and began pacing back and forth behind his desk.

"For God's sake!" he exclaimed. "Even New York is not the same as New Jersey. So what makes them think that Argentina, or Peru, or Venezuela is just like New Jersey? Don't they realize that it's a big world out there, and that every country has to be dealt with on its own terms? You need specialists for that! That's what a region is: a team of specialists. And the longer we work here, the more effective we become! So you can tell them for me, Mr. Consultant, that's why we've got to have regions!"

COLOMBIA

In Bogota, I met with the general manager, and later with those who reported directly to him. Some of them spoke English. For those who did not, I was provided with an interpreter. (The less said about my meager abilities in Spanish, the better.)

In this instance, the general manager was a Colombian himself, rather than a third-country national. He had a graduate degree from a U.S. university, and we had no difficulty understanding each other.

I began by asking him to tell me about the working relationship between Schering Colombiana and both the region and the division.

"With the region, it's OK," he said. "You met my boss in Miami. He's a nice guy, and I like him. But to tell you the truth, I also like the idea that my boss is a thousand miles away. That gives me some freedom. If I need him, all I have to do is pick up the telephone. I can talk to anybody on his staff directly, without asking permission. If something really important comes up, I can always jump on an airplane and be there in a few hours. So with the region, I would say that we get along all right."

But his relations with the division were more indefinite. He had been in New Jersey a few times and had the impression that to the division's staff, Colombia was just one small piece in a big jigsaw puzzle that they were constantly trying to fit together. He had to explain to them things that his boss already understood. They listened politely, but when he visited again, several months later, he had to explain all over again.

"It's better with my boss, frankly," he said. "He speaks Spanish. He's been here. He understands."

I had not yet met his staff, so I asked him to tell me about them.

"They're all right," he said. "They work pretty hard. They're honest. When I travel to other cities, things usually run all right without me. Most of them have been here a long time. I would say they're well trained."

"Would you say that any of them would be capable, one day, of replacing you, if that should be necessary?" I asked.

"Frankly, I don't think so," he said. "We hire them for what they do, not for their potential. When the time comes to replace me, Schering will probably look for a Colombian who is a university graduate and who has already been a successful manager in this country. If they can't find such a person, they will send in a Schering manager from another country."

"You mean you have no management succession plan?" I asked.

He replied that they had no need of one. It cost less not to have too many highly paid people in a subsidiary of this size. If he needed someone with specialized skills, he could always pick up a telephone and call Miami. His boss would send whomever he might need, for a week, two weeks, or even longer.

"So you rely on Miami; is that it?" I asked.

"That's right," he said. "They have excellent people in Miami. And for that reason, the people I have here are perfectly adequate for what needs to be done."

"When you send your monthly report to Miami," I asked, "how many of your employees are needed to prepare it?"

"I don't really know," he answered. "You can ask my personnel manager. But I would say that this task would involve about half of our administrative staff. Possibly more. I know that must sound like a lot, but you must remember that our wage costs are lower here than in the States."

EUROPEAN HEADQUARTERS

During the following week I found myself in Europe. I began with two days of interviews at the regional headquarters in Switzerland, after which I made a whirlwind trip through three other countries.

The regional director was a highly respected older gentleman who was regarded with a certain awe by everyone—even Rick Swaak. I found him to be serious, courtly, and correct. He spoke with the authority of someone who knew just about all there was to know about the pharmaceutical business in Europe, and no one doubted that he did. He took me to dinner at a lovely restaurant, discussed the wine list at some length, and made several excellent selections. Then he held his wine glass up to the light, and as he examined it he finally got down to business.

"Now, Herr Consultant," he said, "your job, as I understand it, is to be concerned with duplication between what the region does and what the division does. That danger would exist only if the division were to attempt to take upon itself an operating role, instead of limiting itself to a conceptual and planning role. That is the proper division of labor between them. If you think about it carefully, I believe you will see that no other arrangement makes sense."

"Why is that so?" I asked.

"Because," he said, "to make a plan is one thing, and to implement it is quite another thing."

He explained that Europe generated about 60 percent of the division's revenue, and to accomplish that in so many different countries was a full-time job that could only be done by experts. He had experts at his headquarters, for example, who knew the market in Greece or in Finland in a depth that would be impossible for someone who had not been close to these markets for years and years. These were the logical people to make sure that Schering's plan was implemented correctly in Greece, in Finland, and everywhere else. The division's headquarters in the United States, he stressed, simply did not have that capability.

"Also," he said, "we must not lose sight of some practical considerations. If my country general manager in, say, Italy wants to speak to me, he can do so at any time during the day, because we are in the same time zone. But if his boss was not here, but in the United States, there would be only two hours during the late afternoon when both of them would be in their office at the same time. And if he wants to see me, he can fly up and be back home that same evening. But if he wanted to see his boss in New Jersey, even for only an hour, at least two days would be wasted, just in traveling back and forth. Not to mention the problems with jet lag.

"For all of these reasons," he concluded, "I would suggest to you that there is really no practical alternative to the way in which the division is structured now. I am sure that after you reflect on all of this, you will agree."

I decided to get his reaction to some of the arguments I had heard in New Jersey. So I asked him about the exchange rate and how the division could generate the cash it needed after converting all those local currencies back into dollars.

"Ah, well," he said, "there is really nothing new about that, is there? Exchange rates fluctuate all the time. We have been through this many times before, and we will be through it again many times. It is not wise to overreact to these things. I assure you that one of these days, the dollar will turn down again, and then we will have the opposite problem. A company should not reorganize itself every time the dollar jumps up or falls down."

Then I asked him about the decision of the "respected competitor" to centralize its international operations.

"I have a great deal of respect for them myself," he said. "They have done so many things right in the past that it is difficult for me to believe that they could have made a big mistake this time. Of course, I do not know why they arrived at this decision, but I believe that they will regret it. In any case, they are responsible only for themselves, and we are responsible for Schering. They do not lead us, and we do not follow them."

SPAIN

The general manager of the Spanish subsidiary took me to dinner at what to him was the awkwardly early hour of 9:30 P.M. We had the restaurant to ourselves, and the local customers did not begin to arrive until we were about to leave. "Normally," he said, "I do not dine so early, but for your sake I will compromise. I realize that this is late for you."

I was famished. So I said, "As far as my stomach is concerned, this is a very convincing demonstration of cultural differences."

He laughed. "It's not just your stomach," he said. "There are many other differences. A more important one is the way we do business. In this country, for example, there are strict controls on the prices we can charge for our medicines. So most of my work is really with the government."

His first task with a new product was to get it approved. Then he had to justify the price that Schering wanted to charge. Since the bureaucrats nearly always insisted on lower prices, he was more or less constantly lobbying them.

"You have a much simpler system in your country," he told me. "You get the product approved by your FDA, and then the pricing is up to you."

I asked him whether American executives usually understood those differences.

"My answer may surprise you," he said. "It is not a question of nationality, but of where the executive is based. It is almost as if you adopt the point of view of the country where you live."

He told me that he had seen Europeans who were based in New Jersey for a few years who after a while seemed to forget the realities of doing business in their home countries and to adopt an American view. He had also seen Americans who had worked in Europe for a few years who began to see things as the Europeans did. When that happened, their European colleagues considered them to have become sophisticated, but their countrymen in the United States tended to criticize them for having changed their views.

"I think the common term for that is 'going native,' " I said. "Perhaps there is a fear that if an American stays in another country too long, he will lose the perspective he was sent there to impress upon the locals."

"Yes," said the general manager, "but as you can see, the same thing happens in both directions. You can bring a European to work in New Jersey, precisely to bring that European viewpoint to headquarters, but after a while it turns into an American viewpoint."

"Then what's the solution?" I asked.

"Solution?" he asked. "If you need a solution, there must also be a problem. But I don't see one."

For him, it was desirable to have managers who could see things from both a local point of view and a global point of view. In an international company like Schering, he felt, there would be an inevitable tension between the viewpoints of the corporation and the subsidiary. But he also felt that it would be a big mistake to let either of these triumph completely over the other.

"You have to keep them in balance," he told me. "But with balance, you also have tension. And is that not what management is all about, anyway? You manage the tension, to maintain the balance."

I asked whether he was more likely to maintain that balance in Spain if he had a boss in Switzerland, or if he had one in New Jersey. And in either case, would the nationality of the boss matter?

"Nationality? No, I don't think so," he said. "It is more a question of the individual, of personal strengths and weaknesses, than the color of his passport."

He conceded that it was more convenient to have his boss on his side of the Atlantic. But he also noted that the average European already knows more about Spain than the average American is ever likely to know.

"So if I could choose any boss," he said, "and put him anywhere, I would have to tell you that I would choose a European, and I would put him in Switzerland."

"So you favor the status quo?" I asked.

"I do," he answered. "Not because it is ideal, but because it works better than any of the alternatives."

HONG KONG

A week later, in Hong Kong, the various pieces of the puzzle began to fit together for me. The regional director was away, so I met with one of his deputies, an Englishman who had spent most of his adult life in the Orient, working for various pharmaceutical companies.

"Do you find these companies very different?" I asked. "Or are they all pretty much the same?"

"Both," he answered. "Of course, there are many similarities. But there are other ways in which each company has its own—shall I call it a 'signature'? In other words, its own characteristic way of doing things."

I asked whether Schering had a "signature."

"Oh, my, yes," he said. "All these bloody controls. All these armies of people putting numbers on paper, for other armies of people to ask questions about."

To illustrate his point, he spoke generally about a company he had worked for several years earlier. In that company, he said, if a manager in Hong Kong wanted to do something that he thought was right for Hong Kong, he didn't have to get an approval from on high.

"He just bloody well did it," he told me, "and put it in his monthly report that he had done so-and-so. He'd tell them why he did it, and what the result had been. I always felt that was the right way to run an international business."

I asked whether that company had armies of people putting numbers onto paper.

"Heavens, no," he answered. "We had our accounting people keeping track of things, of course. But not in such exhaustive detail."

I asked whether there was a danger that, absent strict controls, things could get out of hand? I raised the possibility that some subsidiaries might get their records so mixed up that they literally wouldn't know whether they were making money or losing it.

"I understand that did happen in a few countries," he said. "That was a long time ago, I think eight or ten years. I'm told that Schering's top management was horrified. They were absolutely determined not to let that happen again. But to tell you the truth, in our case at least, the cure has been worse than the disease."

"How?" I asked.

The problem was, he told me, that the company had clamped these controls on everyone, including subsidiaries where there was no problem with their record-keeping.

"Now, if you ask me," he said, "that's an expensive way to do business. You can go into any of these subsidiaries and look at their costs, and you'll see that a bloody big part of it is salaries paid to people who count every pill, so to speak."

By now I was playing devil's advocate, hearkening back to the arguments I'd heard in New Jersey. "But isn't it worth the cost," I asked, "to know exactly where you stand at all times? To know whether you're performing according to plan? And if you're not, knowing right away where the trouble is, and what has to be done?"

"It's a question, is it not," he answered, "of your tolerance for uncertainty? Some people can't sleep at night if there's the slightest chance that something, somewhere, isn't precisely as it should be."

But there were others, he told me, who figure that as long as they've taken reasonable steps to prevent catastrophes, they can sleep like a baby tonight, and deal next morning with anything that needs to be dealt with.

"Do you think that's why some other companies have shut down their regional offices, and pulled all of their management back to the United States?" I asked. "Is it because they can live with uncertainty?"

"I don't know the answer to that," he said. "I'm not privy to what other companies think and don't think. All I know is that when I worked in other companies, they each ran a very profitable business in a lot of countries, and without the kind of detailed controls we have here in Schering, and also without the costs of maintaining those controls."

MANILA

The final piece of the puzzle fell into place a few days later, in Manila, where I met with the country general manager and his staff. Ever since my interview in Hong Kong I had been trying to figure out how the other companies did it—how they ran profitable businesses that were often bigger than Schering's, but with proportionally fewer people in the management structure that controlled their subsidiaries.

The general manager was an American. I asked him whether he thought he could be replaced by a Filipino when his assignment there ended. "Are you grooming anyone?" I asked. "Do you have someone waiting in the wings?"

"I've got some bright young people," he said. "Probably one of them could do it, some day. But I think I'll be out of here before any of them are ready."

"But aren't expatriate managers like you rather expensive?" I asked.

He conceded the point. He was paid an American salary, of course, not a Filipino one. And he got various allowances for his family, including home leave. All that added up. But, he noted, the feeling in headquarters was that it was well worth it. "Our little subsidiary," he said, "makes a nice profit for Schering."

I asked about Schering's competitors. Were they also run by expatriates, like him?

"At the general manager level, yes," he replied. "Most of them have expatriates at the top."

Where I would begin to see differences, he told me, was at the next level down. He cited, for example, marketing managers or financial managers. Some of his competitors had rather strong people in those positions.

"I'd like to hire some for Schering," he said, "if I could. Those companies don't have to send for help from their regional office as often as we do. They're more self-sufficient than we are, in that respect."

NEW JERSEY, AGAIN

As soon as I got home, I made an appointment to see Rick Swaak. I wanted to get his views on the diagnosis that was beginning to form in my mind, before I presented my final report to him and the division's president a few days later.

"Try this, Rick," I said. "Schering's strategy has been to make it impossible for any subsidiary ever to lose control of its finances again. And it has an organization structure designed to make that strategy work. You've got three regional offices watching everything that happens in the subsidiaries, and a divisional office that watches everything in the regions. And it works just fine: The problem that caused it all has never recurred. But all that control comes at a cost, and by now the cost outweighs the benefits."

Rick was intrigued. "The cost?" he said. "Tell me more."

"All right," I answered. "The cost is a lot more than just the salaries of all the bean counters in the subsidiaries, and in the regions, and in New Jersey. A more damaging cost is that the system made the subsidiaries dependent on the regions."

I pointed out that, as a result of this system, many of the subsidiaries hadn't matured. That, in turn, was simply because the regions had made that unnecessary. By design, the subsidiaries used the regions as a crutch. And the regions loved that, because it made them indispensable.

Rick leaned forward. "Are you sure of that?" he asked. "This could be important. Can you prove it?"

"I think so," I answered. "You've got some strong subsidiaries, especially the larger ones, that pretty much run themselves, without much help from the regions. But elsewhere the business is run by third-country nationals or by Americans. And below them, with some exceptions, you've got less talented employees. I'm just telling you what your managers told me."

But that weakness in middle management, I told him, was what made expatriate country managers indispensable. Therefore, both they and the regions had a vested interest in maintaining the status quo.

I sensed that Rick could tell what I was driving at, but he urged me on. "Yes, yes, I can see that," he said, almost impatiently. "Please continue. This is very interesting."

Schering, I told him, had installed strong regional offices that did much of the decision making for the country organizations. It had appeared to me that the subsidiaries did whatever the regions told them to do. "You don't need a lot of managerial talent in the countries to do that," I said.

What happened next, I told him, was that the regions started providing expert help for problems that were too specialized for the subsidiaries to handle. That made the regions even more essential. The result was what is sometimes called a self-fulfilling prophecy. That is, the regions got stronger because the countries were weak, and the countries got weaker because they could lean on the regions.

"And what about the division headquarters?" asked Rick.

"I would say that the division has been using its airtight control system as a security blanket," I answered. "Some of your executives were so shocked by the nightmare of a few out-of-control subsidiaries that they'd pay any price to avoid having to go through that again."

Rick smiled and shook his head. "I have to tell you," he said, "that this is what I was afraid you'd find. But I needed an independent view, like yours."

"Rick," I said, "you're a human resources manager. I think that what you've got here is not a financial problem. That's just the symptom. At the bottom, what you've got is a human relations problem. You've got overprotected subsidiaries kept in perpetual adolescence by overly cautious executives who can't tolerate risks. Can you see that?"

Rick leaned back in his chair, put his hands behind his head, and thought for a moment. Then he smiled and explained that politically he had needed to be careful.

"Sometimes that's why we use consultants, you know," he said. "There are people who would say, 'You run human resources, so of course you see everything as a human resources problem.' But now you've arrived at this conclusion, too?"

"Look," I said, "don't get me wrong. I'm not against financial controls. Obviously, you've got to have them. But it's a question of degree. You cured the old disease, but now the cure is not only unnecessary: it's causing a new disease."

Rick asked about other companies that seemed to be running their businesses with fewer people in management in proportion to their sales. "What's the explanation for that?" he wanted to know.

"They don't need as many people as you do," I answered, "because they probably don't do as much controlling as you do. They seem to live with more risk than Schering does, but that doesn't bother them."

Those other companies were not daredevils, I explained. Rather, by their own standards, they were as prudent as they needed to be. The problem, as I saw it, was with Schering, not its competitors. "Schering," I said, "didn't want to let go of its security blanket."

Rick nodded. "But there's a reason for it, you know," he said. "It goes back to our previous crisis, when we had all of the control problems. Management here in the division had a low opinion of some of the people who let that happen in the subsidiaries. That's why they decided to control the subsidiaries from the regions. That's also why they decided to do any complicated work for them, by sending in specialists from the regions."

"Right," I said. "And that just perpetuated the problem, instead of solving it."

I told him that Schering was going to have to force those subsidiaries to grow up, to find their own professionals locally, and to develop their own managers. That would cost money, obviously, but I could tell him where to find a lot of it. It was in the salaries of all those people who pushed paper for those subsidiaries and all of the people in the regions who read those reports.

"If the subsidiaries acquire the talent to manage themselves," I said, "you wouldn't need big, expensive regions to baby-sit them."

Rick began to probe for weak spots in my argument, because he didn't want me to get shot down in the president's office. "And what about the favorite argument of our European director?" he asked. "Should not Greece report to someone who really understands Greece, and Finland to someone who really knows Finland? What about the need for knowing each country thoroughly?"

"He's right," I said. "But a Greek knows Greece better than any non-Greek, no matter how sophisticated he might be. And the same is true anywhere else, regardless of whether it's a Finn, or an Argentine, or a Thai."

If Schering concentrated on building real strength locally, I explained, it wouldn't need all of these highly paid specialists flying all over the world. A few would still be needed, of course, but only a handful, compared to what they had now.

Rick nodded. "Then you're going to recommend," he said, "that we shrink the regions back, drastically, and order the subsidiaries to make themselves self-sufficient?"

"I'm not going to recommend anything," I answered. "The decision is your president's responsibility, not mine."

I explained that I would simply lay out the pros and cons of each alternative, as I saw them. I admitted that the one that made the most sense to me, which I would favor were I in his shoes, would be to change the division's strategy.

"This division met the old challenges successfully," I told him. "But now it's got new challenges to deal with. I'll tell you what the textbooks say, Rick. Structure should follow strategy. Right now, your problem is that the two are disconnected."

"I'll be with you in the president's office," said Rick. "This is certainly going to be an interesting session. I'm looking forward to it."

REPORTING THE RESULTS

"Well," said the division president as Rick and I entered his office, "you've been to about a third of the countries where we do business, and you've spoken with about a fifth of our managers. What do you have to say?"

"Well, sir," I replied, "it seems to me that there are only five alternatives that make any sense at all. Sooner or later you're going to have to go with some version of one of them."

"Five?" he said. "Is one of them clearly better than the rest?"

I told him that all had their good sides and their bad sides. It was a classic trade-off. He would have to choose the one that he thought did the most good and the least harm.

"But there's no easy way out of this," I said. "They all do some kind of harm."

The president had been making that kind of decision ever since he got his job, so he knew all about trade-offs. "All right," he said, "let's begin. Which alternative do you want to talk about first?"

"Well, the easiest course would be to do nothing," I said. "Just live with the status quo."

Admittedly, that wasn't a very dramatic solution, but a lot of Schering executives had favored it. They had urged me to "Just let the storm blow over" and "Not make a mountain out of a molehill." They had noted, no doubt correctly, that sooner or later the dollar would have to decline again. Besides, they had argued, any other alternative was too risky.

"What do you see as the advantages of just doing nothing?" the president asked.

"First of all," I said, "the results are predictable. What you'd get is what you've got. With every other possibility, there could be surprises, and some of them could be nasty."

"Any other advantages?"

There were. I pointed out that there'd be no bloodshed. Nobody would have to be terminated or relocated. Families would not be uprooted. In brief, there'd be no turmoil.

"And the disadvantages?" he asked.

There were two, I told him. First, no one really knew when the monetary situation would correct itself. It could begin soon, or it might still be years away. Therefore, unless he was prepared to endure a big squeeze on the division's profits for a long time, just doing nothing made no sense.

The second problem was that the current situation was intolerable. The parent company needed to pump huge amounts of cash into product development. So he had to find a way to come up with not just more cash, but a lot more.

"Unfortunately," I said, "you can't do that the easy way, by just converting the same number of francs or deutschmarks into more dollars. You've got to find a way to earn more francs and more deutschmarks. Just sitting tight isn't going to do that."

The president nodded. I sensed that he had already reached the same conclusion, albeit reluctantly. He knew that whatever he did was going to cause pain. "All right," he said. "What's alternative number two?"

"That," I said, "would be to get out your pruning shears and look for every job, anywhere in the division, that doesn't need doing and just eliminate them all."

In every one of my interviews, I had asked the manager to tell me what the people who reported to them actually did. Even in a superficial look like that, I'd found nineteen jobs that were not strictly necessary. "And that," I added, "was the managers' opinion, not mine."

The president didn't like that alternative. He agreed that unnecessary jobs should be eliminated. But even if I had found only half of the dubious jobs that were really there, and assuming that I had taken a fair sample of the entire division, that would still work out to only a 1 percent cut, or possibly 1½ percent.

"That's just not enough," he told me. "We'll do it, of course, but it doesn't solve our problem. So you can go on to number three now, please."

"Number three, " I said, "is to do what most of the people here in headquarters want you to do. Shut down the regional offices and run the world out of New Jersey. And it's feasible. Some of your biggest competitors are doing it already."

"The advantages, as you see them?" he asked.

"First, a huge saving in personnel costs," I said. "We're talking about something like 170 jobs, most of them highly paid. That's about 2 percent of your people, but a lot more than 2 percent of your payroll. Put that together with cutting out those questionable jobs, and you're talking about real money."

The president was more accustomed to "talking about real money" than I was. "Maybe," he said. "But we're not going to save our way out of this situation. The problem is too big for that. We're going to have to earn our way out of it. What does this alternative do to bring home more money from overseas?"

That depended, I told him, on how strongly he believed in global marketing and global finance. Some leading academics had argued that with a few minor adjustments, a single marketing policy and a single financial policy could work well enough all over the world. If the theory applied to Schering, it would certainly get more out of such a one-world approach if it centralized everything in its New Jersey headquarters.

He sighed. "I've been struggling with that question for a long time," he said. "Should each country be treated as if it were one of a kind? Or should you overlook the differences and just concentrate on what they all have in common? The best answer I can give, after all these years, is that you treat them all the same whenever you can, and you treat them individually whenever you must.

"All right," he said, "please continue. What would be the disadvantages of shutting down the regions?"

There were two. The first was that in some cases, the legal, cultural, and marketing differences between countries could be crucial for foreign companies trying to do business there. The big danger in centralizing was that somebody in New Jersey might not know when a country really required individual treatment. That could result in a major blunder, damaging Schering's ability to continue earning a profit in that country.

"That's the standard argument," said the president. "I've heard it before. What's the second disadvantage?"

"Well," I said, "if you're going to cut away the support of the regional staffs, a lot of your subsidiaries are going to flounder. They're nowhere near being self-sufficient."

The president would have to recreate at least part of the regional staff in New Jersey, in order to provide that support. That, in turn, would cancel out much of the savings from shutting down the regions. It would also be a less convenient, costlier way to provide that support.

He nodded. "All right. What's number four?"

"That would be to go in the opposite direction," I said, "and do what a lot of the people in the regions say should be done. Beef up the regional staffs to where they don't need any more specialized support from headquarters."

In that case, the president could pretty much shut down New Jersey, with its two hundred sixty high-paid jobs. He would then create three new divisions to replace the present worldwide division, all of them reporting directly to the parent company, Schering-Plough Corporation. There would be one division running Europe, another for Latin America, and one more for Asia.

"Sounds radical to me," said the president.

"It's different, all right," I said. "But if it's true that you can maximize profits by treating each country as if it were special, this might work."

"I'll tell you what I don't like about it," he replied. "It's too uncertain. If it doesn't work, the results would be catastrophic. I'm paid to take intelligent risks. That one isn't intelligent. Let's go on to number five. I suspect that you've been softening me up for this one anyway, because I don't like any of your first four very much."

He was right, of course.

"Your present organization was designed to keep very close tabs on what the subsidiaries do," I said, "and to make sure that none of them get out of line. It works very well for that purpose. But in today's circumstances, with a squeeze on currency conversions and a parent company that's desperate for cash, maybe that should no longer be your main purpose."

I suggested that perhaps the division's main purpose, at this juncture, should be to make its subsidiaries more profitable. Possibly, if Schering were willing to pay for the best local talent, those full-time locals could solve the profit problem better, and faster, than the expatriates who flew in occasionally for a quick visit.

"Maybe," I said, "you could afford to buy the best talent in Venezuela, for example, by applying the savings from folding up the regional office in Miami. Maybe you could afford the best talent in Indonesia if you folded up your regional office in Hong Kong. Maybe Schering 'controlled' its way right into this problem. Maybe the way out is less control in New Jersey, and less in the regions, and more entrepreneurship out there in the subsidiaries."

The president smiled. "Maybe" was all he said.

WHAT SCHERING DID

For the next several days, the president agonized over the decision. He sounded out some of his closest advisers. Then he did what he had to do. He called in Rick Swaak and told him to prepare a detailed plan for reducing the regional offices to a mere handful of people and for investing in better-qualified people to work in the subsidiaries.

After Rick's plan was approved, he flew to each of the regional headquarters and had a face-to-face meeting with each person whose job was to be eliminated. Most found jobs with other pharmaceutical companies and did not have to relocate. Unfortunately, some of the executives whom Schering had hoped to retain did not like the new plan and left for other jobs in other companies. That was probably unavoidable. It was part of the cost of reorganizing.

Then a meeting was held in New York, to which about one hundred twenty-five managers were invited from all over the world. These were the key people whose cooperation would make or break Schering's new strategy. The president spoke to them about the importance of developing self-sufficiency in each country.

"We haven't lost interest in financial control," he told them. "But now the responsibility for control will be mainly in the subsidiaries. We'll keep tabs on you from headquarters, but you won't have two layers of control over you anymore. And you won't have a free consulting company in the region to get you out of trouble, either. You'll have to stay out of trouble yourselves. You all know what will happen if you can't. And by the way, we're going to reorganize headquarters, too. Under the new plan, we won't need nearly as many people there. All of the growth will be in the subsidiaries, where the money is made."

The changes reduced the four headquarters staffs by about 38 percent. More important than the savings, though, was a speed-up in decision-making, because the subsidiaries now had fewer bosses to convince. Profits did not improve immediately, because a lot of managers had to adjust to new ways of managing. But in time, Schering's international subsidiaries did resume their profit growth, despite adverse circumstances.

Rick Swaak still feels that Schering did what had to be done in time to save itself. Last time I saw him, I told him about Louis Sullivan, an American architect who had coined the phrase "form follows function."

"That was our problem too," said Rick. "An organization usually does what it is designed to do. Your problem is always to make sure that it is designed to do what really needs doing."

AFTERTHOUGHTS

One can make a case that many companies reorganize too infrequently, after too much hesitation, and with too little analysis of what is really at stake. Over the years, or more likely decades, a typical pattern runs something like this:

A company runs into a problem, gradually recognizes it as a threat, and devises a way to cope with it. The new method works and becomes enshrined in the company's folklore as "the strategy that saved us." So it is preserved. Over time, however, the problem that it solved recedes and is replaced by new problems that the old strategy does not solve.

Some managers recognize this new reality and argue for a new strategy. Initially, they are treated as heretics. Eventually, when a crisis looms, the company dumps the old strategy and adopts a new one. This starts the cycle all over again. It's quite natural, and the only thing wrong with it, usually, is the timing.

We usually face unwelcome new realities too slowly and end up reacting to them too suddenly. In this sense, companies are not much different from people who put off buying life insurance or who get around to preparing tax returns late in the afternoon of April 15.

Companies do not necessarily need consultants to sort these things out for them. Often, however, there is no one in the company whose views are not suspected of being self-serving. That is why most consultants are brought in as impartial outsiders, as I was, rather than as "gurus" possessed of unique skills or uncommon insights.

Chapter Four

U.S. Railway Association: Motivation Meets Politics

In order to explain how I found myself in a Senate hearing room at a meeting of the Joint Economic Committee, I'll have to take you through a four-part preamble about (1) the politics of Senator Long, (2) the economic theories of Louis Kelso, (3) the mechanics of Employee Stock Ownership Plans (commonly known as ESOPs), and (4) the bankruptcy of the eastern railroads. I'll be as brief as I can, and I promise you that once we get through all of that, the plot will thicken and the tension will rise. What was involved here, in my opinion, was nothing less than the mother of all government boondoggles, and how it was headed off.

THE SENATOR

During the incident I'll describe here, Russell Long, a Democrat from Louisiana, was chairman of the Senate Finance Committee. Arguably, that made him the third most powerful person on Capitol Hill. Because the chairman can block appropriations, other senators are usually willing to humor him when he wants a small favor. One of those small favors involved ESOPs, and that is why my path crossed the senator's, briefly but memorably.

Long was a populist, an advocate of breaks for the little guy. But he was also very much in favor of private enterprise. He found a way to reconcile those causes in the writings of Louis Kelso, a San Francisco lawyer who specialized in setting up ESOPs and was by far their number one booster. Kelso wrote a book, *Two Factor Theory: The Economics of Reality*, in which

hat employee ownership could eliminate unemployment, raise
, and prevent inflation.

leas were never taken seriously by mainstream economists.

d the book, I considered it wildly unrealistic. (Of course, I am
not an economist, but then, neither was Kelso.) However, the opinion that
mattered in this instance was neither his nor mine. It was Senator Long's,
and Kelso's ideas suited the senator just fine. And that, in a nutshell, is why
the episode recounted here happened, and why we have many more ESOPs
today than we did then.

KELSO'S THEORY

The essence of "two-factor theory" is that capital (in the form of tools,
equipment, and factories) has become far more important than labor in the
production of goods and services. As a result, said Kelso, the rewards for
production go disproportionately to the owners of capital, and that causes
workers to be alienated from their work. They then demand "more pay for
less work," which in turn leads to inflation. By making themselves overly
expensive, workers give employers an incentive to eliminate their jobs,
thus increasing unemployment.

The cure for all that, according to Kelso, was simply to give an ownership
interest in each company to its employees. Once they were possessed of
some shares, their "natural acquisitive instincts" would cause them to
change their attitude and do everything they could to increase the value
of their shares. Productivity would rise because they would now do more
work, not less. With unit costs declining, employers would not need to raise
prices. Therefore inflation would ease. Since employers would have no
incentive to lay off such highly productive workers, unemployment would
also decrease.

The theory itself is easily demolished.

First of all, the relative importance of capital and labor may be of
academic interest, but it has no *practical* importance. That's because each
is indispensable to the other. To raise their productivity above eighteenth-
century levels, workers obviously need technology. But capital is useless
without labor, and that point seems to have escaped Kelso altogether.
Nevertheless, until someone invents a machine that can build, maintain,
operate, and control itself, and then invent an improved new model of
itself, all by itself, machines will depend on people even more than people
depend on machines.

Second, although worker alienation is real enough, it's far from universal and is not primarily due to differences in income. People are turned off by their jobs when they think their work is boring and meaningless. That's a fixable problem. Income inequality is also real enough, but it's primarily a political problem that affects voters, not a motivational problem that affects workers' productivity.

"More pay for less work" is a common stereotype about union bargaining demands. But if you look at what's actually on the bargaining table, the demand is not so much for bigger paychecks as it is for steadier paychecks, and not so much for less work as for work that is less exhausting and less dangerous. In the real world, unions moderate their wage demands precisely because they have learned, the hard way, about the dangers of pricing their members out of the market.

Kelso claimed that workers had natural acquisitive instincts that would be ignited by owning some shares in the companies that employed them. But when you look for evidence of those "instincts," you find that they are barely detectable in most ordinary working people and are notable mainly among the already affluent. In fact, instances of people knowingly acting *against* their own financial interests, for the sake of a nonfinancial goal they consider more important, are by no means rare. (The strike at Caterpillar, described in Chapter 7, is a case in point.) There is no solid evidence that workers who own stock for which they have not paid will work any harder, or become more productive, than they were before they owned it.

As for inflation, Kelso overrated the relatively minor effects of pricing decisions and underrated the major effects of money supply and interest rates. Labor costs are only one of many factors that influence prices. In fact, prices often rise for reasons having nothing to do with labor costs, such as shortages of raw materials or increases in demand. When fuel oil prices go up in winter, it isn't because refinery workers have demanded more pay for less work.

Finally, what about unemployment? It is mainly cyclical, and there is no reason to believe that employee ownership will end the business cycle. When business booms, there are "help wanted" signs in every shop window, and when business sags, there are long lines in the offices of the unemployment commission. Jobs are also eliminated when the workers' skills can be replaced by technology, or when foreign workers can do them just as well for less pay; both reflect inadequate U.S. educational levels rather than rapacious pay demands.

So much for "two-factor theory," which I consider little more than a flimsy rationalization for promoting ESOPs. What matters, however, is that Senator Long bought it, because he had his own reasons for promoting employee ownership. He saw it as a way to build popular support for private enterprise. So he became an enthusiastic exponent of Kelso's theory, and the rest is history.

ESOPs

ESOPs had been around since 1956, but they didn't really catch on until Senator Long became their champion about twenty years later. At that time there were a few hundred of them at most, and most of those were in small companies. From his vantage point on the Finance Committee, Long saw a way to fix that. He wanted to give favorable tax treatment to ESOPs, thus giving companies a financial incentive for setting them up. Kelso enthusiastically agreed, and they became allies.

The rationale for ESOPs was spelled out by Kelso in a 1989 op–ed piece in the *New York Times* (January 29, 1989, section 3, page 3):

It is a financing device that gradually transforms labor workers into capital workers. It does this by making the corporation's credit available to the employees, who then use it to buy stock in the company. The company's reward from an ESOP—in addition to a motivated work force of worker–owners—is the low cost financing of its own capital needs.

In practice, this meant that a company would set up a trust for the purpose of acquiring shares of its stock for the benefit of its employees. The company also committed itself to funding that trust annually. Note that the money it spent for this purpose escaped taxation. This was Senator Long's indispensable contribution to the popularity of ESOPs.

With the company's commitment as collateral, the trust borrowed money, which it used to buy as many shares of stock from the company as the loan would pay for. As the company paid into the trust, the trust paid down the loan, and new loans were taken out to fund still more purchases of stock. The company then used the proceeds from these sales of its stock to buy capital equipment. You don't have to be an accountant to see that the company was able to use money for its own purposes that would ordinarily have been paid to the Internal Revenue Service.

The effect was to lower its cost of capital, relative to what it would have been had there been no ESOP. Senator Long reasoned that a competitive advantage like that would not escape the notice of corporate treasurers and that they (of all people!) would then become the most enthusiastic fans of employee ownership. He was right about that. And the government, by forgoing what would otherwise have been tax revenue, subsidized every company that adopted an ESOP. Whether that amounted to corporate welfare or employee welfare is still being debated.

THE GREAT TRAIN WRECK

The newly enacted tax advantages of ESOPs were not yet widely known when eight of the big eastern railroads went broke: the Penn Central, the Erie, the Reading, all of them. This calamity had several causes.

One was a crushing burden of labor costs. Before they went belly up, wages and benefits were consuming more than sixty cents of every dollar the railroads took in. That didn't leave much to spend on all of the other costs, and it led to some fancy bookkeeping. In order to keep showing a profit, the railroads continually pared down their maintenance budgets. Consequently the tracks and the rolling stock fell into disrepair, and that meant that trains were compelled to travel slowly, so that trucks gained a competitive advantage and grabbed market share from the railroads, and that loss reduced the railroads' revenues. And that, of course, just exacerbated all of the other problems.

Congress also did its share to do in the railroads. It refused to let them abandon unprofitable branch lines, because every unprofitable branch line was in some congressman's district. The railroad bankruptcy was, in sum, a grand and glorious fiasco, with plenty of blame to go around for all parties involved. The government had to do something to keep the railroads running, so it set up an agency under the Department of Transportation called the United States Railway Association (USRA), which was essentially a receiver of the bankrupt properties. USRA was authorized to run the railroads while Congress wrestled with the problem of what to do with them.

That's where Senator Long saw his chance to give ESOPs a big push forward. He wanted USRA to set up gigantic ESOPs and, in essence, turn over the ownership of the railroads to their employees. He argued that an industry that had been plagued by featherbedding, strikes, and excessive wage demands would benefit if workers had an incentive to make their companies profitable.

So the small favor he asked for, and got, from his Senate colleagues was a provision for an ESOP that would acquire ownership of the railroads on behalf of their employees. The Senate wrote that into its version of the legislation that mandated USRA into existence. However, the House of Representatives would have none of it. The congressmen considered it too risky to turn such a vital part of the economy over to a relatively untried, controversial, ill-understood device. So the House version of the bill was silent on ESOPs. In the conference committee that reconciled the two bills, the best deal the Senator could get was a provision that USRA would "consider the feasibility" of turning over the eastern railroads to an ESOP.

Russell Long was a senator for thirty-eight years, and he did not get to be chairman of the Finance Committee without being a very savvy politician. He must have known, even before he went to plead with the conference committee, that his proposal was dead in the water. But he had at least two incentives for pushing it anyway. The first was to publicize ESOPs, which most Americans (including senators and congressmen) had never heard of and which were regarded skeptically by many who had heard of them. He got his way with that one.

His second incentive for pushing the ESOP plan for the railroads was to be able to say, "I told you so," if whatever solution Congress approved for the railroads didn't work out. In that case, he could put the major part of a basic industry under an ESOP on his second try. That would have been a giant step toward the long-range goal of converting most of the ownership of American industry to ESOPs.

He never got that chance, because Congress created Conrail out of the bankrupt railroads and sold it off to private interests in 1987. Conrail never foundered, so what would have been the biggest ESOP ever was never created. Although Senator Long probably would not agree, I will argue here that this nonevent was one of the best things that ever happened to this country.

Anyway, it was all of these schemes and maneuvers that took me to Washington for my first and only encounter with Congress and the way it works. Quite a lot of taxpayers' money was spent, some of it on me, to placate Senator Long. Here's what happened.

VARIETIES OF EMPLOYEE OWNERSHIP

USRA had recruited a private-sector executive whom I'll call "J.T." (I have been unable to locate this gentleman. Rather than identify him without his approval, I will simply use his initials.) to deal with the management aspects of the bankrupt railroads. To carry out the congressional mandate on ESOPs, he decided to seek the opinion of three different consultants. He asked E. F. Hutton, the investment banker, to consider whether the railroads could raise the capital they needed if they were owned by an ESOP. He asked Towers, Perrin, Forster & Crosby, an employee benefits consulting firm, whether an ESOP would be compatible with the existing benefit plans in the eight railroads. And he asked me to estimate whether employee motivation and cooperation would improve if the railroads were owned by an ESOP.

I was given three months to complete the assignment and told that my travel budget would be extremely restricted. That turned out to be no real problem, because only one railroad—the Chicago & Northwestern—had an ownership pattern that even approximated an ESOP, and I was able to visit it. At that time, there were several dozen known ESOP companies scattered around the country, but all were very small and none was a railroad. Even if I had called on them, their relevance to my mission would have been questionable. So I didn't consider my limited travel budget to be a handicap.

This was when I began to learn that there are several varieties of employee ownership and to suspect that they might have different effects on motivation. The oldest and most widely used were profit-sharing plans. Next, in both age and usage, were employee stock purchase plans. The newest, and at the time the least widely used, were employee stock ownership plans. (There are now several varieties of ESOPs, but they differ mainly in their tax provisions, not in their treatment of employees.)

In a profit-sharing plan a portion of profits are set aside for distribution to employees, usually in amounts that are proportional to salaries. When the company does well, the employees get a nice bonus. When the company does poorly, employees get none. The bonus consists of cash, not stock. Ownership remains entirely with the stockholders. Employees as a group have no ownership rights. Of course, individual employees are free to buy their company's shares if they want to, but they seldom do.

In a stock purchase plan, employees can elect to have part of their pay (usually up to 10 percent) withheld, until the sum withheld is at least equal to the closing price of the company's stock on that payday, minus 15 percent. In other words, they buy their company's stock with their own money but receive a 15 percent discount. Legally, they own a piece of the company and have the same rights as other shareholders.

In an ESOP, each employee becomes the beneficiary of a trust that buys and owns company stock with the company's money, not with the employee's money. The trust, not the employee, votes the shares. When the employee retires or leaves, he or she is paid off in cash for the proportional value of the shares in their overall trust. If the ESOP has been in place for many years, the payoff could be substantial.

THE CHICAGO & NORTHWESTERN

The Chicago & Northwestern (C&NW) had a stock purchase program. It was "employee-owned" in the sense that only employees could own shares, but they had to buy them. Only 26 percent had elected to do so, and ownership was directly related to income. It was heaviest among managers and then fell off sharply among the crewmen and other lower-paid workers. The same pattern is found in other companies that offer stock purchase programs, with or without restrictions on ownership.

When employees buy their company's stock, they're not motivated by loyalty, but by a bargain. It's the discount that does it. Studies have shown that the participation rate is roughly double the discount rate. You could probably get at least 90 percent of the workers to buy in if the stock price were discounted by 50 percent. However, most companies would consider that much too steep a price to pay for employee ownership, and the rest of the stockholders would probably howl.

This was precisely why Senator Long favored making an outright gift of stock to all employees via an ESOP. There was no other feasible way to make every employee an owner.

The C&NW was a profitable railroad. It had been bought from its previous owners by a group of its own managers, who then offered all employees an opportunity to buy into it. From this I inferred that these were rather innovative managers. However, when I spoke to C&NW executives, it became clear that the ownership plan wasn't their only innovation.

For example, they had hired industrial psychologists to look after both managerial selection and employee morale. They had decentralized labor relations by assigning specialists to field positions, so labor–management disputes could be settled on the spot. They had sought out, and fired, heavy-handed foremen who had been repeatedly accused of unfairness. They had made it clear to unions and managers alike that they would insist on courtesy and dignity in all dealings with employees. In brief, they had upgraded and modernized *all* of their personnel operations.

As a management consultant, I like to see clients try lots of new ideas. My theory is that if you do enough good things, some of them will probably work. But as a psychologist, I am frustrated by the use of multiple methods, because it's impossible to tease out the effects of each. You can't say which of them is influencing the results, and which are simply getting a free ride on the backs of the others.

For example, the C&NW's profits were going up, in part because its labor costs (per dollar of revenue) had declined by almost 6 percent since it changed ownership. But it's impossible to say that employee ownership or any of the other measures taken by management caused the operating improvements. Even if they did, there's no way to figure out the relative contribution of each, unless you run a costly, inconvenient and disruptive experiment—and that is why psychologists are often reduced, as I was in this case, to making the most of whatever data was at hand.

SLIM PICKINGS IN THE LIBRARY

Most of what little information there was (at that time) on the effects of ESOPs was in the library, in various journals, magazines, and even newspaper articles. So off to the library I trudged. Now that there are many more ESOPs, there are also more studies available, but they are far from conclusive and have not substantially altered the opinions I formed when I first worked on this case. And what I found then gave no support to the possibility that Kelso and Long had hit upon a panacea.

Three findings showed up in most of the published reports: First, employee motivation was usually a secondary reason (at best) for starting an ESOP. The primary reason was to enable the original owners to sell out at a favorable price or to gain the tax advantages that had been pushed through by Senator Long. Management would probably have created these ESOPs anyway, even if they had anticipated no improvement at all in worker productivity.

Second, it seemed to take a long time for workers to understand the advantages they had gained under an ESOP. They received periodic statements showing their proportional share in the trust accumulation, as well as the financial reports issued to stockholders. But they didn't see any money until they retired, so they tended to think of the ESOP as a rather complicated supplement to their pension. In their own unsophisticated way, they had arrived at a fairly accurate assessment. ESOPs, to them, were just another benefit program, so their enthusiasm was understandably muted.

Third, no systematic attempt had been made to measure any of the overt markers of motivation, such as changes in effort, cooperation, or productivity. Aside from some vague reports about a "better feeling" or an "improved spirit," there wasn't much evidence that the ESOPs had made a tangible difference in work results. If there actually had been any such gains, they were subtle.

I also attempted to contact every ESOP company I could find and received replies from about a third of them. Most were smallish companies whose ESOPs had been in effect for only a few years. Most had good employee relationships before the ESOP, which remained unchanged after the ESOP. And most confirmed the three findings of my library survey.

ESOPs, I was told, were an effective way of cleaning up corporate balance sheets. They converted tax liabilities into assets, and that's why management liked them. But if they had any effect at all on employee performance, it was not obvious. And that's what made me increasingly dubious.

GOING IT ALONE

However, the issue I had to deal with was not whether ESOPs in general had, or ought to have, a positive effect on how well employees did their jobs. It was whether they would have such an effect in the particular case of the bankrupt eastern railroads. At the time, no organization that even approached the size of the combined railroads had used an ESOP. And railroads, of course, have their own peculiarities. They have multiple unions, their own labor law, their own retirement law, and their own contentious issues with management.

So it was clear that the available data had already carried me as far into this inquiry as it could, and that I would have to navigate the rest of the way by applying my judgment and experience as best I could to the particular situation of the railroads. So I decided to look for characteristics in the railroads, and in the ESOP planned for them, that had a known relationship to employee cooperation and effort. The ones I eventually focused on were the number of employees in a company, their age distribution, their financial sophistication, and the ratio of their ESOP stake to their other assets.

Large organizations have two well-known handicaps. Their internal communication is often difficult, and workers often see little or no connection between what they do and the company's profits. If explaining the intricacies of ESOPs to employees is hard to do right in smallish companies, it would be that much harder in a huge company. And if workers didn't perceive that today's extra effort would make them wealthier tomorrow, they would have no financial incentive to make that extra effort. So I concluded that ESOPs would probably fare better, at least as far as motivation was concerned, in companies that were a great deal smaller than Conrail.

A benefit that enhanced retirement could motivate older employees, if it had a large enough effect on their retirement income. The railroads had an unusually high concentration of senior employees (46 percent were over age fifty). However, the value of any employee's stake in an ESOP grew only as fast as the ESOP's stake in the company also grew. Eventually it could be worth a lot, but initially it wouldn't be worth much. So about half of Conrail's workers would have received only a minor pension improvement, if that, from an ESOP. As for the younger employees, it would be a long, long time before their additional benefits would amount to much.

There are at least three reasons why managers participate much more heavily in stock purchase plans than workers do. Their income is higher, so they can better afford the investment. They are in a better position actually to influence the value of the stock they buy. And perhaps most important of all, they are likely to have a better understanding of investment-related issues, such as price/earnings ratios. In the absence of that kind of sophistication, stock ownership is not especially attractive.

Kelso himself made a presentation on ESOPs to the leadership of the railroad unions, but he got a cool reception. The union officials had been hardened by years of confrontation with management and expected some kind of trick. They were suspicious of "getting something for nothing." That, plus the relative indifference of employees in the existing ESOP companies, did not bode well for ESOPs in the railroads.

Having seen Kelso in action, I can attest that he was as smooth and persuasive as they come. But more than just a good selling job was needed to convince the union leaders. Their problem was not so much with Kelso's salesmanship as with the product he was selling. They did not consider that owning a small piece of a big business would be a great bonanza for their members. The prospect of receiving free stock did not arouse their "acquisitive instincts" or convert them into instant entrepreneurs.

Yet the idea that ownership, all by itself, could work motivational magic was the fundamental premise of ESOPs. If that didn't happen—if there was no link between an unspecified amount of extra income in the indefinite future and the effort one was willing to expend today—then there was no basis for claiming that ESOPs would induce workers to work harder. And though I looked everywhere I could for incontrovertible evidence of such a link—not just vague feelings that morale had improved, but hard evidence of behavior change—I couldn't find it.

The effect of asset ownership on behavior is not well understood, but it seems to have a lot to do with proportions. For example, if you own a diversified portfolio and you are more heavily invested in certain assets than in others, you will probably be more attentive to your larger investments and less concerned about your smaller ones. Unless one of those smaller investments amounts to a certain minimum percentage of your total portfolio, it may actually be somewhat neglected.

The average working person's largest asset, by far, is the equity in his or her home. The older he is, the greater that equity is likely to be. So the key question with regard to the motivating power of an ESOP for railroad workers was, How long would it take for any worker's stake in an ESOP to become a significant fraction of his home equity? The answer for the older workers was clearly longer than they would actually work for the railroads. For the younger workers, it was many years.

(I've been deliberately vague here about what constitutes a "significant fraction," because that's one of the issues that research has not yet illuminated. Probably it varies from person to person as a function of total wealth, as well as other factors. In any case, it's probably substantial, perhaps on the order of at least 15 to 20 percent.)

The bottom line is that I found nothing in my contacts with ESOP companies, or my review of the available literature, or my analysis of the psychological factors involved in ESOPs to support the hope that they would solve the motivational problems of the bankrupt railroads. I must admit that in my heart of hearts, I was a bit disappointed. The idea of workplace democracy had a certain intuitive appeal, but I was being paid for my professional opinion, not my intuition. So I sat down with mixed feelings to write my report.

ESOPs TAKE THREE DIRECT HITS

When the three consultants submitted their reports to USRA, the results were devastating for Long and Kelso. Hutton concluded that an ESOP could not provide for the railroads' capital requirements. In TPF&C's opinion, ESOPs could not be readily integrated into the existing benefit plans of the eight bankrupt railroads. For my part, I concluded that once the novelty had worn off, there would be little change in the motivation of railroad workers under an ESOP, compared to the levels observed under shareholder ownership.

I took pains not to issue a blanket rejection of ESOPs under all circumstances. For me, the problem with Long's proposal was that under the specific circumstances of the eastern railroads, ESOPs would be operating in an unfavorable environment. In particular, the sheer number of employees involved, and the heavy concentrations of blue-collar workers approaching retirement age, reduced the chances that an ESOP could be effective. It would be like planting a palm tree in northern Maine, or a maple in southern Florida, and expecting it to flourish.

ESOPs, I argued, would be very unlikely to stimulate motivation in these particular railroads, although they might very well have that effect in other organizations with quite different characteristics. In effect, I was telling Long and Kelso to find a more promising place for their experiment in social engineering.

However, they had their own agenda. From their standpoint, the motivational power of ESOPs did not need to be proved, since it was obvious to anyone who accepted their premise: that ownership, no matter how minor or powerless, would work motivational miracles all by itself. I didn't buy into that premise, so from their standpoint I was just another of the many so-called experts out there who had to be refuted.

HEARINGS IN WASHINGTON

It was clear that USRA would conclude that ESOPs were not a feasible solution for the railroads. But the issue could still be milked for more publicity, not so much to educate the folks back home as to enlighten the Congress. So Senator Long arranged for the whole USRA–ESOP issue to be aired at a special two-day session of the Joint Economic Committee (JEC), the highest-level unit in the legislative branch dealing with economic issues. When the JEC spoke, Congress usually listened. Even if the hearings changed nothing (as was foreseeable), they would give ESOPs high-profile exposure among the congressmen and senators who would ultimately decide what to do about them.

J.T. was invited to appear before the committee to present USRA's conclusions. Not wanting to be sandbagged by Kelso, who was also invited, he took the precaution of asking me, as well as representatives of Hutton and TPF&C, to sit behind him as he testified. Our mission was to whisper rebuttals into his ear if Kelso or his cohorts threw any curve balls at him. As it happened, that was never necessary. But I spent two fascinating days in a Senate hearing room at taxpayer expense, all to humor the senior senator from Louisiana.

Hubert Humphrey chaired the first session. He was one of my icons, and I was awed. But on that occasion he was merely genial. He beamed at everyone. I suppose that when your main purpose is to do a favor for another Democratic senator, elaborate courtesy is the order of the day. He was clearly skeptical, but he contented himself with a gentle jab at the "hype" in some of the claims made for ESOPs:

Proponents who will be testifying today (have) said that widespread adoption of Employee Stock Ownership Plans will accomplish acceleration of economic growth to unprecedented levels, create legitimate full employment for two or three decades, and lay the foundation for arresting inflation. I must confess that these are some claims. Certainly no one since I have been chairing this committee has come before us with any program that promises that much.

Senator Javits of New York spoke next. As a Republican, he didn't have to be gentle. He began by saying that employee stock ownership could improve both the financial condition of American workers and the pro-ductivity of American industry, *if* it were properly developed. Nevertheless, he said,

With specific regard to the Kelso model, I am as yet unable to perceive how workers can suddenly become more productive upon the receipt of stock by an encumbered trust, in which they have no voting rights and no financial relationship.

I have no reason to believe that Senator Javits ever saw my report. Nevertheless, I was glad to hear his comments, because he and I were singing, as they say, from the same hymn book.

The opening assault on Kelso's ideas continued with a report from the Congressional Research Service, a branch of the Library of Congress. It noted that the rail unions had listened to a presentation of the Kelso plan and rejected it, partly because they were suspicious of getting something for nothing. The report continued:

For large corporations concerned about the morale of rank and file production workers, it seems doubtful that dispensing what would have to be a relatively few shares of stock to each employee would mean greater loyalty and higher produc-tivity. More important would be the company's record over the years in dealing with its employees.

I had made the same point in my report, when I recommended that the railroads follow the example of the C&NW, by making their personnel departments responsible for measuring and managing morale.

So far, Kelso and Long had been taking it on the chin, and the senator felt that the time had come to intervene. He asked for, and got, permission to question the next witness, an assistant secretary of the Treasury. He wanted to know whether any of the government's witnesses would present any of the anecdotal evidence that supported ESOPs. The assistant secretary replied that "the people in the Conrail analysis will be presenting material to the committee."

Long knew perfectly well that meant J.T. and his three henchmen, including the author of the by-then infamous "Gellerman Report." He was not happy to hear his pet project being lambasted, but he was also pressed for time, so he had to content himself with one remark:

May I say for the Conrail people, in case I am not here, that they indicate the same philosophy of the railroad executives that caused that firm to be bankrupted.

When J.T. testified, Kelso remained silent, apparently preferring not to risk return fire. He would get the floor soon enough. J.T. summarized the three consultants' reports and said that this was why USRA felt that ESOPs would be inappropriate for the railroads.

Finally it was Kelso's turn. He put many documents into the record, including his economic theories and a string of anecdotal reports on ESOP companies, none of which was at all similar to the railroads. It took a full twenty pages of the Committee's published minutes to record his denunciations of me for "bias against ESOPs," "not wanting to be bothered by the facts," and "misrepresenting two-factor economics"—among many equally unkind cuts. Evidently I had struck a nerve, and my best guess is that I did it with a comment in my report that ordinary workers "just don't think about money the same way that lawyers do."

Setting aside the tirades, the substance of Kelso's case against my report was that since I didn't buy into his theories I wasn't qualified to evaluate ESOPs. That's like saying that you have no basis for disagreeing with me unless you agree with me. It's a neat little device for those who don't want to consider the possibility that they might be wrong. But it's still a fallacy, neat or not.

Long and Kelso got their two-day hearing, which filled two volumes of the *Congressional Record*. But in the end, Congress had the good sense to realize that ESOPs were impractical for the railroads, so it set Conrail on its path toward eventual private ownership with no ESOPs attached. I remain convinced that in heading off Senator Long's proposal for the railroads, J.T. probably spared the nation one of the great governmental gaffes of all time.

Suppose that proposal *had* passed. Suppose, too, that a way had been found to deal with the problem of raising capital, and with the equally tricky problem of integrating an ESOP into the benefit plans of the various railroads. That still would have left the problem of reducing worker resistance to measures that would have improved their productivity.

If my analysis was right, the workers would have seen very little difference between their situation under an ESOP and their situation when the railroads were owned by stockholders. In that case, all of that new capital would have been utilized just as inefficiently as the old capital had been. There would have been little, if any, gain in productivity or profitability.

Financially, the railroads would still have been a basket case. And ESOPs themselves would have gotten a black eye and might not have been tried at all in situations where they had a better chance to succeed. The disaster, in other words, would have engulfed the railroads, the nation, and ESOPs themselves.

But Senator Long found other ways to bring ESOPs to America. After his run-in with USRA, he sponsored numerous bills that granted favorable tax treatment to companies that would set up ESOPs. The result is that they have proliferated. Some large, well-known companies, such as United Air Lines and Avis (until it was sold to outside investors in 1996), have resorted to ESOPs, along with many other companies that are less well known.

Russell Long retired from the Senate in 1987. Louis Kelso died in 1991. Today, the legacy of their collaboration includes more than ten thousand ESOP companies that employ, altogether, about eleven million people or roughly 8 percent of the U.S. labor force. Whether this form of employee ownership has been beneficial to those companies and those people, or to the country as a whole, is another question entirely.

ESOP EFFECTS

The problem that J.T. presented to me boiled down to this: If a railroad were owned by an ESOP, would the work-restricting practices of its unionized employees be diminished? My answer then was "probably not."

My answer today, with ESOPs now commonplace and with more research available, would be that an ESOP would have about the same effect on a railroad, or any other large, unionized company, as a somewhat enhanced pension plan. Ultimately, that's what an ESOP is, and no amount of propaganda about "employee ownership" can change that. Once the initial hoopla had settled down, the ESOP would probably have a mildly positive effect on the attitudes of some employees but would be unlikely to transform any entrenched habits or prejudices in the majority. In brief, there is nothing magical about an ESOP.

The extent of even that limited effect would depend on how close a given individual had come to retirement, and on how much the ESOP would actually improve his or her life after retirement. But that vast majority of employees who are not close to retirement would probably be indifferent. That's because most people give little thought to pensions until they are within a few years of having to live on them. That may be shortsighted, but that's the way people are.

The bottom line is that you can't buy beliefs. You can modify them, perhaps, by changing what people experience on the job. That is evidently what happened on the Chicago & Northwestern. But most people's beliefs are not for sale. That's why ESOPs *by themselves* are unlikely to break the grip of work-restricting groups on blue-collar workers.

I am not against ESOPs. At best they may help productivity somewhat, and at worst they don't hurt it. Under the right circumstances (i.e., in a small company with a history of good employee relations and an enlightened management) I might even recommend one.

But ESOPs should not have tax preferences. We don't offer them to companies that use much better-proven techniques for improving their productivity, such as employee participation in management decisions. Nor should we, because those companies get their rewards on their bottom lines. Research has yet to show that ESOPs, *without* the aid of other management techniques, have a positive motivational effect of their own. Even if that were to happen, we would still have to ask whether that improvement was worth its enormous cost. Are the taxpayers, who ultimately foot the bill for ESOPs, getting their full money's worth? I doubt it.

POSTSCRIPT: LESSONS IN PSYCHOLOGY, FROM TWO RAILROADS

The contrast between the executives I interviewed at the Chicago & Northwestern and the Penn Central was striking. Some of that, of course, was situational. The C&NW was doing well, and the Penn Central (which has since been merged into Conrail) wasn't. In such situations, it can be difficult to disentangle cause from effect.

Still, there were lessons to be learned from both.

The C&NW executives had hit upon one of life's subtlest truths: that the behavior we object to in those whom we criticize is often a reaction to our own behavior. We seldom realize the extent to which we provoke, or at least contribute to, the actions that we complain about in others.

In their soul-searching prior to taking over the railroad, these executives achieved a psychological breakthrough. They dared to face the possibility that the antagonism between them and the employees was at least partly the result of their own distorted vision. Managers, especially those who dealt directly with workers, had viewed the workers' attempts to assert their own importance as being, somehow, a challenge to their managerial masculinity. They responded with tough talk and threats. The employees, feeling challenged in much the same way, had responded in kind.

What both sides discovered, after one of them had made the break-through, was that when you stop provoking your enemy he may become merely your opponent, someone with whom you can sit down and work out a settlement. Did that breakthrough contribute to the success of the C&NW? No one can say for sure, but it would make good psychological sense if it did.

The Penn Central executives were understandably defensive. They felt they had been made scapegoats for the sins of others. So they fired back, and the interesting point is that everything they said in their own defense (about congressional interference, for example, or union intransigence) was true.

But they were also telling the truth selectively, emphasizing the parts that might exonerate them while ignoring or discounting those that left them open to criticism. Thus they illustrated a common psychological gambit in which we draw a phony moral distinction between a partial truth and an untruth. We all favor the truth to the extent that it also favors us, but it takes a certain largeness of mind to pursue truth into regions where we may be at fault. Most contentious issues are argued in this way; that is why we need arbitrators, judges, and even juries to settle them.

Chapter Five

Würth Fastener: How to Excel at Selling

I used to go to Brussels two or three times a year to present seminars for the European branch of the American Management Association. At one of those seminars I noticed a participant who focused intently on everything I said. He took careful notes and asked a series of penetrating questions. After a while it dawned on me that he was sizing me up.

At lunch on the second day, he carried his tray over to my table and asked to join me. "Of course," I said. "Please do."

He sat down and introduced himself. "My name is Reinhold Würth," he said. "I am managing director—what in America you would call the 'CEO'—of a company in Germany that distributes fasteners. These are the things that hold cars together: clips, screws, nuts, and bolts, things like that. We sell tools also, and other auto parts."

He handed me his card, which identified his company as Adolf Würth GmbH & Co. KG." I had never heard of it. He seemed to sense this and said, "Unfortunately, we are not yet very big in your country. Unless you are very interested in foreign cars, you may not have heard of us."

I confessed that I wasn't and that I hadn't.

He nodded. I was not the first American he had met who knew nothing of his firm. Still, it was a major company by almost any standard. It employed more than twelve thousand people in forty-three countries and had annual sales that were then approaching $2 billion. In North America, however, the company had not yet achieved the kind of market penetration that had made it such a success in Germany and elsewhere.

"Your products themselves are small," I said, "but I assume the market for them must be big."

It was, so big, in fact, that the Würth company concentrated on only part of it: the "after-market" of repair shops and the service departments of car dealerships. It did not focus on the "primary market," which consisted of the big auto manufacturers themselves.

"You know," he said, smiling, "in Germany we are a little bit car-crazy. We want our cars to run perfectly, so we are always taking them in to be fixed. And the repair shops use lots of fasteners."

"Sounds like a good business to be in," I said.

"In a way it is too good," he answered, "because it attracts a lot of competitors. So we have to fight them very aggressively."

Würth salesmen were sent out to virtually every repair shop and auto dealership in Germany. Their aim was to keep their customers' supply bins filled exclusively with Würth products. If the strategy was carried out effectively, competitors would encounter little demand for their products.

"That is aggressive," I agreed.

"You have to be realistic," said Reinhold Würth. "Our competitors are very tough. So we have to be always just a little bit tougher."

"But I take it you are successful," I said.

He smiled again. "We are successful at least in Germany, and some other countries also," he said. "But as I told you, we have a problem in your country. And this is why I want to talk to you."

"You sell fasteners in the States, too?" I asked.

He explained that in the United States, Würth salesmen called mainly on garages that serviced foreign cars. It was a highly specialized market. But because America herself was so large, that specialized market was enormous. So it was understandable that Mr. Würth wanted to improve his American business, and was vexed by the contrast between the achievements of his American subsidiary and those of its sister companies in Europe, especially Germany.

I asked what the problems were in the United States.

"That's what I want you to find out, Herr Doktor," he said.

Würth-USA had tried several top executives, he told me. All but the current one had been Americans themselves. The current general manager was English. He had done such a good job of running the company's British subsidiary that Reinhold Würth decided to see whether he could do as well on the other side of the Atlantic.

"Is it a management problem, then?" I asked.

"Of course, everyone has a theory," said Würth.

His was that the American subsidiary was not being sufficiently aggressive. But the manager on the scene in the United States had another explanation. He had concluded that the huge market was covered too thinly and that more salespeople should be put into the field to get more complete coverage. But Reinhold Würth told me that he was skeptical of this approach. He watched expenses very closely and had come to a different conclusion.

"Unless we can raise the average production of each salesman," he told me, "simply hiring more of them would not solve the problem. I could spend such money better in Germany. Our problem in America is what you call, I believe, 'productivity'—how much we can invoice from each salesman's work. I came to your seminar to hear what you have to say about this subject."

"Then you've heard me say that productivity depends on two things," I said, "methods and motivation. You've got to do the right things, but you've also got to do them persistently."

"Exactly," said Reinhold Würth. "Now we have to take your formula and see how it applies to our American business."

Würth-USA was still a small company, operating mainly on the East Coast, with about two dozen salesmen. Each of them was assigned to a territory in or near a major metropolitan area. Würth told me that if the American salesmen could penetrate their markets as well as their German counterparts did, he would gladly hire many more.

"But they don't," he said. "It is very frustrating to me to have such a tremendous opportunity, and also such a modest result."

"What did the previous general managers say about this?" I asked.

"They wanted instead to find better people," he answered. "So they kept trying one psychological testing company after another, hoping to find one that could tell them who would sell the most screws and the most clamps. Do you have any ideas about that?"

Because there were only two dozen salesmen, I told him, I should be able to spend a full day in the field with nearly all of them. Even though their average production might not be very high, there must be some who were better than the others. I would try to find out what the best salesmen were doing that was different. Then, instead of searching for stronger salesmen with tests, Würth-USA could teach its average salesmen to do what the better ones were already doing.

"And please tell me how much that would cost?" he asked.

My fees are based on the time it takes me to complete a project. So I began a quick mental calculation. But Reinhold Würth was calculating, too. At the instant I arrived at a figure, which I was about to tell him, he named precisely the same figure. It was uncanny. "I will pay you only that much," he said, "and not one dollar more."

I told him that he had a deal. He shook my hand and said, "Good. When you get back to the States, I want you to see our manager in New Jersey. Here is his telephone number. Meantime, I will also send him a fax, so he will expect you."

WÜRTH-USA

The American subsidiary had its headquarters next to its warehouse, not far from the docks. As containerized loads of Würth products arrived by ship from Germany, they were trucked straight to the warehouse. From there, as orders came in, they were shipped to customers all over the East Coast.

When I met the manager for the first time, he seemed a bit harried. "Whatever Reinhold wants me to do for you," he said, "I'll do. I'll answer your questions and arrange all of your meetings. But I also have a lot of other things to do. Can we be brief?"

I said, "Sure. Just tell me what you think this company needs."

He sighed. "I've been trying to convince Reinhold that things are different over here," he said. "They get away with some things in Germany that just wouldn't work in this country. Like 'selling packages.' That's what he means when he says he wants us to be 'more aggressive.'"

"What's 'selling packages'?" I asked.

He told me that if a German customer ordered a box of a particular item—say, a screw of a certain size—the salesman could decide the number of screws in that box. It could contain three hundred, five hundred, or even a thousand of that particular screw. If the customer objected, you would say that these screws are normally packed in these quantities and you would suggest that the customer should just pay for them now, because sooner or later they would need the extra screws anyway. He said that a lot of German customers would agree to that, since it was easier than returning the surplus items.

"In fact," he said, "a lot of them just pay for whatever you send and never object."

"That's how they keep the customer's bins filled up?" I asked.

"That's one way," he said. "I've told Reinhold that if we tried to do that to an American repair shop, our salesman would be thrown out the next time he walked in the door. Reinhold understands this, intellectually. He's been all over the world, so he knows that every country is different. But in his heart he wants to use the same methods everywhere."

Next, I asked him about performance differences between various salesmen. He told me that there was a wide range between the best and the worst. A few were very good, and he wished he could find more like them. The rest were mostly mediocre. They had reached what he called their "comfort level," earning enough to get by and unwilling or unable to exert themselves to earn more. He said he would replace those, if he could find more ambitious salespeople. And then there are always one or two who were not going to make it. Usually, he told me, the most hapless salesmen simply gave up before he had to fire them.

OBSERVING SALESMEN IN ACTION

The manager arranged for me to spend a full day in the field with each salesman. In the end, difficulties with my schedule or theirs prevented me from observing all of them, but I did ride with about 80 percent of the Würth-USA sales force.

I asked the manager *not* to tell me about their sales records in advance. I wanted to be open-minded about what I saw. After I'd seen them all, their records would be disclosed to me, and I could go through my notes to look for differences in their sales tactics.

I would meet each salesman at 7:00 A.M., usually in a coffee shop near his territory. Over breakfast, he would brief me on his plans for the day. Then we would get into his car and start calling on repair shops. I was always introduced to the owner rather vaguely, for example, "This is my friend; he's working with me today," or "I'm just showing him the ropes." During the call I just stood to one side, out of the way, and kept quiet.

I am sometimes asked whether having a third party present makes the sales call artificial. Of course it does, but probably not enough to matter. Once the salesmen got to work, both they and the owners usually ignored me. They both had more important things to do than worry about a silent stranger, and whatever novelty my presence may have had soon wore off.

I would concentrate on memorizing the details of the call: on who said what. As soon as we returned to the salesman's car, I would execute a quick "memory dump," scribbling down on a notepad everything I could remember about what had taken place. Then, as we drove on to the next customer, I would ask the salesman for his analysis of the call and write down what he said. By the end of the day, I had a full notebook and virtually a blow-by-blow account of one day in the life of that salesman.

Here are summaries of some of the sales calls that I observed, as I reconstructed them from those notes.

A BATTLE OF WILLS

It took a while for Andy, the salesman whom I accompanied that day, to find Lou, the owner of the first shop we called on. It turned out that Lou was in the back of the shop, under a car. When Andy greeted him, Lou called out, "All right, I'll be with you in a minute." But it was more like ten. Andy waited patiently, studying his price lists and the record of his last visit to Lou's shop.

Finally Lou emerged, wiping his hands. "What do you want?" he asked. I thought he was a bit grumpy.

"Hi, Lou, it's good to see you," said Andy. "You remember me, don't you? I'm Andy, from Würth Fastener."

"Yeah." Lou glanced back at the car he had been working on, a German import. "You want to know what's wrong with this country?" he suddenly asked. "I'll tell you."

He launched into an impromptu denunciation of people who bought cars they could not afford and then drove them ostentatiously all over town. Then when they brought them into his shop, they complained about the high cost of repairs and about all of the other bills they had to pay. So Lou had to accept partial payment and extend credit for the balance, in effect subsidizing his customers' extravagant lifestyles.

Andy listened sympathetically. "I sure hope you don't have too many customers like that one," he said. He had taken out his sample board and was about to steer the conversation toward the products he was selling. But Lou was just getting warmed up. He had a captive audience of two, neither of whom he had to pay. One of the mechanics walked behind Lou and winked knowingly at us. He seemed to know what his boss was up to. And ironically, Lou's next target was his employees.

"I also think the people in this country forgot what it's like to put in a full day's work," he expounded. "Did you ever see mechanics who didn't want to get their hands dirty?"

He complained that he often had to go searching for his employees, who could be out behind the shop smoking, or lingering in the rest room, or even on the telephone placing bets—anywhere, in other words, but where he said they belonged, which was under a car. And worst of all, he told us, he still had to pay exorbitant wages just to prevent them from going to work elsewhere.

Andy sympathized again, but Lou was warmed up now and was hardly listening to him. Next he denounced politicians, from the mayor to his congressman, whom he blamed for making it too easy for workers like his not to work and for nonpaying customers like his to stay out of debtor's prison.

Finally Andy managed to get a word in edgewise. "Lou," he said, "you've got to be running low on these clips by now, and I've got a special on them this month."

"Clips? I don't need no clips," said Lou.

"I've got a special on fan belts, then."

"Fan belts? Nah. Listen, I'm busy. I've got to go."

Andy began to plead. "Aw, come on, Lou, give me a break. Let's go through your bins, you and me together, and we'll see what you need. It won't take but a minute." He began to steer an obviously reluctant Lou toward the parts bins.

The sales call now turned into a battle of wills. Andy was determined not to leave without an order from Lou. He went doggedly through every item on his product list, but Lou wasn't buying. Instead, he proclaimed his obstinacy with body language, folding his arms across his chest. But in the end, it was Lou who finally blinked.

"All right," he sighed, "send me a box of those. Now get out of here. Can't you see I'm busy?" I had the distinct impression that Lou had placed his order mainly to get rid of Andy.

In all, Andy had spent close to half an hour in Lou's shop and emerged with perhaps a thirty-dollar order. His commission would be a scant reward for a half hour of hard work, and Würth wouldn't have much profit to show for it, either.

Afterward, as I mulled over that sales call, three aspects of it seemed important. First, Lou was mad at the world that morning. He had used Andy as a dumping ground for his frustrations. And Andy had let him do that.

Second, throughout the call, Lou had signaled his lack of interest in buying, beginning with keeping Andy waiting, and culminating in the lengthy standoff in front of the parts bins. Andy read those signals as a challenge to his pride, not as a warning to keep away.

Third, Andy had spent a great deal of his most precious resource—more than twenty-five minutes of it—with not much to show for it. He had done the wrong thing well. He had certainly been persistent, but he hadn't been productive. He had squandered his time on an unpromising prospect—time that he might have put to better use elsewhere.

ON WORDS AND DEEDS

From my discussions with Andy, I concluded that he was *capable* of making sound judgments, because what he said made sense. But I had also seen that all-too-familiar discontinuity between words and action. In this particular instance, he simply hadn't exercised an ability that he possessed. Andy's mismanagement of his call on Lou illustrates a common, highly practical question for psychologists: Why do smart people do dumb things?

It would take another book to answer that question, and someday a smarter psychologist than I am may write it. I will confine myself here to an analysis of Andy's unfortunate sales call, and what it may reveal about not just Andy, but human nature in general.

Clearly, possessing an ability is no guarantee that you will use it. If it were, the correlations between psychological test scores and job performance would be a lot higher. Therefore, something else must be present that can interfere with the exercise of that ability. That "something else" has no established name, but since it can, in effect, override the use of an ability we can call it the "veto factor."

In Andy's case, the veto factor was a misperception. He somehow managed to endow this sales call with a psychological importance that exceeded its business importance. To walk out empty-handed would have been a blow to his self-esteem, even if it would have been the smart thing to do. So emotion overcame reason. That is a glib way to put it, but it has the advantage of being concise. Freud himself wrote of an unfortunate rider who was obliged to guide his horse in the direction in which the horse wanted to go. We still don't know very much about how to predict or prevent that.

What we do know is that to be able to detach one's self from hopes and fears, to deal with one's situation rather than with one's demons, is a valuable skill. In some fortunate people, it has become a habit. For the rest of us, it is a daily struggle to prevent our private veto factors from depriving us of the full use of our abilities. Thus, writers like me are familiar with writer's block, actors know all about stage fright, and salespeople know about call reluctance. The settings differ but the effect is the same: something within you—your own private veto factor—prevents you from doing what you've done successfully in the past.

THE BETTER PART OF VALOR

Ed, another Würth salesman, entered a shop with me and asked for Harvey, the owner. "He's in his office, behind that door," said one of Harvey's mechanics.

Ed tapped on the partially open door, then peered inside. Harvey was on the telephone. Occasionally he held it away from his ear. He nodded at Ed and gestured with his hand to mimic a jaw that opened and closed rapidly.

Evidently his caller had more to say than Harvey wanted to hear. Now and then he said, "Right," or "Yup," into the mouthpiece. Ed grinned and pointed at the chairs in front of Harvey's desk, his arched eyebrows asking silently whether we could sit there. Harvey nodded, and we sat down.

Finally the call ended. Harvey hung up the telephone and rubbed his ear. "All that gabbing over a tune-up, would you believe?" he said. "Some people you can never satisfy."

"Hi, Harvey, good to see you," said Ed. "After all that grief, you deserve a break. Let me show you what I've got for you here."

But Harvey jumped to his feet and headed for the door. "I've got a lady waiting out in front who wants to talk to me," he said. "You can't keep a lady waiting, you know. I won't be but a minute."

Ed frowned, glanced at his watch, and began to drum his fingers on Harvey's desk. He waited about two minutes, stood up, and glanced out the door. Harvey had evidently completed his conversation with the lady, had returned to the shop, and was bending down beneath the hood of a car with one of his mechanics.

"All right, let's go," said Ed. He walked up to Harvey and said, "Harvey, I can see that you've got a lot to do today. Why don't I come back next week? What about nine o'clock Wednesday? Would that be better for you?"

Harvey emerged briefly from beneath the hood. He looked apologetic. "Yeah, I'm sorry. But that really would be better."

"OK, no problem, Harvey. Wednesday at nine. See you then."

We returned to Ed's car. "That's typical Harvey, to tell you the truth," he told me. "Nice guy, but he's got to be the most disorganized man in the world. Something is always interrupting him. The trick is to catch him early, before too many things start to happen, because that's when he starts getting confused."

Ed's call on Harvey had produced no revenue at all—thirty dollars less than Andy's call on Lou. But he had spent twenty minutes less in Harvey's shop than Andy had in Lou's, had seen the same poor prospects for a worthwhile sale, and had cut his losses early. Ed's philosophy was simple: "The more customers I see," he told me, "the more chances I have to sell something." Now he could take the time he had decided not to spend with the easily interruptible Harvey and invest it in other customers.

As if to prove his point, Ed's next call was a winner. Rocky, the owner, was a short, taciturn man who wasted no words. When Ed walked in, he looked up and asked, "You got any specials this time?"

"For you, I've always got specials, Rocky," said Ed, pulling out his list of discounted items. "You're going to love this." They went through the list together, and Rocky barked out his orders. "I'll take five dozen of these. Give me two dozen of those." He spoke so rapidly that Ed, who was entering the figures on his order sheet, had trouble keeping up with him.

After they had gone through the list of specials, Ed said, "What about something else, Rocky? You know my regular prices aren't so bad either, don't you?"

"No. My business is lousy. I buy only specials."

Ed pulled out a sample board of electronic items and pointed to a small part that I couldn't identify. He said, "Rocky, you know you've got to have these. In a shop like yours, with so many foreign cars, you can't run your business without them. Can I ship you some of these, too?"

"All right," said Rocky, conceding that Ed was right. "Give me whatever is your smallest order on that one." He reflected for a moment and then said, "Maybe I forgot something. What else have you got?" That was Rocky's way of acknowledging that Ed knew a lot about his business. When we walked out of Rocky's shop after a fifteen-minute call, Ed had written an eight-hundred-dollar order.

One does not make sweeping generalizations on the basis of a single example, or even a few. Instead, you look for trends that keep showing up in a large part of your sample. But as this study progressed, I gradually realized that what I had witnessed between Ed and Rocky was the rule, rather than the exception. Most big orders were placed in a few well-spent minutes, because the customer was ready to buy. To my surprise, there was almost an inverse relationship between the size of an order and the amount of time and effort that salesmen put into their calls.

That puzzled me. I was thrown off, at first, by the familiar stereotype about so-called salesmen who were really just passive order takers. Unlike aggressively persuasive salesmen (another stereotype), the order takers were not supposed to produce very much. But my data seemed to refute both stereotypes.

As I observed more salesmen making more sales calls, the explanation began to dawn on me. Very few of these sales calls were first-time visits; in most cases, the salesmen had seen the customer several times already. To a large extent, the impressions made in those earlier calls had a major influence on the outcome of the calls I was observing.

A SALESMAN'S THEORY OF INTERPERSONAL BEHAVIOR

Some of the salesmen I rode with expressed a fatalistic attitude toward their work, as if their relationship with any given customer, and their results on any given day, were somehow predestined. A salesman named Charley had a belief about his customers that seemed to be fairly typical:

You go in there on the first day, and the owner doesn't know who you are. You tell him you're from Würth, but most of them don't know one manufacturer from another. They can tell their salesmen apart, but not their products, or the companies they sell for. So you have to start making an impression on him, to show him you're his friend, and that he can work with you. And I'd say you've got about three, four, maybe five chances to do that.

After that, Charley was convinced, that particular customer already knew all he wanted to know about you. He had made up his mind about you, one way or another, and was unlikely to change it, ever. Charley likened this to the customer's having assigned you to a little mental box, somewhere inside his brain. If you're lucky, he said, you'd be put into his "good" box, in which case he would save most of his business for you. That would happen if the customer had decided he could trust you, and that you knew what you're talking about.

"And if you're not so lucky?" I asked.

"If you're not so lucky," said Charley, "you'll go into his 'maybe' box."

That would mean that you've got to call on that customer at just the right time to get any business at all, either because you happen to catch him in a happy mood or because he needs a part so badly that he can't wait for his favorite salesman.

"And if you're really unlucky," said Charley, "and you're in his 'bad' box, forget about it. He'll only talk to you to make sure the other salesmen aren't overcharging him. But no way will you get an order out of that customer."

"So the bottom line," he concluded, "is that you've got to get into enough 'good' boxes in your sales territory to make a living. If you don't, you'd be better off in another territory, or maybe selling something else for some other company."

I asked Charley whether it was really just luck that put a salesman into one "box" or another.

"That's part of it, for sure," he answered. "But you know, there's also this 'chemistry,' I guess you'd call it, that goes on between people."

"Chemistry" is a commonly used item for a hard-to-describe phenomenon. It's the almost instant comfort, or discomfort, that two strangers sometimes feel with each other the first time they meet. Most of the salesmen with whom I spoke about this were convinced not only that it existed, but also that it could be a huge advantage or an insuperable obstacle.

"Doesn't the salesman have any control over which box he goes into?"
I asked Charley.

"I suppose so," he answered. "You've got to read each customer and figure
out how he likes to be treated. They're all different, that way."

But in other ways, he noted, most garage owners had a lot in common.
They nearly always wanted to be sure that you knew about cars and about
their business. If they lacked confidence in your knowledge, they'd be
doubtful that you could be of any use to them.

And then Charley got to the most important lesson that his many years
on the road had taught him. "Most of all," he said, "they need to know if
they can trust you, that you're really going to do what you say you're going
to do, and that you're not going to feed them a line of bull."

As an amateur psychologist, Charley hadn't done badly at all. We tend
to make up our minds about each other quite early in our relationships, and
on the basis of rather pragmatic criteria. Is this person reliable, inoffensive,
and useful? (For "useful" you could also read "entertaining" or "interesting.") Those are the screens that we pass each other through. In the case
of a salesperson, getting through those screens successfully is more important than having a lot of clever sales tactics up one's sleeve.

From what Charley said, and from similar remarks by others, I concluded
that it was by no mere stroke of luck that Rocky was ready to buy from Ed
the moment he walked into his shop. Actually, Ed had done all of the real
selling long before I arrived on the scene. He had convinced Rocky during
his first few visits that he was knowledgeable and reliable, and he would
cater to Rocky's preference for visits that were brief and to the point. It was
precisely because Ed had impressed Rocky with his usefulness early on that
he could act as a "mere" taker of orders (big orders) during his subsequent
visits.

THE "EARLY OMEN" SYNDROME

The other fatalistic attitude among these salesmen was even more
revealing, because it seemed to divide those with the best record from the
rest. This concerned whether a given day was going to turn out well or
badly. They claimed that by nine thirty or ten o'clock, it was already clear
how the entire day would turn out. Customers were either in a welcoming
mood or in a foul mood. If the morning customers were glad to see you, you
would get big orders all day long. But if your first few calls ended badly, so
would the rest.

I asked a salesmen named Rick, who had voiced that theory, to explain
it. "Why do you think it happens?" I said.

"Who knows?" he answered. "Maybe I should read the horoscope in the newspapers. Whatever it is, I can tell you this: You can't fight it. That's just the way it is. I wake up in the morning, and I go out to find out what kind of a day is waiting out there for me. And once you know, there isn't much you can do to change it."

By his own estimate, the day I spent with Rick was a bad one. His first few calls were frustrating. After that, we began to stop for coffee between calls, and as the day wore on he kept finding ways to prolong those stops. He began driving to distant customers, instead of calling on nearby ones. We went to lunch early and got back on the road a bit late. He talked about many things but only talked about his job when I steered the conversation in that direction. Plainly, Rick was avoiding his job.

You might suspect that Rick was an unproductive salesman. Actually, he was an average salesman having a below-average day. After observing many other salesmen, I became convinced that for most of them, the first few calls of the day were not a foretaste of what awaited them, but a mood setter. If they went well, the salesman felt good, and his upbeat attitude was reflected in his sales tactics. If they went badly, he was discouraged. Some then became desperate (as Andy had), and others were reluctant to press on, as Rick had been. Either way, a bad beginning had the effect of tilting the salesman away from effective tactics and toward ineffective ones. The reluctance to face more rejection became, in effect, a "veto factor."

This "early omen" syndrome seemed to affect most Würth salesmen. But there were exceptions. Some of them simply kept a tight rein on their disappointment and went on to score big successes later in the day. These salesmen had better overall performance records, mostly because their results didn't vary much from day to day. But those who were susceptible to the outcomes of their first few calls usually had more erratic records: dismal on some days, spectacular on others, but overall mediocre.

From an emotional standpoint, selling is an especially tough way to make a living. Disappointment is *the* defining feature of the job. But at least some of Würth's salesmen knew how to manage it. So the key question was whether this ability to circumvent the veto factor was an inborn gift or a teachable skill. If it was the latter, some worthwhile productivity gains could be produced by anyone clever enough to teach it.

CONVERSATION FOCUS

As I went through my notes, another factor emerged that seemed to distinguish the more effective salesmen from the rest. This was simply what the salesman and the customer had talked about during most of their time

together. In a "focused" call, most of the conversation was on topics that
would be of little interest to anyone who was not in the automobile repair
business: part specifications, quantities, prices, and delivery dates.

But that, after all, was precisely what the salesman was there to discuss.
By keeping the conversation focused on what he was selling, he used both
his own time and the customer's efficiently. Of course, a certain amount of
small talk, joke sharing, and comments on the fortunes of local sports teams
was expected. But in a focused call, the salesman managed to keep these
digressions brief. After sharing a laugh or a reminiscence when the customer seemed to want that, he would return adroitly to the products on his
sample board. Focused calls usually produced substantial orders.

An unfocused call, on the other hand, consisted mainly of digressions.
Most of the conversation dealt with anything *but* auto parts. Some favorite
topics were the weather, current scandals, and criticisms of the managers
of local sports teams. Some unfocused calls were mainly monologues, such
as Lou's tirade with Andy. In most cases, however, the salesman participated
actively in discussing whatever the customer wanted to discuss. He was
trying to sell by pleasing the customer, instead of by discussing what he had
to sell. The tactic was usually ineffective.

These salesmen knew full well that a sales conversation should stay
focused on the products being sold. When I asked them for a self-appraisal
after unfocused calls, they usually were aware of what had gone wrong and
berated themselves for it. They had reverted to an ineffective tactic because
they felt that the customer was not taking them seriously, and they were
hoping to gain some small measure of sympathy, if not respect, that might
somehow become the basis for an order. One salesman, Jack, explained it
this way:

No matter what you are selling, you know, you're really only selling yourself. To
the customer, let's face it, a fastener is a fastener. One set is not much different from
another. So he's going to buy from the guy he likes, the guy he's glad to see, the guy
who brings a little sunshine into his life. So, if he wants to talk about some show
he saw on TV, that's fine with me.

"So you go in there to make him a little happier?" I asked. "Is that it?"
"I guess you could say that," said Jack. "Sooner or later, he's going to give
his business to his pals. And I want to be one of his pals."

For all his attempts to ingratiate himself, Jack was not an effective
salesman. He did not earn enough in commissions to pay back the advances
he had received from Würth. A few months after the day we spent together,
he left the company.

To understand why some sales tactics work and others don't, you have to look at the characteristics of the customers. The owners of auto repair shops are a varied lot, but those whose businesses survive tend to have certain features in common. They are tough-minded and shrewd and recognize that if they don't take care of their own interests, nobody else will. To them, a salesperson is someone from whom they will derive no income, but who makes a claim on their time.

Therefore, a salesman is someone to be used if he is useful now, kept hopeful if he might be useful later, exploited if he can provide some comic relief, or disposed of if he is none of the above. (If you detect an echo of Charley's "box" theory in this explanation, you are quite correct. And so was Charley.)

The point is that a salesman can focus a conversation on his products only if the customer lets him do that. With customers like these, that will happen only if they expect to benefit from it.

REPORTING RESULTS

When I reported to the manager, I told him that he could upgrade the overall productivity of his sales force by teaching them to do certain things that the best of them were already doing:

- Cut short their unpromising calls, but give customers who are buying all the time they want.
- Impress customers early with knowledge of their business, but also with their reliability and trustworthiness.
- Shrug off rejection, especially when it occurs early in the day.
- Keep the sales conversation focused on what they are selling.

The manager studied the list. "Some of this makes sense," he said, "like keeping the conversation focused, and using their time more intelligently. But some of it won't be so easy, like impressing the customers early on."

"Why is that?" I asked.

He was very candid. These were the people he could afford to hire, and they were mostly run-of-the-mill. They were willing to work for a straight commission of 20 percent. Some could do very well indeed on that. The rest were willing to try, mainly because they could not do better elsewhere.

"Now those are the economic facts of life," he said. "So, how many of those kinds of salesmen are going to make a positive initial impression on customers?"

I asked how new salesmen were trained.

"It's usually three days in a hotel room with the regional manager that hired them," he answered. "Mostly they go over the product list and the ordering procedures. After that, they're given a list of places to call on, and they're mostly on their own. The regional managers ride with them, as you did, from time to time. But mostly, they're busy hiring replacements for the ones that leave."

"I take it the regional managers were once successful salesmen themselves," I said. "Do you think they could teach some of these things, if you gave them more time? And perhaps you could call in some of your successful salesmen to help with the training?"

He studied the list. "I think so," he said. "But it would take a lot more time. I'd say, five or six times as much time. And it would cost a lot more. Still, it might be worth it."

"If it cut your turnover and increased your productivity, would it be worth it?" I asked.

"It might. It depends on the actual numbers, of course. But to spend that much on training would be a radical change, and I'd have to talk Reinhold into it. Also, to tell you the truth, I don't think that this is our biggest problem just now."

"Then what is?" I asked.

He explained that Würth-USA had been using a model that had been successful in Europe, where the area in any given country wasn't so vast and the competition was different. In the United States, his competition came from a swarm of small local suppliers. They could deliver tomorrow, because they were located close to the customer. Würth-USA was in New Jersey, trying to cover the whole East Coast. To keep his costs competitive, he couldn't afford air shipment, except for small orders. He viewed that as a severe competitive disadvantage.

"What's the answer?" I asked.

"More warehouses," he said. "Regionalize the company. But that would be a major decision, believe me. We're talking about really big money if we're going to do that. And Reinhold is cautious."

"Well," I said, "if you're asking Mr. Würth to make a major decision on training, maybe you can throw in a radical change in warehousing, too."

"I'm willing to try anything that I think can help this company," he said. "It's been one almighty struggle, I'll tell you. But I'm going to have to think this over. Your report makes sense, but I have to fit it into the overall picture."

OUTCOME

Several months later, Würth-USA introduced a six-week training program for newly recruited salesmen. The first week was spent at the New Jersey warehouse, learning the product line and being coached in sales tactics. The next week was spent in the field with a manager who coached the salesmen before and after each call. During the third and fifth weeks, salesmen were on their own, but their managers accompanied them again during the fourth and sixth weeks. In time, the turnover of salesmen declined, and their productivity improved.

A few years later, Mr. Würth felt sufficiently encouraged to expand his U.S. operations, although not as radically as he had suggested when we first met in Brussels. The company was reorganized into four units, each with its own warehouse and sales force. By then, the manager I had met had left to pursue his career in another industry, but the changes he had argued for had finally been implemented.

As for Würth-USA, its sales during the past ten years have increased by more than 600 percent. And Reinhold Würth, who is now chairman of the parent company's advisory board in Germany, still thinks it could do better.

Chapter Six

Baffling Behavior
in the Beverage Business

My old friend Jim invited me to lunch one day in a New York restaurant. He sipped his drink and told me, "Launching a new product is a crap shoot. In fact, it's a multimillion-dollar crap shoot."

Jim was a marketing executive with one of the big beverage companies and had invited me to lunch because he was looking for a competitive edge. (The company referred to in this chapter declined to be identified, citing "unflattering references" to some of its distributors. Jim is retired.) As I munched on a sandwich, Jim explained that there were three levels of the industry's distribution system. At the first level, bottlers would ship their products to wholesalers, who were the second level in the chain. In addition, they advertised their products to create demand in the retail stores, which were the third level.

"Sounds simple," I said.

"It is, but only up to a point," he answered. "We know pretty well what goes on between us and the wholesalers. But we don't know much about what goes on after that, between them and the retailers. And there are some trends in there that worry me."

"Trends?" I asked. "Can you give me an example?"

"I'll give you two examples," said Jim. "The first is those new product launches."

He explained that launching a new brand was one of the biggest expenses his company faced. But it had to be done, from time to time, because some old brands died out or because opportunities arose to increase market share. But every new brand was a high-stakes gamble. It cost a lot of money to find out whether the public would accept it or ignore it. His company would do the market research, design the packaging, and invest heavily in advertising.

"And then," said Jim, "we hold our breath and wait to see what's going to happen."

"How do the retailers fit into this?" I asked.

Jim shook his head. "That's the big problem," he said. "I just don't trust the feedback we get from them."

Initial product placements were nearly always good. A "placement" occurred when a product went onto a retailer's shelves. Sometimes the retailer would reorder, and it would appear that the brand was taking off. But the real test came much later. Thus, for several weeks, or even months, it wasn't clear whether to increase production to meet a burgeoning demand or just sit tight and hope.

"If we gear up," said Jim, "but the brand stops moving, we're stuck with the inventory, and the production cost, and a humongous advertising expense. But if we hold back, and the demand keeps up, we get backlogged. Then we've got a lot of unhappy customers switching to other brands. To me, as a marketing man, that's even worse."

What troubled Jim was that no one really understood what a retailer had in mind when he agreed to take a new product from the wholesaler, or why he ordered a particular quantity, or why he sometimes kept ordering the brand even though it wasn't really moving off his shelves. There were, of course, a lot of theories, but few if any had much factual support.

"So we sit here in New York," he continued, "making multimillion-dollar decisions, and all we've got to go on is some very dubious information. Frankly, I'm not sure the retailer knows what he's doing. And I'm not sure that the wholesaler knows what the retailer is doing, either.

"So that's my first example," he said. "Are you ready for the second?"

"OK," I said. "Tell me."

Jim explained that his industry was being affected by the same trend that was impacting the retail trade in general. Big, well-financed chains were beginning to crowd out the independent neighborhood stores. Typically, these were small shops that were owned by an individual entrepreneur or by a family. If that trend continued, he felt, it could change his industry drastically.

"You see," he said, "it's the old story of who needs who the most. When you've got a lot of retailers and a few bottlers, which is the way it has been, the retailers need the distillers more than the other way around. That's fine for us."

But he was concerned with what might happen if the ownership of the retail end of the distribution system were to become concentrated in a relatively small number of chains. Would they then attempt to bypass the wholesalers and cut their own deals with the bottlers? And would those deals be as favorable for bottlers as the ones they had now with the wholesalers?

"So what you want to know," I said, "is what is really going on in the distribution chain, beyond the point where you lose control of it: in other words, between the wholesaler and the retailer. Is that it?"

"That's it," said Jim. "And now, if you can give me a good answer to my next question, I'll pay for your lunch. If we were to ask you to go out and find some answers, how would you do it?"

I answered by describing my research technique. It was based on the principle that the best way to find the answer to any question about people was to talk to a lot of them. To a large extent, the reliability of your conclusions would depend on how many people were in your sample.

"It's a numbers game," I told him. "The more people you talk to, the more likely you are to find some good answers. Probably we ought to talk to a lot of retailers. And not just around New York. It's a big country, and sometimes you get regional differences."

Jim peered at me skeptically. "Talk to them? What do you mean?"

I recommended that we hold a series of focus groups. We'd bring together four or five retailers for a morning session, and another four or five in the afternoon. We'd tell them that this was going to be a bull session, a kind of informal discussion among themselves, except that we'd like to listen in. There'd be no "agenda." They could say whatever they wanted. The only restriction would be that it had to be connected in some way to their relations with wholesalers.

"That's our 'focus,' Jim," I said, "relations with wholesalers. And we'll never disclose their names, so the meeting will be 'off the record' in that sense. Once they get started, they usually keep talking for a good two or three hours."

"How do you know they're telling the truth?" he asked.

"Jim," I said, "that's not really a practical question. It's a philosophical question. For that matter, how do you know that I'm telling you the truth right now, or vice versa? But let's be practical. We can each believe what the other says, if it makes sense and doesn't contradict what we already know.

"And that, my friend," I continued, "is as close to 'the truth' as you and I are going to get in this life. What's more important, it's as close as we need to get. We can take that information, and work with it, and get results. What more do you want?"

Jim grinned. "I think we can work together," he said.

A few weeks later, Jim arranged for ninety retailers from nine different cities to meet with us. Jim sat in on the interviews, which I led. We both took notes. (I've developed a private shorthand that captures about 90 percent of what I want to record, verbatim. I prefer not to use recording devices, because too many people are inhibited by them.)

The study turned out to be a plus for everyone concerned. The company got the answers it needed, and I learned some things that surprised me about the psychology of running a retail business.

THE PERILS OF INSTANT PSYCHOANALYSIS

But first a few words are in order about the pitfalls of drawing sweeping conclusions from what you hear other people say. That's because you're about to see me read a lot into the remarks of ninety people who were, and still are, complete strangers to me.

You have to be cautious—very cautious—about what a stranger's comments may, or may not, "reveal" about the kind of person he or she may be. Before you start finding "meaning" in what they say, you have to make sure that you have more than just a few remarks to support your conclusions. In other words, you have to be certain that you've found a real pattern, and that the pattern is in that person's own words, and not just in some wild guess that you've concocted yourself, out of thin air.

You also have to limit your inferences to the context of those remarks. For example, even if you think you understand why a given retailer runs his store the way he does, that still doesn't tell you what kind of husband, father, or friend he might be. And finally, as Sigmund Freud himself would have warned you, you've got to be on guard against simply reading your own meanings into someone else's words—that is, of assuming that his or her mind works just like yours.

But having said all that: When someone makes several remarks in the course of a few hours, which taken together suggest a consistent view of his or her situation, you can justifiably draw the commonsense conclusion that, knowingly or otherwise, that person has revealed something genuine to you about his or her self.

And that's about as far into that person's psychology as we need to go. Knowing even this much about him, we can work with him more effectively than we could if we didn't know it. There is still, of course, a great deal about him that we don't know, but that is his business, not ours.

All of the remarks quoted here were drawn from a much larger set, precisely because they are fairly typical of the rest. To draw sensible conclusions about the way these retailers viewed their work, you would have to find some consistency in that larger set. I did.

WHAT WE HEARD

As we traveled around the country, three themes recurred in our focus groups, and each of them shed some light on Jim's two basic questions: What really went on between retailers and wholesalers? And how did that affect the retailers' buying decisions?

The first theme was how the retailers saw themselves. The second was how they saw the wholesalers. The third was the prices that they paid for their merchandise. Although all three are interrelated and were often presented together, I'll review them separately for the sake of clarity. What we heard in the focus groups led me to conclude that with respect to Jim's questions, there were really two kinds of retailers out there.

Of course, the real world isn't that simple: Seldom (if ever) does everyone fit neatly into either one set or another. In this case, however, a majority consistently expressed one of two attitudes with respect to how much control they had over their own business. Only a minority did not fit readily into either group. So to the extent that these retailers could be sorted out at all, it was in terms of how much leverage they felt they had on factors that determined how profitable, or unprofitable, their business would be.

TWO KINDS OF RETAILERS

Consider, for example, this initial set of four comments, which I have selected from a much larger set of similar remarks. Each is followed by my "instant analysis" of what it may mean. Then, to see an altogether different approach to the same topic, compare the first set with the second set, which follows immediately afterward. The topic of these remarks was the wholesaler's salesmen:

A good salesman should come in and shoot the bull with you for a while. You know, to get you in the right mood. Then he should ask you for your opinions about different things. You know, what do you think about this, and what do you think about that? And only then, when you're really in a good mood, should he get down to business.

This man is telling us that he wants to be treated as a person of consequence. He knows that he wields some power over the salesmen who call on him, because they desperately want the order that he can give or withhold. So he uses that power to extract something from the salesmen that he probably lacks in the rest of his life: deference.

The pandering salesmen probably make him feel, at least for the moment, that he amounts to something. Thus the sale, when it occurs, has little to do with business considerations, such as profitability or demand. It has a lot to do with massaging the retailer's tender ego. But after being buttered up as thoroughly as he seems to want, is this retailer likely to resist a plea to buy a product he might not be able to sell? Probably not.

In the same vein, consider this comment by another retailer:

I'm tired of doing favors for my salesmen. They come in and beg me to save their jobs for them. My customers don't do favors for me.

One wonders, of course, why this retailer continues to tolerate whining salesmen, if they are really as tiresome as he claims. In fact, most wholesalers will send another salesman if the retailer asks for one. At some level, this retailer would probably rather whine than do something decisive about the problem.

Here's another comment, by another retailer:

Like us, the wholesaler is trying to cut costs, so they don't pay enough to get good salesmen. They take people off the street who know nothing about the products. What can you expect from such people?

Is this retailer so resigned to the "inevitability" of poor service that he won't even try to get it improved? Is he really that helpless, that overwhelmed? The answer, if we were to base it on his behavior, rather than on what he tells us, is yes.

One more comment to illustrate the point that emerges from this first group:

Most of the salesmen who come in here are nice guys. You know, like everyone else, they are just trying to make a living, and they have families to support. But they are in a tough spot. Their boss threatens to fire them if they don't make their quotas. I would hate to be in that situation myself. So I do what I can to help. I order a few items that maybe I don't need, just to help the poor guy keep his head above water.

Was this fourth retailer a compassionate Good Samaritan, as he portrayed himself, or did he identify so closely with a fellow underdog that he could not defend his own interests? In everyday language, was he a sucker for a hard-luck story? Evidently so.

Taken together, remarks like these began to suggest that a subgroup of the retailers we interviewed had taken a passive, resigned approach to running their stores. This subgroup was more concerned with the psychological purpose of the store (which was to make them more comfortable) than with its economic purpose (which was to provide their customers with products they wanted at a price they would accept and still yield a profit). Given the highly competitive nature of their industry, they were also following a formula for failure, or at the most, marginal success.

Taken together, this first group of retailers was kind, tolerant, and forgiving. Most welcomed the visits of ineffectual salesmen as an opportunity for both to commiserate with each other. However, the underlying assumption of a free market is that all players will competently defend their own interests. Unfortunately, those otherwise admirable qualities do not provide much protection when the other players in the game (including the ineffectual salesmen) are prepared to victimize you if you let them. And the independent retailer is in exactly such a game.

For simplicity's sake, let's just refer to people who have this submissive outlook on life as "softhearted." Now, compare the remarks of the softhearted retailers with those of an altogether different type, whom we encountered in the same focus groups:

I am that salesman's customer. If he comes into my store, it should be to help me, and not just to do what his manager told him to do. He should come in and say to me, "Let's make money together." He should know my stock, and point out to me what is profitable to me, and what isn't. But only the best of them do that, and that's very few.

This retailer has some sensible things to say about the ways in which a wholesaler's salesman can earn his business. But he also wants us to believe that he has banished from his mind anything, such as compassion or sensitivity, that has no direct effect on his ability to make money.

He wants us to know that he is one tough customer, and that attempts at casual conversation will be futile. He probably learned long ago that the best defense is a good offense, and by now that defense is perhaps impenetrable. This is a man whom you take on his own terms if you want to have a relationship with him.

Here's a similar comment from yet another retailer:

Ninety percent of my clerks know more about these products than the average salesman who comes in here. I have yet to have a salesman come in here and ask me, "Jack, why don't you try this merchandising idea, or that one?"

He is saying that a salesman who merely goes in to collect orders is close to useless. To an enterprising wholesaler, who is more interested in building market share than in merely loading up the retailer's shelves, he is offering an invaluable clue. The more knowledgeable about the customer's business a salesperson is, the more welcome he or she will be in the customer's store. The quid pro quo in this case is not sympathy, but sales.

Here's a related comment, from another retailer:

I have no use for the kind of salesman who sticks his head in the door while I am talking to a customer, and calls out to me, "You don't need anything today, do you?"

He is saying that a salesman who doesn't contribute to the success of his store is irrelevant, and one who actually interferes with the store's purpose is worse than irrelevant: He is contemptible.

This second group of retailers was much more demanding of the sales representatives who called on them, whom they expected to make themselves useful by checking the inventory or advising them of impending price changes. A salesperson who was willing to earn his orders by providing services like these would usually do well with this type of retailer. On the other hand, those who went in solely to pick up an easy order were likely to leave with little to show for their scant efforts.

This second group of retailers was highly focused on the economic function of their stores. They were there to sell products to their customers and to make money, period. For them, the stores had no "psychological" function. To them, a store was simply a link in the distribution chain, from which a shrewd merchant could extract a profit. So an equally accurate label to pin on this group of retailers would be "hardheaded."

Here are some of the pet peeves of hardheaded retailers:

What ticks me off is a salesman who comes in here to introduce a bum item, and tries to sell it by telling me that it does fantastic in Los Angeles. Doesn't he know that I don't care how it does somewhere else? Tell me how it does here!

Believe it or not, some salesmen will actually come into my store, and stand around and talk to my clerks, or feed their face, instead of going up and down the aisles checking for what I need. Or they will take an open spot in the customer's parking area, instead of parking in the employees' area, where I park my own car.

But the same tactics were not only tolerated by softhearted retailers, but actually welcomed, as in these examples:

These salesmen are nice guys, but what can they do? The wholesaler controls their income to within a hundred dollars. They are supposed to bring me promotional materials, but they seldom do, because they don't have the time.

I try to be a nice fellow, and buy from a lot of salesmen that I've known for years. But I'm annoyed that even so, I now have to make larger purchases than I can afford in order to get discounts. I feel there should be some consideration for my past loyalty.

Recently we were pressured by a wholesaler to take a new brand that my father had turned down, because he thought it wouldn't sell. But their managers came down to our store, and they caught my father on the floor with customers. And he is such a nice man that he bought it. He felt he had to say "yes," because of his relationship with the managers.

The hardheaded retailer, however, is a much tougher customer:

I'll take it if I think I can make money. Otherwise, even if my customers ask for a new item that I don't carry, I'd rather sell them something I can move. Ninety percent of my customers will take another brand if I don't have what they want.

Four out of five new products fail. So if I say "no" to all of them, I'm right four times out of five, am I not?

From these and many similar remarks, I drew the conclusion that softhearted retailers made irrational buying decisions, not because of any lack of intelligence, but rather lack of self-respect. Those flawed decisions found their way into computer models that assumed, erroneously, that all retailers were hard-headed.

And therein lay a big part of Jim's problem. Much of the sales data going into his computers was unreliable. And as any computer specialist can tell you, if what goes into a computer is garbage, what comes out is going to be, to the same extent, garbage.

WHOLESALERS

The difference in perspective between softhearted and hardheaded retailers also affected their perception of wholesalers. The issue that arose here was about how much freedom of action retailers and wholesalers should have, relative to each other.

The softhearted retailer did not resent being dominated by the wholesaler, because that relieved him of a great deal of decision making. The wholesaler made the decisions and the retailer accepted them, whether he liked them or not, as if that were the wholesaler's prerogative.

But there was an unspoken understanding between them: The softhearted retailer, like a medieval serf, expected to be protected in exchange for his servility. He would take products from the wholesaler that were probably unsalable, and the wholesaler in turn would not cut off the retailer's supply of the products that he could sell.

So the softhearted retailer went along, passively or with only token grumbling, with whatever decisions about his store, his merchandise, and his money his patron, the wholesaler, made for him. Even when those decisions hurt him, the softhearted retailer did not blame his patron. On the contrary, he sympathized, because he felt that the wholesaler must surely be just as dominated by the bottlers as he was by the wholesaler:

I have no gripes about new products, really. If one doesn't sell, I can generally get rid of it at cost. But I don't know why the wholesaler takes some of these new brands. Often they are just trash. Still, I realize that they have no choice if they want to keep their bread-and-butter products.

When told of pressure from bottlers for more placements of weaker products, the softhearted retailer willingly sacrificed his own business interests to rescue his patron. But the consumer seldom rescued the compassionate retailer. So one ill-fated product after another found a permanent home for itself in the back of his store:

In this industry, market trends are dictated by the big bottlers. They tell the wholesalers how many cases of each product they have to get rid of, and I wind up with cases that I can't get rid of!

This man's world, it would seem, consists of puppeteers and puppets. He evidently considers himself one of the latter, dancing helplessly to the string pulling of others. His role in life, he seems to be telling us, is to make life more convenient and more profitable for those who are more powerful than he is, at whatever cost to him.

Another retailer had this to say:

The idea is supposed to be that the guys in the ivory tower on Madison Avenue can make no mistakes. So they say to the wholesalers, "To hell with the retailers, you just make them take it." And what the hell, I'm an easy mark. Who knows, maybe this one will sell.

In this way, the softhearted retailers absorbed what the market would not. To ensure that they would continue to receive favors from the wholesalers, they agreed to let their stores become a dumping ground for the bottlers' mistakes. They regarded exploitation as the price of security and considered that about as good a bargain as they were likely to get.

Contrast that attitude with these remarks, on the same subject, from hardheaded retailers in the same focus groups:

If I let him do it, the wholesaler would make me into a warehouse, which is his job, instead of a retail store, which is what I should be.

The wholesaler is going to have to learn to respond to demand, instead of thinking that he can manipulate it by just dumping products onto my shelves.

I make my living by giving my customers what they want, at a price they can afford. The wholesaler should make his living the same way, by giving me products I can sell, at a price that lets me make my profit. The wholesaler's job is to help me make money. If he won't do that, who needs him?

If the big bottlers try to manipulate the wholesaler, and get him to make a big push with some bum product, that's the wholesaler's problem, not mine. If he is stupid enough to go along with that, I won't bail him out.

To the hardheaded retailers, the wholesaler was a convenience, not a necessity—and a dispensable convenience at that. They felt that the proper function of a wholesaler in the distribution system was not to dominate, but to serve. When wholesalers would not play that role, hardheaded retailers were willing to circumvent them. They would band together to place large orders with more distant wholesalers, making up for the shipping costs with bigger volume discounts.

The effect of their resistance to products that would not sell was to hasten the demise of those products. And in what economists call an "efficient market," in which products that do not meet a demand do not survive, that is exactly what a retailer is supposed to do.

If hardheaded retailers should find themselves at a disadvantage under the existing "rules of the game," they would simply try to change the rules. To them, nothing is etched in stone, and there is nothing sacred about the status quo. They consider themselves sovereign, in the same sense that no nation is bound by any other nation's rules unless it consents to them.

To the softhearted retailer, that kind of audacity would be presumptuous. It also raises the frightening prospect that one might be responsible for one's own fate. That's a scary thought for anyone whose basic premise is that life is a raw deal and that its only saving grace is that its rawness wasn't his fault, or hers.

The two types of retailers also disagreed over whether wholesalers should have exclusive distribution rights for certain products. Not surprisingly, the hardheaded retailers were against it, because it decreased their bargaining power. They preferred being able to play wholesalers off against each other, so they could push their own costs down as far as possible. They wanted wholesalers to be exposed to the same competitive forces that they had to face with their own customers. That is to say, they were behaving exactly as economists assume that rational market players would behave.

But if the "price" was right, the softhearted retailers were willing to act against their own economic interest. In this case, they were willing to trade away some of their profits in exchange for comfort and convenience. They favored exclusive distribution for wholesalers, because that would minimize the number of decisions they had to make. It also minimized the number of competing salespeople whom they would have to risk disappointing. They were more interested in minimizing their headaches than in maximizing their profits.

Thus the softhearted retailers played havoc with those economic models that do not allow for the irrationality and eccentricity of real-world decision making. The hardheaded retailers did fit the economists' assumptions, but they clearly had enough softhearted colleagues to produce the forecasting problems that Jim was trying to solve.

PRICES

Back to the focus groups: Another topic that the retailers discussed at length was the prices they paid for their merchandise. Many suspected that the wholesalers were discriminating against small independent retailers like them, charging them higher prices in order to make up for much lower prices that they offered to the big chain stores. Softhearted retailers considered that just one more unfortunate fact of life, something that you simply have to endure, whether you like it or not. One of them put it this way:

I have the power in my store to give some people one price and other people another price, and I suppose the wholesaler has that power, too. That's just the way it is.

But the hardheaded retailers were not about to let themselves be victimized. Instead, they took charge of the situation:

I decide myself what prices I will pay. First, I check the ads. Then I decide what profit I want. Then I call the wholesaler and make my bid, just like at an auction. Very seldom do they turn me down, because I base my bid on the lowest competitive retail prices.

If I buy it, and then there's a discount announced afterward, I'll have the salesman's head. Either that, or the wholesaler will just have to back up and make an adjustment.

In some cities, the hardheaded retailers tried to unite with their soft-hearted colleagues into buying pools, for their mutual advantage. But those same colleagues often squabbled with each other, and this caused the pools to fall apart. Their dissension left them unable to fight together for better treatment from the wholesalers. One hardheaded retailer observed:

Our local retailer meetings are just a circus. They all have such low esteem for each other, and probably for themselves, as well. They just cut each other down, and complain about the wholesalers. The wholesaler probably figures that he can afford to wait them out, because they'll just collapse into their usual apathy. I hate to say it, but he's probably right.

But the hardheaded retailers also felt that the wholesalers were being shortsighted by favoring the chain stores:

It's in their self-interest to help us. Why can't the dummies see that? If the small independent is driven out, buying power will then be concentrated in the hands of a few chains, and any one of them could make or break a wholesaler. Their attitude is, we need them and they don't need us. But they're wrong.

It hurts all of us when another independent retailer closes his doors. That just increases the concentration of the market. That's bad for the wholesalers, too. If they had any sense, they would try to prevent small retailers from overbuying. That just plays into the hands of the big chains.

It appeared that in this industry, at least, Leo Durocher was right: Nice guys finished last. The softhearted retailers were easygoing, accommodating, agreeable—the quintessential nice guys. But they not only allowed themselves to be exploited: They even managed to thank their exploiters. What kept them in business was their willingness to tolerate low profits indefinitely. In brief, they were everyone else's doormat. They were the ultimate schlemiels.

For their part, the hardheaded retailers were not nearly as likable. They were tough-minded, driven—even pugnacious. But they ran profitable businesses, mainly because they were so consistently focused on that single, overriding goal. They were much more likely to survive, and even prosper, in the rough-and-tumble of retailing than their softhearted colleagues. They also provided a much more reliable source of feedback for executives like Jim, who have to decide whether or not to pump more money into new brands.

Jim's instinct was correct: Certain retailers were not running their businesses rationally. They were an important reason for the proliferation of more brands than the market would support, and for the prolonging of the inevitable demise of products that could not pay their own way. Now we knew what kinds of people were likely to run their businesses in a way that fed false signals into the distribution system.

THE MYTH OF THE SELF-RELIANT ENTREPRENEUR

The self-employed businessman or businesswoman has been almost as idealized in American mythology as the cowboy. We have romanticized people who run their own small businesses, assuming that they are rugged and self-sufficient. And indeed, many of them are.

But there are millions of people who are in business for themselves, and it should not be surprising that there are all kinds of individuals among them. So what I'm about to say applies only to a subgroup of entrepreneurs, not to entrepreneurs in general. No one knows for sure how many retailers fit the "softhearted" pattern. But to judge from this sample, there are probably enough of them to make a difference in this industry, and probably many others, as well.

Some retailers—perhaps most—open their own stores because they want to be their own boss. Others seek unlimited opportunities to enrich themselves. But for at least some of the others, running a small business is more of a refuge than an opportunity.

If the business happens to make them rich, that would be welcome—an added bonus. But even if it doesn't, the business can still serve its primary purpose of protecting them from things they want to avoid, like being employed in a company where they don't feel welcome, or being managed by someone they don't trust, or having to endure the disciplines of organizational life.

This next point may violate another of our cherished stereotypes about hardworking entrepreneurs. Some people really go into business for themselves because they are lazy. They like being their own boss mainly because they are more tolerant and less demanding of themselves than a corporate boss might be. And their businesses survive because (contrary to economic mythology) a marginal business can scrape by for a long time if its owner considers low profits to be a fair enough trade-off for low pressure.

For those with the right inclinations, running one's own barely profitable business has its compensations. No one tells you what to do. The business itself is usually steady and predictable, albeit not very lucrative. You have plenty of time for reading newspapers, watching television, or chatting idly with whoever happens to come in. It is rather like being semiretired on a modest pension, except that it lasts for most of your career. The prerequisite for tolerating such an existence is a sufficiently low level of self-esteem.

The life-style of those with less-than-heroic notions of who they are is to settle gratefully for whatever comes along with the least hassle and the least risk. Instead of trying to maximize their income, they maximize their comfort. Their position may be economically precarious, but it is psychologically stable. They may grumble a bit, as we all do, but they are nestled into a cozy niche on the margins of retailing, and they like it that way. They may not fit our preconceptions of what entrepreneurs are supposed to be like, but they don't get many ulcers—or give many, either.

WHAT MAKES THE DIFFERENCE?

A good concept to explain the differences between softhearted and hardheaded retailers is called "locus of control." What it boils down to is whether people feel that life is a participant sport, in which you call your own shots and take your chances with the outcomes, or a spectator sport, in which life just happens to you, and there isn't much you can do about it except hope for the best.

In real life, of course, most people are mixtures of both patterns. What matters is the mix itself: whether one is more likely, in a given situation, to act or be acted upon. For clarity's sake, I'll oversimplify and speak as if everyone fit one pattern or the other—to be active or passive—which is really the same simplification I made in classifying most of the retailers in this study as either hardheaded or softhearted.

In this case, the "softhearted" retailers seemed to have an "external" locus of control. To them, life was something you watched with mixed anticipation and dread, but that you couldn't really do much about. They were convinced that whatever was going to happen to them was going to happen, whether they liked it or not. Most of them had learned long ago to accept their fate philosophically. You hope for the best, but if the worst arrives instead you are not surprised.

People who feel that their lives are controlled by forces external to them will wait passively for events to unfold. To them, attempting to steer those events, other than through hopes and prayers, would be futile. So they spend their lives on the receiving end of other people's decisions, much as servants wait patiently for their masters to tell them what to do.

On the other hand, the hardheaded retailers seemed to have an "internal" locus of control. To them, life was a daily opportunity to outwit fate, not to mention their competitors. They reckoned that if they played the game cleverly, they could make their own luck. They could win wealth, independence, and, best of all, the exhilaration of being in control.

An analogy would be the marvelous feeling, however brief, while you are skiing, or surfing, or sailing, of making the world do what you want it to do. For a few moments, anyway, you can make the mountain or the wave or the lake take you where you want to be taken. The difference is that for someone with a strong internal locus of control, you can get that thrill at work as well as on vacation.

This sense of being able to run the world is like an opiate. People who have experienced it once want more. That's precisely why they tend to be very successful. Hardheaded retailers work at staying in control of their lives, and their businesses, for the same reason that softhearted retailers are content to leave their lives and their businesses in the hands of fate: They both like it that way.

This is an industry with thousands of independent retailers. Obviously, there are many kinds of people there. But if we could trust our sample, the industry attracted two kinds of people disproportionately to all other types, and those two were very different from each other.

Softhearted retailers, with their external locus of control, live at the mercy of forces they cannot cope with alone. So they seek protectors and try to appease them. That is why the wholesalers could so readily call the tune with this type of retailer. Keeping the wholesaler happy was a far more important consideration for the softhearted retailer than making or losing money on a particular order.

But hardheaded retailers, with their internal locus of control, had no need of protectors. On the contrary: They saw the wholesalers as threats to their independence and schemed to neutralize their power by playing them off against each other. To find themselves dependent on anyone, be it the wholesaler or anyone else, would be the ultimate indignity. They would do whatever they had to do to prevent that.

DOING SOMETHING ABOUT THE RESULTS

After our nine-city tour, Jim and I sat down to go over the results and decide what could be done about them.

I'm pretty sure that your sales information is being biased," I told him, "by certain retailers who make dumb decisions about new products. Eventually, reality catches up with them, and they have to stop buying. But until that happens you don't know whether they really know what their customers want, or if they just caved in to the wholesaler."

"That's what I suspected," said Jim.

"The problem is," I continued, "that we don't know how many retailers make bad buying decisions, or how often they make them, or who they are. And they're not going to just die off, because they are content with making marginal incomes. So they'll probably be with you for a long time."

"Well, those are the facts of life," said Jim. "But we can still make smarter decisions if we get better data. I want to call in our computer wizards and tell them to filter out the phony sales. Is there a way to do that?"

"The only practical way," I answered, "would be to go on past records. Look at your previous launches of new products. Any store that takes a big initial order and then fizzles out is suspect. A store that keeps buying consistently is probably reliable. It's the same logic they use to predict elections. Some counties usually go the way the whole state goes, so you use those counties to make your forecast."

"What can we tell the wholesalers?" asked Jim.

"First of all, tell them that they're not really holding their costs down when they hire the cheapest salesmen they can find. A sales rep who can't help a small retailer to survive is simply helping the chain stores to take over the market. The best way for them to protect their market share would be to spend a few extra bucks on better people."

"Amen," said Jim. "But they've also got to spend more money on training. Some of these salesmen walk in with nothing but an empty order book."

I agreed. "Make them understand," I said, "that training isn't an expense. It's an investment, because in the end, it pays off. If they want to move their product off the retailer's shelves, to make room for what's sitting in their warehouse, they have to give that retailer the information he needs to sell it. Only a well-trained sales rep can do that."

Jim grinned. "You're preaching to the choir, you know," he said.

"Yes, but you won't be," I answered. "You've got a bunch of skeptics out there who would rather save money than make money."

"Well, it's my job to change their minds," he said. "And here's something else I'm going to tell them. They should let their salesmen swap customers. All of them have customers they can't do much with, and sometimes it's just because the two of them just don't hit it off. They've got nothing to lose by switching, and sometimes that will solve the problem."

"I'll bet it will, some of the time," I said.

A big company does a lot of things to improve its performance. Consequently, when the results actually do get better, it's hard to say which action, or combination of actions, did the trick.

Nevertheless, in the first few years after this study was completed, I would ask Jim, whenever I ran into him, about what he had done as a result of the study, and what had happened afterward. Of course, he wasn't entirely at liberty to answer. Instead he would just smile and give me a knowing wink. That was his off-the-record way of telling me that he was still happy with what we had done.

Chapter 7

Caterpillar: The Anatomy of a Strike

A Caterpillar executive whom I will call Stan called me in to discuss the devastating strike the company had experienced at its plant in Joliet, Illinois. ("Stan" is a pseudonym for a Caterpillar executive, now retired, who prefers to remain anonymous.) Five thousand workers had stayed out for three months. Most strikes are much shorter and much less disastrous. But when the Joliet strike ended, it was unclear why it had lasted so long or what could be done to prevent a recurrence.

"Everybody in Joliet is still shell-shocked," he told me. "Nobody expected the strike to go on like that, or to do so much damage. The company took a big hit on its bottom line. And the union did, too. Their local is just about broke."

Stan knew that I was not an expert on labor relations, so it wasn't clear why he thought I could be helpful. I had read about the strike in the newspapers, and that was all I knew about it.

Stan explained that as he saw it, the strike had less to do with collective bargaining than with underlying attitudes. The proof, he said was that when the union finally settled, the difference between the contract they finally accepted and the one they had rejected when the strike began was minimal.

"They got a few extra cents per hour," he said, "and some upgrades in their cost-of-living coverage. Nobody in their right mind gives up three month's wages for that."

The main reason why Stan decided to talk to me was that no one on either side had a convincing explanation for why the strike had lasted so abnormally long. There were lots of theories, of course. At corporate headquarters in Peoria, he told me, executives tended to blame the management at Joliet. But in Joliet itself, managers claimed that the real problem had been a factional dispute within the union. The union leadership was at a loss to explain what had happened. They had tried to settle the strike several times to avoid draining their treasury. But each time they tried, the rank and file had voted them down.

"So the real question," I said, "was not what started the strike but why it continued for so long?"

"That's right," said Stan.

He explained that short strikes, lasting only a week or so, were fairly common in the industry. Some managers considered these almost inevitable, because the union had to convince its own members that they had gotten the best possible deal. When these strikes were called, management would typically let them run for a few days and then "sweeten" its offer, thereby making the union look good to its members. The strike would usually end in short order.

"But that didn't happen this time," I said.

"No, it sure didn't," said Stan. "We thought that this would be just another token strike. But they turned down our 'sweetened' offer. Pretty soon, both sides were dug in. And then it became a 'matter of principle' on both sides."

"Why did it finally end?" I asked.

"There were a lot of theories about that, too," he said. "I think that by then, nearly everyone on both sides was simply sick of the strike. They were exhausted."

I asked Stan how I could help.

"If I'm right," he said, "this strike had more to do with people's feelings than with the issues on the bargaining table. It just doesn't make sense that we couldn't settle this with the union a lot sooner. So if you're interested, I'll try to convince my boss that someone like you ought to go in there and figure out for us what really happened."

"But what about the union?" I asked. "Do you think they'd cooperate?"

Stan thought they just might. Their leadership was looking for answers, too. For their own political reasons, they couldn't risk the appearance of having grown too close to management. Stan felt we would have to offer them some kind of quid pro quo to gain their cooperation.

"I'd like to try it," I told him.

"Then tell me how you'd handle it," he said.

Five thousand people were clearly too many for one psychologist to deal with. I told Stan that I would have to put together a team. I knew some professors who could help, and they could bring along some graduate students to help with the interviewing. I figured that we'd have to talk with about five hundred people, and that would probably take us about a week. Then we could put together a questionnaire that could be given to all five thousand. We'd need access to a powerful computer to analyze the results.

"And when you have done all of that, what are you going to have?" he asked.

I told Stan that I didn't know. But if, as he seemed to think, the real reasons why the workers had stayed out so long lay somewhere in their attitudes and perceptions, rather than in the issues on the bargaining table, we could probably find them.

Stan reflected for a moment. "Caterpillar is a conservative company," he said. "We haven't done much of this sort of thing before. Let me think about it, though. You'll hear from me if anything develops."

A few weeks later, Stan had cleared the project with his superiors, and shortly afterward I was in Joliet with nine other psychologists to begin interviewing employees in the huge Caterpillar factory. Our mission was to sort through all of the conflicting opinions and bruised feelings on both sides to try to pinpoint the most likely reasons why so many workers had held out so stubbornly for so long. Then, we hoped, management and the union could look for ways to neutralize those reasons during the three years before the next contract had to be negotiated.

INSIDE THE PLANT

One of the foreman showed me around the Joliet plant. It was easily the size of several football fields. Inside, on any one shift, as many as two thousand people were cutting and welding steel to make parts that eventually went into bulldozers and other heavy equipment. It was a bustling, noisy place.

Heavy pieces of steel were moved about by overhead cranes. As one passed above us, I instinctively ducked, and the foreman laughed. "You'll get used to it," he said. I was glad he had insisted that I wear a hard hat. Potentially, I thought, any of those cranes could become a guillotine. "What keeps that steel from falling?" I asked.

"Magnets," he said. "Big, powerful magnets. As long as the cables don't fray, those cranes aren't going to drop a thing."

"Do the cables fray?" I asked.

He explained that if you put enough strain on a cable, it would eventually fray. But he also said that management would not let that happen. Foremen could tell when a cable began to weaken and would take that crane out of service so the cables could be replaced.

Then we entered one of the welding areas. Joliet was then one of the largest welding shops in the world, with hundreds of welders at work at any given time. The men worked behind protective shields that prevented the sparks from flying. They wore metal masks and heavy gloves. When they used their torches, thick smoke roiled out, obscuring everything. The welders worked by the light of the flames at the tips of their torches. I must admit that the welding shop was the closest approximation of Dante's *Inferno* I had ever seen.

I was being introduced to the blue-collar world and was experiencing a bit of culture shock in the process. My tour was a useful introduction to the world that the Caterpillar strikers worked in. But I knew that I would have to learn to see that world as they did, through their eyes, so to speak, rather than through the eyes of the privileged white-collar professional that I actually was. And I knew that the best way to do that was to listen as intently as I could to as many of them as I could meet.

Our next stop was a small conference room that was used for union negotiations. Inside were the plant's labor relations manager and some of the officers of the union local that had called the strike. Without their cooperation, my project would be futile. Before Caterpillar confirmed my assignment, it had tried to make sure that the union would not obstruct the survey. The union had agreed, but only *in principle*. They wanted to meet me before giving their final agreement. They were not about to take management's word that I could be trusted.

We all shook hands, and then one of the union officers got right to the point. "We want to see your questionnaire before it goes out to our members," he said. "We want to be sure you won't put something in it that's against the union."

"If I did that," I answered, "I could never convince management that you didn't tell your people how to answer. The only way we can get Caterpillar to take this survey seriously as if they believe the results are real."

I pointed out that no one had to fill out a questionnaire and that no one had to answer every question, either. If anyone thought that answering a particular question could hurt the union, he could just leave that question blank. And if too many people left too many questions blank, I would have done a useless survey.

"Why should Caterpillar pay me for that?" I asked them.

The union officers glanced at each other. After a moment, one of them growled, "All right. But what's in it for us?" We had come to the quid pro quo that Stan had warned me about.

I answered that I was willing to give the union officers a printout of the survey results the night before they were released to the employees. They would know the results first and could do whatever they wanted with them.

"You're going to let it all out?" one of them asked. "No matter how bad it is?"

I told him that we didn't expect the results to be good. After all, there had just been a strike. But management knew that it had to rebuild morale. The survey would show them where the problems were that had to be fixed. And, I added, we would publish a summary of the overall averages, so everyone could see for himself how Joliet employees felt about the various issues probed by the questionnaire.

"Won't that be just a bunch of numbers?" asked one of the union officers.

"Only the most important ones," I said. "And the plant manager will comment on what the numbers mean, and what he plans to do about it. That will also be included."

They glanced at each other again. They had already heard most of the points I had made. But they had heard them from management, and their real purpose was to decide whether they trusted me. For a moment they just read the expressions in each other's faces. Then one of them said, "We'll tell the membership to go along with this. But we're going to hold you to your word, Doc."

I felt relieved and nodded at him. "You can," I said.

THE "BLOODY-MINDED" SYNDROME

By the time we got to Joliet, the two sides were like a pair of groggy fighters who had battered each other nearly senseless in a drawn-out grudge match. The particular differences that had started the fight had long since ceased to matter. Eventually, the goals for both sides had narrowed down to not giving in, no matter what that might cost, and to inflicting as much damage on the other side as possible.

The British, who have seen their share of labor–management strife, have a phrase for this kind of impasse: They call it being "bloody-minded." The opponents have already lost more than their cause is worth, but by now the common sense has been beaten out of them. So they suffer even more losses, as if that could somehow justify their previous losses. Each side knows it can't win but fears that to acknowledge this openly would be to "lose." So neither backs down, mainly because the other side is also too bloody-minded to back down.

When people become bloody-minded, more than their sense of proportion is lost. Restraint is also lost. Strikes, like wars, are restraint-releasing events. Some people find it all too easy to believe that a strike suspends the ordinary rules of civil conduct. Under these conditions, things you ordinarily wouldn't think of doing become not only thinkable, but doable. That's why, during long strikes, people who ordinarily know how to behave themselves can do terrible, vicious things.

Of course, not everyone will sink that low. The problem, however, is that a few probably will, and their provocation can erode the restraint of the others. The longer a strike continues, the greater the risk that someone on one side will do something that everyone on the other side considers outrageous and unforgivable. That is how grudges are born that continue to play themselves out long after the strike itself has ended. And that is what we found as we began our interviews in Joliet.

INTERVIEWS WITH MANAGERS

My colleagues and I began by listening to some middle-level managers in groups of three or four. Remarks like these were typical.

"The strike got pretty rough. You expect some of that, but this was really disgusting. They used the strike as an excuse to act like a bunch of animals. They carried these signs on the picket line: 'Cat Doesn't Care!' That was their slogan. They screamed it at us as we drove into the plant every day."

"What do you suppose they meant by that?" I asked.

"I think," replied the manager, "that it was their way of saying that all of us in management were a bunch of bastards, because we wouldn't give in and let them have whatever they wanted."

I had this dialogue with another management group:

"You want to know the truth?" said one of the managers. "All of us think that you and your friends are going to tell Peoria whatever Peoria wants to hear. They bought you and they paid for you. They think that the management here in Joliet screwed up, and that the strike was our fault. But they're wrong."

"Why is Peoria wrong?" I asked.

Another manager replied:

"A lot of the old managers from Joliet were promoted to the corporate staff in Peoria. They claim that in the old days, when they were here, they used to go out with the hourly workers after a shift ended and drink beer together. At least, that's what they say. But I can tell you this: It sure as hell hasn't been like that since I've been here."

"No friendly get-togethers?" I asked.

Another manager answered:

"Hell, no. They live in their little world, and we live in ours. Frankly, most of them are not the kind of people that you'd want to socialize with. That's why I can't believe those guys in Peoria who say that we've 'lost the human touch.' That's bull."

Of course, the remarks presented here are only a small sample of many that we gathered from middle managers. But they are fairly typical of the feelings expressed by most of their colleagues. It was the repetition of similar remarks that began to suggest that middle managers, as a group, felt "besieged": as if they were under attack by both their superiors in Peoria and their subordinates in Joliet.

My colleagues and I knew that our only chance to win them over would be to present them with an analysis that was as impartial as we could make it, based on as many facts as we could gather. And we had to win them over, because without the cooperation of local management, any attempt to change the psychological dynamics within the plant would be doomed.

INTERVIEWS WITH FOREMEN

Next we interviewed a sample of the shop floor supervisors. Here's what a pair of typical foremen had to say:

"We've got two kinds of workers on the shop floor. Most of them are not really here to work. They just want to see what they can get away with, because they know their union will protect them. Then you've got some, just a few, who try to put in an honest day's work. When we get a chance to promote somebody, we move them up."

The other foreman said:

"A good foreman has to be tough. You have to let them know that you won't let them get away with one damned thing. If you do, they're going to take advantage of you. You can lose control just like that." [He snapped his fingers.] "And then you might as well quit, because you can't do your job anymore."

Remarks like these suggested that foremen, most of whom were up from the ranks themselves, thought of their former colleagues as adversaries who were conniving to take home a full paycheck for less than a full day of work. And they saw themselves as embattled defenders of justice—like a few good marshals who were trying to impose law and order on a tumultuous western town.

INTERVIEWS WITH WORKERS

As you might expect, the workers saw things differently. Remarks like these were typical:

"Management here is crazy. They're always pushing for more production. Just make it faster, even if what comes out is junk. They say they'll fix the parts later. So I put in eight hours every day, making junk."

"During the strike, I was lucky. I got a part-time job. Even so, after a few weeks, we couldn't make ends meet any more. It will take a long time to pay off all my bills. But I still say it was worth it."

"Why?" I asked.

"Because Cat lost a ton of money. Maybe that will get their attention! You have to hit those S.O.B.'s where it hurts to make them sit up and take notice."

A welder had this to say:

"They talk about safety, but they don't mean it. These foremen are always trying to win the production prize. They figure, there are two other shifts. So why should they fix a cable? Even if it breaks, it's two chances out of three it will break on another shift."

Another worker told me:

"My boss is always on our backs to turn out more parts than the other two shifts. You know what some of our guys do? They take some tools and hide them at the end of the shift, so the next two shifts can't find them. That way we can beat their production record, and get the boss off our backs. But I think it's crazy myself."

These and similar remarks suggested that the Joliet workers saw management as irrational, callous, and indifferent to their safety. It also suggested a different interpretation of the strikers' slogan. "Cat doesn't care" was evidently the workers' way of accusing the company of not regarding them as worthwhile human beings.

Yet how could that be squared with stories of camaraderie between workers and managers in the not-so-distant past? In the dozen or so years since the Joliet plant had opened, there had evidently been major changes in the way managers and employees thought about each other. At this stage, we were still trying to figure out why.

THE PSYCHOLOGY OF HIERARCHIES

The Joliet plant was organized as a typical hierarchy. Power was distributed unevenly, and had to be, so the work of five thousand people could be safely and efficiently coordinated.

But no hierarchy is *inherently* efficient. They all have internal tensions that can boil over if they are not managed. In a hierarchy you have to live in forced dependence on people who may not have your best interest at heart. Without some degree of trust between people at different levels of power, the powerless will fear exploitation and the powerful will fear revolution. That's why the most basic aspect of managing a hierarchy is to keep everyone reasonably confident that no one else is out to get him.

That basic trust in the civility of others is what had somehow spun out of control in Joliet. When our interview phase was completed, we had at least some clues as to what had gone wrong:

The midlevel managers were oriented upward, concerned about what their superiors in Peoria thought of them, rather than downward, toward the five thousand men and women who worked in the plant. The foremen were contemptuous of the workers, convinced that they had to be tightly controlled. And the workers regarded the foremen as oppressive, self-seeking, and uncaring.

But had these widely differing perceptions actually affected the length of the strike? To find out, we had to learn what the workers would have to say in their questionnaires.

STRATEGY

The technique we used was fairly simple, provided you've got a computer that can crunch a *lot* of numbers—and we did. Our questionnaire included about sixty statements, each with set of multiple-choice answers indicating one's degree of agreement (or disagreement). Then we correlated each of those answers with the answer to this "key" statement:

Despite the hardships during our strike, we were right to hold out as long as we did.

We had the computer search for the four or five statements among the sixty-odd that, taken together, provided us with the best prediction of how the key question would be answered. We reasoned that those few state-ments would pinpoint the worst complaints—the ones that made workers so angry that they would turn down almost any settlement their union had negotiated for them. Once we knew the major irritants that had prolonged the strike, we could look for practical ways to make them less aggravating.

That procedure may seem roundabout. Why, for example, didn't we simply *ask* the workers why they had stayed out so long? The answer is that we did, but in a way that enabled us to make sense out of what otherwise would have been a hodgepodge of thousands of opinions.

So one morning we began asking the workers on each shift to fill out our questionnaire, and within twenty-four hours more than 90 percent of them had done that. Then we fed all of their answers into a computer, which proceeded to crunch all of those numbers. As the printouts came rolling out, we were surprised to see that the issues that correlated best with a reluctance to end the strike were not the usual "bread-and-butter" issues, such as wages and job security. Instead they were promotion, safety, product quality, and relations with supervisors, in that order.

So my colleagues and I headed back to the conference rooms, where we interviewed new samples of employees. This time, instead of encouraging a freewheeling discussion, we focused the conversation on those four issues. Here's what we found:

PROMOTION

For the shop floor workers, most promotions were not into management, but rather to higher paid (and usually more desirable) blue-collar jobs. For example, you could be promoted to the tool room, where the work was less arduous, or to maintenance, where it was less tedious. Once we knew that this was a key issue, we asked the computer to tell us whether any particular group of workers was more upset than the rest about a lack of promotion opportunities. The answer was clear: It was the welders.

We spoke with groups of welders and learned that most of them had begun as apprentices and gradually worked their way up through a series of pay grades as they learned their trade. Most didn't particularly like their work but regarded it as a way to qualify for a better job.

When the plant was new, one could expect to be promoted out of the welders' ranks within a few years. In those earlier days, one's chances of eventually escaping the welding shop were good, so optimism was realistic. That hope made the daily immersion in heat and smoke and sparks easier to tolerate. But when the plant reached its full complement of manpower, promotions slowed. Most of the attractive jobs were already filled. Those welders who started up the ladder too late faced a much slower climb.

This led to a surprising insight about the strike. The *age* of the Joliet plant itself was part of the problem. It didn't actually cause the strike, of course, but it did cancel out an advantage that would have dampened the effects of the other grievances. Cooperation and even camaraderie are possible when everyone has something to look forward to.

But that advantage had disappeared after the Joliet plant reached its full strength. By the time of the latest strike, it had been replaced (especially among the welders) by a sense of entrapment. To make matters worse, they felt powerless to escape. Here's what one welder said about the few promotions that did occur:

I read on the bulletin board the other day that some guy who I don't even know who got promoted to tool room assistant. That's not such a bad job! But I didn't even know they had an opening.

We checked that out with management. A first-level supervisor told us,

If we get an opening, we give it to one of the good guys. Some of the men bitch, and say we give all the soft jobs to our buddies. But some people will complain no matter what you do.

The foremen were convinced that the existing system for adding new colleagues to their ranks not only give the company the kind of first-level supervisors it needed, but also let them see to it that justice was done. And for reasons I was only beginning to understand, they were fiercely protective of that system.

SAFETY

There had been accidents in Joliet, and some of them were bad. But the overall record showed that the accident rate was about average for plants of that type. Statistically, at least, Joliet was not unusually dangerous.

But the workers were unimpressed by statistics. Their perceptions were entirely different. Some even compared the plant to a battle zone. When the mismatch between their beliefs and the actual safety record was pointed out to them, they gave explanations like this:

Those are just numbers. The real problem is that *nobody* should get hurt. What really bothers me is that when something happens out there, it didn't have to happen. The foremen are always pushing for more parts, and some poor bastard gets worn out trying to make them faster. That's when you get hurt: when you're too tired to think straight. It could happen to any of us, any time.

It was not the actual safety record, but the apparent willingness of foremen to run risks with safety, that created the perception of danger. But when this interpretation was presented to middle managers, they defended the foremen. They acknowledged that accidents occurred but blamed most of them on employee carelessness or recklessness. Foremen had to be constantly watchful, they said, to prevent more and even worse accidents from occurring.

When we followed up on alleged risk taking by foremen, we learned that several years earlier, management had introduced an informal competition among the three shifts. The idea was to stimulate production by building team spirit within each shift, so each would try to outperform the other two. It worked: Productivity did improve.

At some point, however, this "friendly" competition underwent a subtle change. Foremen began to suspect that the stakes had escalated and their own chances for advancement would be affected by how their shift ranked against the other two. Accordingly, they became more demanding with their workers. But they adamantly denied that their zeal to outperform each other could lead them to compromise on safety. One foreman said:

That's a lot of crap they told you about letting the cables fray. It was just a rumor that they started, and now they all believe it. I don't believe it ever happened. The real problem in this plant is that a lot of guys don't like to work. So when you make them earn their pay, they bellyache and invent a lot of crazy stories.

With so many contradictory perceptions, who was telling the truth? Actually, both sides were telling the truth *as they saw it*; and both were engaged in a bit of exaggeration, because both felt that they were under attack. The question of whether some of the more outrageous incidents had ever actually occurred (for example, frayed cables and hidden tools) was, for all practical purposes, unanswerable.

Nor did it really matter. True or not, those allegations were symptoms of a severe underlying antipathy that was probably a key reason why the workers had stayed out as long as they had. When people who ordinarily get along begin to demonize each other, it is usually because some very strong feelings have overwhelmed their reason. In other words, the strike had been prolonged because it was a grudge fight that had more to do with self-respect and wounded pride than with a few extra pennies per hour.

PRODUCT QUALITY

Most of the workers in the Joliet plant made parts. They cut and milled and welded pieces of steel into gear wheels and flanges and hundreds of other components that were eventually fitted into rugged earth-moving machines.

The issue here was production pressure. Once again, we encountered two quite different views of the same subject. This was a typical response when we asked workers about product quality:

Don't talk to me about quality. My foreman is all the time counting the finished parts in my bin. The only way to keep him off my back is to just run the pieces through, and never mind if they're right or not. How can anyone turn out good parts, when you're all the time in such a goddamn rush?

Management's all-out push for productivity had two effects on the workers' perceptions—both negative. First, any pride they may have felt in their own craftsmanship was effectively nullified. That loss just aggravated their already foul mood.

Second, the workers took the company's perceived demand (seemingly, for more defective parts!) as an indication that this management was either incompetent, irrational, or both. That only added to the demonic image that the foremen had already acquired in the minds of the workers. It was as if their superiors used their power not to lead, but to torment.

But I got an altogether different perspective on the same problem when I spoke to one of the industrial engineers. He pointed out that when labor cost is high and the product is fairly easy to make, it can actually be cheaper in the long run just to turn out parts as quickly as you can and fix whatever needs fixing afterward. An analogy would be running a spell check after typing a letter: You type as fast as you can and correct the errors later.

But in a larger sense, the question came down to how you did your accounting. If you considered only the directly measurable costs, like labor and materials, the industrial engineer was right. But if you also took into account the effects of the fast production pace on the workers' attitudes toward management, and the way those attitudes fed their determination to retaliate, the policy of producing at top speed became more questionable.

RELATIONS WITH SUPERVISORS

Although the question of relations with supervisors ranked fourth on our list, it was so interwoven with the other three that it was clearly the real crux of our problem.

Nearly all of the foremen had come up from the ranks, having been selected by other foremen on the basis of their work record and their attitude. Here's how two foremen described what they looked for in seeking a prospective addition to their ranks:

I look for somebody who is here to work, who doesn't loaf, who isn't into fraternizing with his buddies. I look for somebody who just tells them, "I'm going to make as many parts as I want to, and if you don't like that, nuts to you."

A foreman isn't paid to be liked. He has to be able to chew somebody out, and you can't do that to a pal. So I look for somebody who doesn't have a lot of pals.

Because of the way foremen were selected, they tended to be more independent and inflexible than most of the people they supervised. They made no secret of their disdain for the shop floor workers, and the workers were well aware of how their foremen felt. In large measure, therefore, the strike had been a payback by the rank and file for the perceived disrespect of their bosses.

The way foremen were selected allowed entirely too many people with chips on their shoulders to gain authority over their fellow workers. Police departments are usually far more scrupulous about screening their would-be officers than most companies are about screening their supervisory candidates. In both cases, people with a grudge against those whom they would oversee are the ones most likely to abuse their authority.

Midlevel managers might have eased the problem by cautioning the supervisors and holding them to higher standards. But they seldom ventured onto the shop floor. They regarded the foremen as strong and demanding and generally felt that these were exactly the qualities needed to keep such a large plant under control. Their perceptions of the workers were largely based on what they had heard about them from the foremen. As one manager put it:

There is a rough element out there. Nowadays the problem is to make sure that they know who is boss. By and large, I think our foremen do a good job of keeping them in line.

Management viewed the workers as potentially unruly, and therefore in need of strong discipline, and they were content to leave that discipline to the foremen. The effect of managerial indifference to shop floor matters was very unfortunate, because with few exceptions the workers and their foremen despised each other. Without the restraining hand of middle management, open conflict was inevitable.

WHY DID THE STRIKE LAST SO LONG?

The Joliet strike revealed a willingness by five thousand people to sacrifice their income and even their assets to preserve their self-respect. They were convinced that their management scorned and threatened them and defended themselves against that perceived threat to the point of exhaustion. Stan was right: The Joliet strike was an intensely psychological event.

There were several contributing factors. The way foremen were selected, and then indoctrinated by their colleagues with derogatory attitudes toward the workers was certainly a key factor. So was the relentless pressure for production, rising to seemingly dangerous and irrational levels. The same could be said for the feelings of entrapment that afflicted those who found themselves unable to advance, especially the welders.

But behind all of these contributing causes, enabling them to exist in the first place and worsening them, was midlevel management's reluctance to become involved in the day-to-day management of the shop floor. The moderating, guiding influence they might have exerted over the foremen wasn't there, at least not to the extent necessary to forestall the gathering disaster.

Most of the middle managers were engineers whose preferred style of working was to immerse themselves in technical matters. They were cautious and reserved and felt uncomfortable among people who were more spontaneous than they were. They expected any prolonged involvement with uncouth people on the factory floor to turn ugly. So they were content to leave the everyday management of those people to the foremen, who were up from the ranks themselves and professed to know how to handle them.

The middle managers had used a common self-protective mechanism that might be called "preventive detachment." It's the same tactic that suburbanites use to minimize their involvement with inner cities. You simply exclude from your life the people and the problems you don't want to deal with. The managers could easily rationalize it: From their perspective, they were simply concentrating on what they did best and leaving other tasks to the people who did them better.

In effect they were practicing "management by not getting involved." But the results were disastrous. The normal reviews and briefings that serve as managerial sanity checks were too rare and too brief to matter. The managers saw no need to demand that the foremen show a greater concern for worker morale, because they had no idea that morale was such a burgeoning problem. It was precisely this lack of middle management intervention that allowed the gut-level animosity between foremen and shop floor workers to veer out of control. That's why the midlevel managers were astounded when the strike dragged on.

PREVENTING A RECURRENCE

I concluded that the best way to head off another drawn-out strike would be to focus on two contributing causes—the employees' safety concerns and feelings of entrapment by unpromoted workers—as well as on what I was now convinced was the primary cause—the tendency of middle managers to distance themselves from day-to-day involvement in employee relations. In the end we only succeeded with one of the three. Fortunately, it was the one that mattered most.

SAFETY REVISITED

By now we were convinced that the workers' overblown fears about safety were a reaction to the apparent indifference of their foremen to risk. So we developed two proposals to counteract those fears. One would relieve at least some of the anxiety about shop floor accidents. The other was aimed at the underlying cause of that anxiety, which was the pressure on foremen for production.

Our first proposal was a quick fix: We proposed that the company buy an ambulance. Since the plant was located several miles from the nearest hospital, an on-site ambulance would cut the response time to an accident in half. It could be parked prominently near the plant gates as a highly visible demonstration of the company's concern for employee welfare.

From an economic standpoint, our proposal was debatable. Ambulances were expensive and were only needed occasionally. Besides, the hospital's own ambulance usually arrived quickly. Nevertheless, the proposal did not conflict with any of management's basic beliefs and was accepted with almost no discussion.

But we also pointed out that the effect of the ambulance on employee attitudes would fade rather quickly. At best, it would buy some time, and we proposed to use that time to get at the underlying reasons for the workers' exaggerated fears. In particular, we focused on the production pressure that resulted from competition between shifts.

But that proposal ran head-on into one of management's core beliefs and got nowhere. Here was one typical comment:

Competition works. It's a proven method. If we give it up, what will we replace it with? If we don't have a substitute for it, we're going to lose a lot of production. And what for? How much happier would the union be if we dropped it? Happy enough that they won't strike anymore? I doubt it.

All this managerial resistance to change had an underlying cause. I recalled the remarks of the first manager I had interviewed, early in the survey: "Peoria bought you, and they paid for you." The Joliet managers felt that they were under attack by their own corporate headquarters and that my colleagues and I were mercenaries in that attack. They were polite and willing to listen. But they were not yet about to budge from their habits or opinions.

PROMOTION REVISITED

We asked some midlevel managers if they had ever considered posting promotional opportunities on bulletin boards, so all qualified workers who wanted to advance could be considered. But we ran into another brick wall. Here's what one of them said:

You don't understand. These foremen have already had most of their power taken away by union contracts. If you're in the union, you can thumb your nose at your boss and get away with it. So you can see why the foremen are going to fight to hold on to whatever power they have left.

In other words, the foremen were caught in a bind that every management textbook warns against: responsibility with insufficient authority. The midlevel managers understood that anything that reduced the workers' frustrations would also reduce the risk of another long strike. But they were also reluctant to deprive the foremen of a privilege that they prized. The result was a stalemate. Nothing changed.

But this was also another clue that the midlevel managers were avoiding tough decisions about the workers. There is a fine line between delegating—in this case, giving the foremen authority to deal with the workers as they saw fit—and abdicating, which is failing to guide or review the tasks delegated. It was increasingly clear that some of the middle managers had crossed that line.

SPEAKING FRANKLY TO MIDDLE MANAGERS

If anyone was going to clear up the labor relations mess in Joliet, it would have to be the plant's own mid-level managers. Most of them most had contributed, albeit unknowingly, to a severe employee relations crisis. The key, I felt, was to get them to accept that they had become a part of the problem themselves. If we could do that, we could leave them to find their own ways of lowering the level of animosity between the foremen and the workers.

We held some long meetings with Joliet management to discuss the results of the survey. I told them that there was some degree of truth in most of the theories that had been advanced about why the strike had lasted so long. But the main reason, I said, was that the relationship between foremen and employees had deteriorated before the strike to a point where workers felt that their self-respect was under daily attack.

In some respects, the strike had been a bid for the attention of middle management, or failing that, of corporate management. The workers wanted them to do something about the foremen. Of course, none of the workers articulated it quite that way. They had their own (often unprintable) ways of saying that the way they were supervised had become intolerable.

The point we stressed was that management had to find ways to back both sides away from confrontation, and toward accommodation. This was not so much a matter of getting committees to negotiate as of getting individuals to examine their own attitudes. I told a group of managers:

A supervisor belittles the people he supervises at his own peril. If they feel that you think they are worthless, that can escalate a simple disagreement into a life-or-death struggle. Like it or not, these are the people you have to work with. You have to find ways to work with them yourselves, and of getting the foremen to work with them, that do not offend them.

The Joliet managers were unaccustomed to such talk, but they understood it and took it seriously. They decided among themselves that they had to become more involved in shop floor relations. Once that corner was turned, recovery became possible.

The managers began to look for ways to defuse the often volatile relationship between the foremen and the workers. They directed Joliet's training department to begin running leadership seminars for the supervisors, stressing the importance of examining one's own attitudes toward the people being supervised. They also had the labor relations department meet informally with the union's leadership, stressing the need for a more professional approach on both sides of the bargaining table.

All of these steps helped. But the most important aspect of Joliet's recovery process was the fact that virtually everyone *wanted* to restore a viable working relationship. The strike had astounded and/or appalled just about everyone whom it had touched. Except for a few diehards, no one wanted to go through such a calamity again. So they had a strong incentive to find ways to prevent it.

Fortunately, the catastrophic strike that brought me to Joliet was not a harbinger of things to come. Instead, both sides came to view it as a terrible warning and had the maturity to treat the warning seriously. Three years later, with Stan himself leading Caterpillar's negotiating team, a new contract was settled without a strike.

Nor was there a strike during the subsequent negotiation. Joliet had a comparatively short strike once after that, but since then it has been strike-free, even as other Caterpillar plants have been hit by some well-publicized strikes.

At one point, Joliet was a textbook example of how awful the relationship between management and labor can get. Three years later, the same management and the same union demonstrated how a focused, determined effort by both parties to a conflict can make their relationship manageable again—not smooth, not idyllic, but manageable. In the words of St. Paul, both sides "put away childish things." That can be an extraordinarily difficult thing to do. But they did it, because they realized that too much could be lost if they failed.

Could all this have been accomplished without the intervention of a team of psychologists? Perhaps. My own view, which may be self-serving, is that we made their comeback easier for them in two ways. One was to direct the attention of both sides away from a fruitless debate over who was to blame, and onto the much more constructive question of how to prevent such a calamity from happening again. Blame is a useless concept when conflicts occur, because it gives each party a handy excuse for not examining its own contribution to the conflict.

Second, we gave Joliet management what it had previously lacked: a clear focus on the issues that had to be addressed that only they could address effectively. That they did so is entirely to their credit.

Chapter Eight

Shop Floor Strategists

I must confess that I have the same feeling about factories that most little boys have about electric trains. So when Bill L., who was vice president for human resources at one of my client companies, invited me to tour his company's main plant, I jumped at the chance. (The company has asked not to be identified. Bill L. agreed to be identified, but in deference to the company's wishes I have abbreviated his last name.) After that day's seminar ended, Bill guided me around the huge multistory factory and showed me how the company's products were made.

There were several hundred people scattered about on each of the factory floors. Most stood or sat in fixed positions from which they kept an eye on the big machines that shredded and sprayed the raw materials and then wrapped and packed the finished products. Clean-up crews and maintenance men moved about, and supervisors (easily identified by their neckties) kept an eye on everything. Because so many machines were in operation at once, it was a rather noisy place.

I knew that Bill wasn't merely indulging my fascination with manufacturing. As we walked back to his office I thanked him and said, "Now, tell me, Bill. What's really on your mind?"

"It's those foremen," he answered. "They're the key to keeping our productivity up and our costs down. And we'd like to do something to help them do their job better."

He went on to explain that the company had invested heavily in the education of its midlevel managers and its top executives but had so far spent relatively little on its first-level supervisors. Nevertheless, he could think of at least two reasons why there might actually be an even bigger payoff from upgrading the capabilities of the foremen, if a way could be found to do that.

The first was their sheer numbers. Supervisors worked on all five factory floors on all three shifts, so they greatly outnumbered the middle managers, most of whom worked only on the day shift. Any impact we could have on the supervisors would be magnified much more than any corresponding effect on the middle managers. Second, foremen were the only members of management who dealt directly with the employees who actually turned out the product. So no one was in a better position to influence their performance, and therefore that of the entire factory.

"So my question for you," said Bill, "is whether you can do something for our foremen. Do you have any ideas? I'd like to hear your proposals."

Since I was due to return to the company during the following week for another seminar, I promised to think it over and have my reply ready by then.

MANAGEMENT'S NEGLECTED RESOURCE

In most factories, first-level supervisors are up from the ranks themselves, have had little or no education beyond high school, and have already advanced as far up the management ladder as they will ever go. Their job is to make sure that nothing particularly exciting happens on their shift. A sure sign that they've done their jobs well is that nothing noteworthy has occurred. Their mission is to maintain that status quo, day after day and week after week.

So perhaps it is understandable that they are often taken for granted. To the ordinary worker on the shop floor, the supervisor is "the boss," the personification of the employer's authority. But to his or her managerial superiors, the first-level supervisor is someone whose job may be necessary, but is also monotonous and leads nowhere. That's why companies with money to spend on making their managers more effective have usually invested more of it in upper-level managers, with their college degrees and their M.B.A.'s, than in first-level supervisors.

But Bill had sensed that this was a mistake, and the more I thought about it, the more I agreed with him. So with Bill's approval, I went looking for some data.

MANAGING A FACTORY

I met with the factory manager and asked him about supervisory job performance. Could he get hold of the actual production records of each department, over months or even years? Yes, he could. And did those records show that some supervisors' departments were *consistently* more productive than the rest? Yes, they did. Could those differences be due to having more experienced workers on certain shifts or to mechanical reasons, such as newer equipment in some departments than in others?

"No," said the factory manager. "This is apples to apples. When you factor out all of those things, some foremen just get more out of the same machines than others do. And they keep their people in line better, too. We know who our best supervisors are, and that's not just my opinion, or anyone else's. It's a hard fact."

"Can you explain it?" I asked. "What makes some supervisors more effective than others?"

"I guess it's like everything else in life," he answered. "Some people are just better than others at whatever they do. But if you're looking for a deeper explanation than that, I haven't got one for you."

"But when you get down to the bottom line," I asked, "does it really matter? As long as those machines keep running, what difference can foremen make?"

"Let me simplify this for you," he said.

To make his plant run profitably. the two main variables he had to control were the rates at which the machines were utilized and the wastage rate of raw materials. The utilization rate was the number of minutes during a shift when a machine was actually turning out products, rather than shut down for repairs. (The labor cost, though it involved a lot of money, was not really variable, because the union contract required him to employ fixed numbers of people at fixed wage rates.)

"So I stay focused on those two variables," he said, "because that's where management can make a difference."

About 97 percent of the raw materials that entered the factory left it in the form of salable products. The other 3 percent was wasted, either in defective products that had to be discarded or in tiny particles that floated up from improperly adjusted machines, settling as dust that had to be vacuumed off the floors, the machines, and even the workers themselves. Of that 3 percent, he estimated that about two-thirds (i.e., 2 percent) was due to employee error, and the rest to mechanical causes.

"Two percent may not sound like a lot," he said, "but when you factor in how much raw material we process here, it can work out to a few million dollars a year. Obviously, anything we can do to cut down on that loss, we're going to do."

I asked him about machine utilization. He explained that the equipment had many moving parts, and therefore a lot of vibration. But the settings had to be kept within close tolerances. Inevitably, the machines would shake themselves out of those limits. The trick was to recognize when that was beginning to happen, and to make small adjustments before a cascade effect set off a chain of breakdowns that would require time-consuming repairs.

"Whose job is that?" I asked.

"Everyone's," he said. "Primarily, it's the employee's job. Sometimes the foreman catches it first. But that's the reason they're both there. To keep the machines running right."

"What exactly do you mean by 'employee error?' " I asked.

"Sloppy habits," he said. "Taking shortcuts. Lack of attention. Boredom. Distraction. Forgetting. Being upset about something. Getting tired. Not giving a damn. All of the things that can happen to human beings during an eight-hour shift."

"And it's the foreman's job to prevent all of those things?" I asked.

"That's the main reason why we need foremen in the first place," he explained. "We need people to watch the machines, because these are machines that still don't know when they're screwing up. But people aren't 100 percent reliable, either. So somebody has to keep them on the ball."

"Who keeps the supervisors on the ball?" I asked. "They're human too."

If you chose the right foremen, the plant manager told me, they were pretty much a self-disciplined group. But there were also midlevel managers above them, and if it came to that, he himself was the last line of defense.

SELECTING A RESEARCH STRATEGY

My first impulse, after listening to the factory manager, was to look at how the foremen were selected. Some methods that had become popular were showing fairly good statistical results. That is, people who got high ratings from these methods were more likely to become highly rated supervisors than those who didn't do as well.

But that still left a considerable margin for error. I felt that we could probably improve productivity as much, if not more, by just improving the work of the existing foremen, than we could by looking for new ones (if any could be found) who were better suited for the job.

Besides, I was bothered by the same question that had prompted the IBM study: Precisely what were factory supervisors doing when they were being effective, and how did that differ from what less effective supervisors were doing?

If we couldn't answer that question, we couldn't pinpoint which qualities to seek when looking for new foremen. We'd have to fall back on the familiar, but not very helpful, generalities that we'd always used in the past. (Supervisors were supposed to be alert, to be "self-starters," and to be reasonably articulate.) The awkward problem with that vague formula was that lots of failed or inadequate supervisors had displayed those qualities.

But if we found an answer to that question, we could teach the methods of the best foremen to the others. That would raise the average level of supervisory performance. I decided that the best way to solve the problem that Bill had presented would be to hunt for what the factory manager had called the "deeper reason": What did the better foremen *do* that made them better?

My strategy was the same as in the IBM study: a search for behavioral differences. But because I was working at the opposite end of the managerial pyramid, and in a very different company, I decided that my tactics would have to be different.

SHADOWING SUPERVISORS

When I saw Bill the following week, I explained that I wanted to see for myself what factory supervisors actually did all day. "Let's start with fifteen of them," I said. "Let the factory manager choose them, based on their production records. I want five of your best producers, five who are average, and five who are bringing up the rear. I just want to know their names. I don't want to be told their production records."

"And what will you do with them?" asked Bill.

I explained that I would spend an entire shift with each of them. About fifteen minutes before the shift began, we would meet in the supervisors' lounge, where I would explain my mission. I would not interfere with their work but would follow them around the factory all day, literally two steps behind them.

I would also carry a stenographer's note pad, on which I would furiously scribble down everything they did. When they indicated that it was all right for me to speak to them, I would ask questions about what I'd seen and scribble down those answers, too. By the end of the day I'd have a minute-by-minute diary of everything that supervisor had done during an entire shift.

"And then?" asked Bill.

I said I would transcribe the notes and study them, looking for patterns of similar behavior. Only then would I ask the plant manager to tell me the production records of the supervisors. Then we'd see whether the patterns matched production. If we found a match, we'd know which "tricks of the trade" had enabled the better supervisors to outperform their colleagues, and we could design training courses around them. If we found no match at all, we'd have to chalk it all up to experience.

"But I really don't expect that," I told Bill. "If some people consistently outperform the rest, there's got to be a reason for it. We might need to add more supervisors to our sample, just to be sure. Fifteen is about as small a number as we can use."

"It sounds good to me," said Bill. "But before I authorize this project, you'll also have to see if the plant manager will buy into this project. You'll have to get his agreement on what you want to do in his factory."

THE AFTERNOON SHIFT

The plant manager readily agreed to cooperate. So a few weeks later I found myself in the foremen's lounge at 2:45 P.M., fifteen minutes before the start of the afternoon shift. The plant manager was there too, and he introduced me to the first of my fifteen supervisors, whom we'll call Carl. I'll describe my observations of Carl and two of his colleagues, because they were more or less characteristic of the other twelve.

A few minutes before three o'clock, Carl strode out onto the factory floor and found the outgoing foreman, who had been running the machines in Carl's area since 7:00 A.M. They huddled together briefly, exchanging a few pleasantries and reviewing the status of some troublesome machines. As they spoke, day-shift employees were streaming off the floor and the afternoon shift was streaming in. Carl had eighteen employees under him, and he greeted each with a nod or a few brief words as they took their places.

"You want a good start," Carl told me, as he walked swiftly down the line. "The first half hour sets the tone. If they get into a good mood, they'll keep up a good pace all day. A bad start puts them in a bad mood. They'll look for excuses to get off the line. There's more relief calls on a bad day, believe it or not."

As Carl and I walked past, one of the machine operators nodded toward me somewhat suspiciously. "Who's this?" he asked Carl.

"Oh, he's only here for today," said Carl. "Don't worry about him."

I thought Carl's reply had been a bit vague, but to my surprise, the operator seemed satisfied. If my presence was all right with Carl, it was all right with him, too. The reason for this became clear later on.

For the most part, Carl was a man of few words. He seldom spoke, and whatever he had to say was said quickly and quietly. But I noticed that he always said something, however brief, each time he stopped by an operator's station and that these stops were fairly frequent—about every twelve to fifteen minutes. He was more or less constantly in motion.

Carl had jotted down some notes when he read the meters on each machine at the close of the previous day's shift. When production exceeded the department's usual average, he would announce the total to each employee at the start of the next day's shift, shake his hand, and say something like "Good running yesterday" or "Nice going." When production was below average, he would announce the figure but omit the handshake and say something like "Let's see if we can beat that today."

Whatever Carl did, he did quickly: a glance at a meter, a brief look at some packs as they emerged from the wrapper, a few words exchanged with an employee. From time to time, he paused for a moment to check a video display unit that kept track of each machine's performance on a minute-by-minute basis. The device tallied the number of rejected packs and the reasons for them, deviations from expected weights, operating speed, and a number of other variables, all of which helped Carl to anticipate when it might be necessary to make an adjustment or even to shut down a machine for preventive maintenance or repair.

He moved so rapidly that I had to make most of my notes on the run. Finally, he stopped at a water cooler, offered me a paper cup, and asked how I was doing.

"Do you always rush around like this?" I asked. "Is there a reason for it?"

He did, and there was. In addition to his eighteen subordinates, each of whom needed varying degrees of oversight and hand holding, there were numerous instruments to check and contacts to be maintained with the maintenance crews and other supervisors. From time to time, he also had to check in by telephone with his boss. Trouble could develop with any of those subordinates, instruments, or contacts.

His strategy was to minimize the interval between the last time he had checked any potential trouble spot and the next. His aim was to head off trouble by dealing with it while it was still minor, or even merely possible. To do that with so many sources of potential mishaps required that he avoid lingering over *anything*. Hence his fast pace and his crisp, no-words-wasted style of relating to his subordinates.

Carl's approach to managing his department was essentially preventive. He didn't want to have to deal with any crises at all if he could help it, and if he couldn't avoid one he wanted it to be small, hence easily managed. Above all he wanted to avoid having to deal with two problems at once, because that could tie up so much of his time that some ordinarily preventable problems might not be prevented. He had never experienced the cascade of operational problems that he most feared but claimed to have seen it in other supervisors' departments.

On any given occasion, he rarely spent more than a minute with an employee, and usually much less. At first, I thought that as a result of this brevity, he might be seen as impersonal and uncaring. But that clearly was not the case. He had an easygoing manner that made his brief visits welcome to those who craved company but also made them tolerable to those who preferred to be left alone.

For example, he played out what was evidently a standing joke with an operator at a packing machine, a lady who was considerably older than he was. She "wouldn't allow" him to inspect more than one pack at a time. When he pretended to grab for a second pack, she pretended to slap his hand, which he promptly withdrew. They both giggled, and he said that he was only checking to make sure she was still alert. They both pretended that she had more authority than she actually did, thus satisfying her need for the dignity due someone her age.

Carl's main concern with his operators was to make sure they followed a checklist of standard operating procedures. Each of them had memorized his or her list, and could recite it by heart. But Carl was well aware that merely knowing the rules was no guarantee of following them. On this shift, most workers were mature, senior employees, so there were few problems with rebelliousness or horseplay.

Instead, the greatest danger was wandering attention, or as Carl put it, "daydreaming." His frequent arrival at an employee's work station repeatedly interrupted any drift of attention away from the ceaseless flow of raw material and the endless march of packs into the wrapping machines. Many work stations were isolated, so except for lunch breaks and relief breaks, Carl's visits were the only social contacts those workers had for eight long hours.

Carl was having a good run, with no breakdowns and steady production. I began to find it rather boring. But Carl, with his constant fear of losing control if he neglected anything for more than a few minutes, wasn't bored at all. The workers, some sitting at their work stations, others pacing within a confined area, had long since made their peace, in one way or another, with an unstimulating job.

Then, just before Carl's scheduled coffee break, one of the lines that fed raw material into one of the processing machines unexpectedly became jammed. The operator quickly threw the emergency switch and stood to signal Carl. But Carl had heard it and was already racing over. "You did the right thing," he said, reassuring the somewhat uncertain operator. "Clean up what you can, and I'll get someone to hand-feed for you."

He picked up a nearby telephone and called maintenance for a repair crew. Then he called the labor pool for an extra worker to hand-feed the line from a big barrel of raw material that had been held in reserve for just that purpose and was quickly wheeled into place. The foreman from the next department, who ordinarily would have covered both his own department and Carl's during Carl's coffee break, arrived on time. But Carl waved him off. "No coffee for me this morning," he said. "Bad timing." Then the repair crew arrived, and Carl told them what had happened. As they got to work, he resumed patrolling the rest of his department.

"These things happen," he told me over his shoulder. "The important thing is to get back into your routine as quick as you can." The breakdown had cost him less than four minutes. Luckily, no other problems had begun to develop while he was distracted by the broken feed line. Later, over lunch, he told me, "The worst time to get a problem is when you've already got another problem."

After I had observed all of the fifteen supervisors in my sample, I learned that Carl had one of the best productivity ratings in the factory. He was one of the few who had actually analyzed his job, identified what was essential, and developed a strategy for keeping those things under control. That, plus the self-discipline to adhere to that strategy, day in and day out, was what distinguished him from most of his colleagues.

When the shift ended at 11:00 P.M., Carl waited until his workers left their work stations, and then quickly jotted down the production figures from the meters on each machine. He reported the total to his boss; he would tell his workers about them when they reported to work on the following day.

THE NIGHT SHIFT

The night shift usually has certain built-in handicaps, including a high proportion of inexperienced workers, comparatively few maintenance people, high turnover and absence rates, and an almost universal desire to transfer to one of the other two shifts. Thus the foreman's task on this shift was in some respects more demanding than on the two daytime shifts.

The foreman, whom we'll call Len, met me in the lounge at 10:45 P.M. We chatted amiably until 10:55, when he headed out for the corridor to watch his subordinates punching in. Each took his card from the "out" rack, inserted it into the time clock, and then put it into the "in" rack. Promptly at eleven o'clock, he pulled the three cards that were still in the "out" rack. Those represented employees who either were absent or would arrive late.

Len walked quickly out onto the production floor, blowing hard on a whistle that dangled from a cord around his neck. That was a signal to his workers to start their machines. He moved rapidly down the line to make sure that each worker was at his or her proper station. Then he went to a telephone to call for replacements for the three absentees.

He was very energetic, sometimes actually jogging from place to place. It became apparent that he was largely concerned with three things: the availability of supplies, the condition of the equipment, and the location of each subordinate on the floor, in about that order. He seemed more concerned with where his people were than with what they were doing. If anyone wandered away from where he was supposed to be, Len promptly told him to return. If workers were in the right place, that seemed to satisfy him.

Len told me later, during a break, that most people didn't like a boss who interfered with their work or who told them what to do. So he got involved with them only when he had to, and otherwise busied himself with making sure that his subordinates had everything they needed to get the job done.

When the three replacement workers arrived, Len showed them where to stand and what to do. He watched them long enough to be sure they had understood and then left them. Next, he made a quick tour of the department to be sure that all was well. For the moment, it was. So he found a place from which he could see most of the department and stood there, watching from a distance, alert but not directly involved.

A cleaning crew was sitting on some stools next to some pillars, not conspicuously busy, bantering with some nearby machine operators. I asked Len about them. He told me that this was all right, because the line was running well and none of the machines had become particularly dirty yet.

As we walked down the line together, we passed a wrapping machine that had jammed. The worker was reaching into the loading trough, pulling out and discarding the packs that were stuck there.

"See that?" said Len. "We had a foremen's meeting about that a few weeks ago. He's not supposed to do that. It isn't safe, and it can make the jam worse."

"Are you going to stop him?" I asked.

"No," said Len. "He's almost got it cleared. If I had caught him when he just started, I would have stopped him. But it's faster to clear it out by hand, *if* you don't get hurt."

Len seldom checked the video display units. When I asked him about that, he explained that he didn't trust them. When the instruments were originally installed, he told me, they had frequently displayed incorrect data. It had taken several months before the technicians could work most of the "bugs" out of them, and even now they could still be unreliable from time to time. Besides, he didn't consider them necessary. He could usually tell when a machine was getting out of adjustment simply by listening to it.

But the plant manager had told me that the video display units had been installed because the instruments they were attached to were far more sensitive than the human eye or ear. Their purpose was to eliminate human error, but evidently they had not eliminated human ego. Len was one of many supervisors who were convinced that they could detect sounds that scientists said no human could detect. The plant manager deplored the foremen's resistance to technological change, but he also offered a psychological explanation for it.

"In the old days," he had told me, "if you wanted the other foremen to respect you, you had to hear it when a machine was just starting to wiggle out of adjustment. Being able to do that was like a status symbol to them. You wouldn't want these engineers to take that away from you with their fancy instruments."

Here was a clash between psychology and technology. Len and his like-minded colleagues were just as intent on preserving their dignity as the company was on improving its productivity. Conceivably, humans could react to subliminal cues of which they were not, strictly speaking, "aware." But the pragmatic test of whether the foremen or the engineers were right about this would be in the production data. If foremen who regularly used the video display units had consistently outproduced those who did not, the engineers would be right and Len and his colleagues would be wrong. And vice versa.

I had to watch my biases here. I'd been indoctrinated in graduate school to favor science over folklore, so it would be easy for me to prejudge Len's claim. But the penalty that scientists and engineers have to pay for working on the frontiers of knowledge is that they are wrong some of the time.

Maybe Len was right. But, flawed human being that I am, I must admit that I was beginning to have my doubts about him.

Being on the night shift, Len had a disproportionate number of younger workers, many of whom were working full-time for the first time. I detected a certain amount of what might be called "latent rowdyism" among them: that is, waiting hopefully for one of the others to act up, which would be taken as a signal to engage in something more entertaining than watching dials and turning knobs. Mostly this took the form of loud banter, vulgar gestures, and hooting at the antics of others. Although the older employees disapproved, they tried to ignore it, and thus had no restraining influence on their younger coworkers.

Len's attitude toward these youthful shenanigans was permissive. The one thing he wouldn't tolerate, he told me, was fighting. Otherwise, as long as a younger worker was situated where he or she was supposed to be, Len took no particular notice of what they were doing. He told me that it was hard for the company to find more mature people willing to work the night shift, and that the younger folks would eventually straighten out. Tonight's three absentees, he noted, were all younger workers.

I had to agree with what he said, but I puzzled over what he seemed to overlook. The central purpose of the jobs he supervised was alertness. These people were hired to pay attention to the way the machines functioned and to react promptly when necessary. Merely being in the right place was no guarantee that they would do that, and engaging in horseplay almost guaranteed that they would not. Len could rationalize his tolerant attitude by saying that, after all, kids will be kids. But that same attitude helped to make his own job more comfortable, by keeping him out of confrontations with resentful young men.

Shortly after midnight, one of the machines on Len's line broke down. At first, he reacted exactly as Carl had. He dashed over, commended the operator for throwing the emergency switch, and called in a maintenance crew. But instead of leaving the scene of the breakdown as quickly as possible, Len lingered. He kept examining the machine, offered advice to the mechanics (who went about their work their own way), and paced anxiously up and down as the repair proceeded. He was obviously concerned about the machine, but he had in fact already contributed all he could to the repair process. Once the repair crew arrived, he had ceased being a supervisor and had become, for all practical purposes, a spectator.

After the machine was back in service, I asked Len why he had stayed there.

"For as long as that machine was down," he told me, "getting her back up again was the most important thing in my department. You've got to do things in the right order. Whatever is the most important thing, that's where you go. After that, you take care of the next most important thing."

If Carl's strategy had been proactive, trying to prevent mishaps, Len's was reactive. Len's aim was to correct any mishaps as quickly as possible. Not surprisingly, he had to deal with more of them than Carl did. Some of that could be attributed to the inherent disadvantages of the night shift, but some was also the inevitable result of Len's strategy. On this occasion, fortunately, no new crises erupted elsewhere while Len was preoccupied with the disabled machine. He had been lucky. But luck, by definition, is fickle.

With about ten minutes left to go in the shift, Len began checking the meters and writing down the production figures for each machine. After he had passed each meter, the operator would shut the machine down. Some stood there idly, waiting for the shift to end, while others headed out into the corridor to get to the head of the line at the time clock. Len's department was effectively shut down before the shift had ended. I did some quick arithmetic on my stenographer's note pad. Those machines were scheduled to run for four hundred eighty minutes per shift. There goes another 2 percent of production, I thought.

After I had finished all of my observations, I learned that Len was in the group of five supervisors who lagged behind the others in productivity. That was no surprise, and by then I knew why.

A key distinction between a foreman's job and that of most factory workers is their freedom of movement. Workers are told where to stay and as a rule can only leave that area with permission. But foremen can go wherever they feel they can do the most good. How they elect to use that freedom is one of the major distinctions between the most and the least effective supervisors.

Effective supervisors—some of them, at least—adopt a disciplined approach to their use of time. They deal briskly with everything, cover all important bases frequently, and if they are interrupted get back into their planned routine as quickly as possible.

Less effective supervisors are more likely to treat their liberty as a license. After all, life is more fun when you can fill it with variety and surprises. So they contrive to have a lot of both by simply waiting for them to happen— as they will, if you don't manage a complex operation proactively.

But the reactive supervisors get more than their share of negative surprises. That's because they will sooner or later face a cascade of preventable disasters on a single shift. When that happens, their productivity takes a big hit: so big, in fact, that it's difficult to restore their record by averaging that one bad day against subsequent good days.

After I had completed about half of my observations, I began to detect an interesting pattern. From time to time I'd be separated from my foreman, either to get to a telephone or to a men's room or for whatever reason. So I had to relocate a foreman who could be anywhere on the floor of a very large factory. Those with a tendency to stay in one place for an extended period, like Len, were fairly easy to find. Those who were constantly on the move, like Carl, were much harder to locate.

I wouldn't suggest this as a "rule of thumb" for evaluating factory supervisors. After all, I had only a small sample, and many other aspects of supervisory performance have to be taken into account. But it does highlight one of the underlying principles of staying in control of any multifaceted managerial task. It can be summarized conveniently in two words: Keep moving.

Anything that is worth managing should be managed briskly, so it does not rob time from other management-worthy tasks. If a particular responsibility requires considerable managerial time, it is better to revisit it frequently than to concentrate on it to the exclusion of other tasks.

A corollary is that when a process is supposed to produce a predictable result, the most convenient and stimulating way to manage that process is probably *not* the best way. In other words, technology dictates the appropriate psychology for a supervisor. Sorry about that.

THE DAY SHIFT

I met the day-shift supervisor, whom we will call Ed, in the lounge at 6:45 A.M. This was toward the end of my observations, so I had already developed some insights into what foremen had to do. Therefore I was perhaps better able to appreciate the nuances of Ed's performance than I had been at the beginning of my study.

Ed began by conferring with his predecessor, the night-shift supervisor. The day shift has many more maintenance people than the night shift, and therefore it commonly inherits maintenance problems that the night shift has not been able to solve. For this reason, the day shift seldom gets off to as smooth a start as the other two shifts.

The trick to running the day shift successfully, Ed told me, was to preserve the workers' morale until the repairs were made and the machines could start running again. Waiting for repairs made the workers feel helpless, and operating machines at reduced speed (to forestall break-downs) made them feel ineffectual. So he had to be prepared both to cheer up his workers and to figure out how to minimize the repair time.

Sure enough, the night-shift foreman looked haggard and reported a rough night. Three machines were down, and several others were in a borderline status.

"We'll take care of it," Ed told his colleague, who seemed grateful to leave.

Ed moved quickly down the line, telling each operator the speed at which it was safe to run the machine. In some cases, of course, that was zero. "I'll get you up again, just as quick as I can," he told them. "It won't be long. Just hang in there."

When the maintenance crew arrived, Ed told them which machines to deal with first. Some required lengthy repairs, while others could be fixed quickly. I thought he might want to get right to work on the lengthier repairs, to minimize the delay in bringing them back into service. But he chose the opposite strategy instead. Later, he explained it to me this way:

If two machines are down, one with a big problem and one with a little problem, and you fix the big problem first, you'll have both machines down for as long as it takes to fix the big problem. But if you fix the little problem first, you'll have one machine back in operation fast, and the second will be ready only a little later than if you'd done it first. Meantime, that first machine will be producing for you all the while you're working on the second one.

As the repairs got under way, Ed spent much of his time with the workers whose machines were shut down or running at reduced speed. He offered encouragement and tried to make himself useful, for example, by rolling a stack of containers a short distance or picking up debris. One operator seemed quite agitated, and Ed engaged him in conversation for several minutes, out of earshot. Later Ed told me, "He gets upset real easy. You just have to hear him out and jolly him along. He'll be all right, once we get going."

Another operator looked up as I walked by, smiled sadly, and said "We're all running bad today." I tried to be encouraging. "Don't worry," I told her. "We'll get it fixed pretty soon." Of course, I knew full well that I hadn't any idea of how long it would take. The operator seemed to sense that, because her only answer was another forlorn smile.

But I could see Ed's point about the psychological reaction to a bad start-up. These people were facing the possibility of eight hours of unavailing effort to overcome problems they had not created. Some were downcast, some were angry, and some were grim. Ed's main concern was that some of his people might just give up and try to get lost in the rest rooms and that others might just sit sullenly at their machines, oblivious to the dials and meters, but ready to snarl at anyone who came close to them.

As the more easily repaired machines came back into service, Ed called out the good news to those who were still shut down or running slowly. "Here comes old number eight over there," he announced cheerily. "Look at her go! We're moving again! Just keep on hanging in. We'll get to you, too!"

The gloom began to lift a little. Ed continued to spend most of his time with the operators who were still unable to operate at full speed, leaving those whose machines were already repaired to their own devices. He looked in on the maintenance crews only often enough to be sure they were progressing more or less as he had anticipated. As lunchtime approached, the entire department was up and running again. The crisis had passed.

By now, Ed's style of supervision had changed. Instead of providing close support to the workers who were awaiting repairs to their machines, he moved quietly about the line, speaking mainly when he was spoken to. He was very visible, but for the most part he left his operators alone. He noted with satisfaction that some of his operators had begun to help each other in small ways, though they were not required to do so.

At lunch, he told me that his priorities would be different that afternoon than they had been that morning. During the morning he had been conducting a holding operation, trying to keep the department together until all the repairs were made. Now he would switch to a preventive mode, making lots of routine checks and preventive inspections, hoping to turn over a clean operation to the afternoon shift.

"We inherit a lot of problems from the night shift," he said, "because we have lots of maintenance capacity that they don't have. But that also means that sometimes we start off slow, like we did this morning. No way are we going to have a good production run on a day like this. But if we can set things up right for the afternoon shift, they should do real good. So that way, we can average it all out."

With his urgent tasks out of the way, Ed spent most of the afternoon attending to deferrable tasks. He ordered supplies and put the maintenance crews onto preventive or elective work. Then, with about thirty minutes left to go, one of his machines developed an intermittent malfunction. He could have run it until the end of the shift, simply discarding any defective products and leaving the machine for the afternoon-shift supervisor to fix. Instead he shut down the machine, and assigned a maintenance crew to begin the necessary repairs, which would have to be completed by the next shift.

I asked him about that. "Don't you guys compete with each other," I asked, "to see who can have the best run?"

He acknowledged that they did. "But in this case, I lost less production by shutting that machine down than the next foreman would lose if I left him with a worn-out machine. You can't look only at your own shift; you have to look at what's best for the company."

As the afternoon shift filed in, Ed briefed the incoming supervisor about the partially repaired machine and then thanked his own subordinates for a good day's work as he passed down the line reading their meters.

Despite the handicaps he encountered when the day began, Ed had done a virtuoso job of managing his department, adjusting his tactics to meet its changing needs. He had provided whatever his people needed to maintain their productivity, which included leaving them alone when they regained their self-sufficiency. Ed was, of course, one of the top-rated supervisors in the plant.

ON EFFECTIVE SUPERVISION

I don't know whether the company had ever tested the intelligence of these fifteen supervisors. But I did spend the better part of eight hours with each of them and had an ample opportunity to form an opinion of their comprehension and reasoning powers. That's not the best way to measure intelligence, but it's the best way I had. On that admittedly fallible basis, I'd say they were all fairly bright and that they didn't differ very much from each other in raw mental capacity.

But they did differ in their effectiveness, because that's the way the sample was selected. Does this mean that there's no relationship between a person's intelligence and his supervisory performance? No. It means that if a company selects only reasonably bright people to be first-level managers, there probably won't be enough difference between their intellects to explain any other differences between them. So the practical question that we face is, Why are some reasonably bright supervisors more effective than other reasonably bright supervisors?

I think the answer is that for whatever reason, the best foremen have formed more effective *habits* than their colleagues did. Their superiority wasn't built into them beforehand, and therefore it couldn't have been detected or predicted by tests. Instead, it was learned after they were selected.

Foremen learn, probably in their first few months in their new capacity, to approach their job in ways that presently become, for better or worse, habitual. Some learn their way of managing by trial and error, and others learn by following the counsel or example of other supervisors. Whether they learn habits that make them into highly effective supervisors or other habits that make them into not-so-effective supervisors is, I think, largely a matter of chance. That's the best explanation I have for why there are so many supervisors who do their jobs tolerably well, but seldom much better than that.

Habits themselves are inevitable, but less-than-highly-effective habits are not. The obvious antidote to first-level managerial mediocrity is training. To be effective, training has to be given both early and often. And what should supervisors be taught, besides the technical and paperwork details they are already taught?

They should learn how the best of them manage, especially how they manage their time. There will be some differences, I think, from company to company, and from industry to industry. But there will also be a core of principles on supervising effectively anywhere. There are things, in other words, that every supervisor should know.

MANAGING THE UNFORESEEN

The foreman's job exists, in part, because production involves too many variables ever to be completely predictable. Therefore, someone has to be there to deal with the unanticipated. It's the supervisor's main responsibility to keep production flowing smoothly, regardless of what may crop up to impede it. That's the key word in a supervisor's job description: *regardless*.

Thus, the key distinction I observed between the most effective foremen and their less effective colleagues was in how they managed unforeseen events. Carl, for example, was forever trying to forestall the unforeseen—to outwit fate, as it were. Len, on the other hand, relied on his coping skills to deal with emergencies that were already upon him. Instead of fending off the unforeseen, he tried to beat it back—to counterpunch against the blows of fate, so to speak. Ed's strategy had to be different, because his worst problems arose on the night shift, literally while he was still asleep. He had to master the art of the holding action, of keeping his department from losing its will to work while he improvised ways to restore its full capacity.

What's the best way to manage unforeseen events? There is probably more than one best way. The important thing is to get newly appointed foremen to think about them as early as possible, before their habits get too encrusted to be easily changed. Here's how it was done at this company.

RESTRUCTURING THE FOREMAN'S JOB

When I presented these findings to Bill L., he studied them for a few days and then called me. "It makes a lot of sense to me," he said, "but what really matters is whether it will make sense to the foremen. We have to get them to buy in to any training we want to put them through."

He was right. All we had so far was one nonforeman's observations of a handful of foremen in one plant. Whether I had pinpointed the habits that enabled some of them to supervise more effectively than others was, like it or not, a secondary issue. Foremen, like most people, are as concerned with the messenger as much as, if not more than, they are with the message. Inevitably, the primary issue with them was going to be, *Who says* that we need to change in these ways?

Unless the findings rang true to the foremen themselves, they'd get a polite hearing and then be quietly forgotten. Bill proposed to finesse the "Who says?" issue altogether, by appointing a committee of the most respected foremen to interview all of their colleagues, searching for effective ways of dealing with common problems. The idea was to pool the collective experience of all of them. That way, the answer to the crucial "Who says?" question would be "You did."

"They'll probably come up with plenty of good ideas," he said. "And if your survey was at all accurate, some of their ideas will be the same as yours, anyway. But this way they'll own the results themselves. They won't be indebted to some out-of-town consultant."

I thought it was a brilliant answer to the "not invented here" problem. As it turned out, Bill was right. The supervisors, after interviewing all of their colleagues, zeroed in on what they considered to be their own worst habits, including many that I had identified. For example:

- Reluctance to correct employees who used convenient but forbidden procedures (such as reaching into a jammed machine). The foremen's committee brushed aside the rationalizations (such as, "it's the quickest way to clear a jam") and focused on the real problem: their own reluctance to confront someone whom they didn't want to offend. The committee's prescription: Confront him anyway, and after a few repetitions, he'll get the message.

- Tolerating employees who ignored quality and concentrated only on the volume of production. The supervisors admitted that they were ambivalent about this issue themselves. It was similar to "just push cases down the chute," since most cases had no defects in them anyway. The problem was that whatever caused a defect would keep on causing it until it was detected and stopped. The committee's conclusion was blunt: As foremen, they were paid to make sure that employees were constantly vigilant. The implication was clear: This should be a do-or-die issue for supervisors.

- Reluctance to use the video monitors. The supervisors recommended, and got, some plain-language explanations of how the devices worked and how to interpret them. Although these largely duplicated their initial training on the monitors, their attitude this time was more realistic. After discussing the matter among themselves, they recognized that the retraining would replace an antiquated expertise ("hearing" the onset of mechanical malfunctions) with an up-to-date one (analyzing the video displays).

- Taking good work for granted. They regarded this as the worst of their own "bad habits." They acknowledged that the best way to prevent poor workmanship was to recognize good workmanship. Otherwise, management's initial investment in training employees to do their work properly would be lost, as good habits eroded from lack of reinforcement. Their prescription: Take the few extra seconds to tell people who are doing their work well that somebody noticed.

I'll close this case by noting that Bill L. was an executive who knew how to use consultants. He respected my findings, but he used them as a source of ideas to be combined with other ideas, not of answers that were complete in themselves. He made it a habit to seek good ideas wherever he could find them, and I was pleased that he turned to me for that purpose.

Chapter Nine

U.S. Home: A Motivational Pressure Cooker

One day, I was glancing through a copy of *Business Week* when a familiar name caught my eye: mine.

It was in an article about U.S. Home Corporation, which was then the country's largest builder of one-family homes. The chairman, Guy Odom, was a voracious reader who usually finished several books a week. When he found one he liked, he assigned it as required reading to employees who had signed up for the company's management development program. The article listed a few of those books, and one of mine was among them.

So I sent Mr. Odom an appreciative note, and in due course he sent me a courteous reply. One thing led to another, and a few weeks later I found myself in the Houston headquarters of U.S. Home, because Guy Odom wanted to talk about the company.

A COMPANY OF MANAGERS

My purpose in this chapter is to focus on a particularly important aspect of employee motivation: the performance of highly motivated individuals under high stress. That turned out to be one of the few areas in which Guy Odom and I had differing views. However, we saw eye to eye on most other issues, and in the end he accepted the majority of my recommendations.

In all of my dealings with Guy Odom, I have found him to be a man of strongly held convictions. I must also admit that people who know me well have made the same observation about me. So it should not be surprising that when he and I differed, we differed emphatically. The case presented here will focus on those differences, even though they represented only a small part of the many issues that he and I worked on together, and even though we agreed on most of the others. I should add that even when we disagreed, our relationship was always cordial.

When I got to Houston, Odom began by explaining that U.S. Home was a company of managers. "We have no roofers, no painters, no masons of our own," he told me. "Instead, we farm out all of the work to individual subcontractors."

The people who were directly in charge of building houses were being trained for jobs in upper management. Functionally, they were called "superintendents"; in effect, each of them was a general contractor. He or she would sign up the subcontractors, as needed, to work on a particular house. They hired, fired, paid, and generally rode herd on them. "These management trainees," Odom told me, "are the key to our success."

The superintendents were bound by the company's financial guidelines and quality standards. But within those limits, they ran their own construction projects. It was their job to find the subcontractors they needed, to schedule their work, and, above all, to make sure that they showed up when they were supposed to and did their work properly.

At the time, I was still a bit naive about the building trades. So I asked whether all that was particularly difficult.

"It is if you want to deliver a good house when you said you would, and still make a good profit on it," said Odom.

He explained that most subcontractors—the carpenters, plumbers, and so forth—were self-employed. Many of them had other jobs, too, and also did their construction work for other companies. They tended to be *very* independent and did their building work when and if they pleased.

At the time, U.S. Home had hundreds of active construction sites, all over the country, each with its own team of superintendents. All of them had their hands full, looking after myriad details and trying to keep everything moving ahead on schedule. But Odom assured me, with evident pride, that virtually all of those projects were on schedule and under tight control.

"There are two reasons for that," he said. "This will interest you, as a psychologist, because both involve motivation."

The book that Odom had assigned to his managers was called *Management by Motivation*. I had been expecting some kind of reference to it, and here it was. "Tell me more," I said.

Odom smiled. "First of all," he said, "our managers are a bunch of tigers."

He explained that U.S. Home sought out people who were aggressive, demanding "self-starters." The company wanted management trainees as superintendents who simply would not accept someone else's failure to perform, regardless of circumstances. No excuses were accepted for missing a deadline or for poor workmanship.

"Of course," said Odom, "every other company would like to hire the same kind of managers. But we happen to know how to find them."

He had me intrigued. People with those characteristics are relatively scarce, so I asked him to explain.

He told me that in 1967 he had assembled a team of key executives who had proved themselves under fire, time and again. They had withstood the job pressures that caused the careers of many other executives to derail. Seeing this pattern repeat itself many times, he became curious and began to read whatever psychological research he could get hold of that addressed the problem. Why were some people consistently effective under trying conditions, while others were not?

"Are you familiar with the Guilford–Zimmerman Temperament Survey?" he asked me.

I was. It was a well-known paper-and-pencil personality test that had been around for a long time.

"In 1969 I decided that the top executive team should sit down and take the G–Z together," he said. "And sure enough, we all had a similar profile. Almost all scored high on ascendancy."

The authors of the test had used the term "ascendancy" for a pattern of responses that was perhaps better translated as "dominance." It referred, broadly, to gaining influence over others by self-assertion and willpower.

I saw what Odom was driving at. "So you took that pattern," I said, "and made it the standard for hiring all of your management trainees."

"That's part of it," said Odom. "We're also looking for intelligent people who can sort out complex problems. But yes, we do want them to be hard-driving and uncompromising, like us, because that's what it takes to build a quality house on a tight schedule."

I was not as convinced as Odom seemed to be that you could actually homogenize the behavior of hundreds of people simply by selecting them according to their test scores. A lot can happen between answering some test questions on one day, and then, on another day, dealing with a roofing subcontractor who is disinclined to work. I suspected that U.S. Home's managers were less alike than Odom seemed to think. But to debate the point then would have meant a lengthy digression, so I decided to postpone it.

"What's the second reason?" I asked.

"Asset appreciation," said Odom, "financial independence."

Newly hired superintendent–management trainees started with just a few houses to put up. If they did well, they became "lead superintendents" and their responsibilities increased. And so did their pay—geometrically. "The higher you go," said Odom, "the bigger those increases get." He mentioned some impressive figures. "If you can go high enough," he said, "you're looking at significant sums of money."

"And if you don't go that high?" I asked.

He conceded that the company had some attrition. "The majority of those drop out voluntarily," he said. "Others we have to let go, after fair warning. After all, this is a tough, competitive business."

U.S. Home was using a classical "high-risk/high-reward" motivation system. The rewards were so great for those who succeeded that most superintendents willingly accepted the risk side of the trade-off.

"So you've got a bunch of tigers chasing a pot of gold," I said, "knowing full well that some of them will make it and some won't."

"That's the formula," said Odom. "But there's also our management development program. It's voluntary, but most of our management trainees sign up for it."

Odom explained that he read every management book he could get his hands on, in the belief that this made him a better manager. When he came across one that he considered appropriate for training purposes, he sent a copy to all enrolled superintendents. They met in discussion groups once a month to talk about how these books were related to their work.

I noted that the superintendents had to put in long hours to get all those houses built. "Then on top of that," I said, "you expect them to read a new book every month and meet with each other to discuss them?"

"Absolutely," said Odom.

He explained that the superintendents were all in training to become division presidents. They had three or four years in which to prove themselves, and in that time he wanted them to reach for their own limits: to become the most effective managers they could be. He would settle for nothing less and was convinced that the best way to make that happen was to lay heavy demands on them.

"Sometimes," he said, "I expect more from them than they ever thought they could accomplish. My aim is to prove to them that they have potentialities they didn't even know they had."

The core of Odom's strategy for getting all of those houses built on time, within budget, and up to specifications was to use hefty rewards to lure the most ambitious people he could find and then challenge them with prodigious demands. He sought individuals whose internal motivation was set permanently on "full speed ahead." Then he maximized their external motivation. They could fall by the wayside, which was the risk, or they could succeed and grow rich, which was the reward.

Motivation has three sources. One is embedded uniquely in each personality, and for reasons we don't fully understand it induces behavior patterns that can last for a lifetime. That is what we try to discern with tests like the G–Z. The other two sources are external, out there in the world in which the individual lives and works. One external source consists of various attractors: things we seek, like the big income opportunities at U.S. Home. The other external source includes the deterrents: things we wish to avoid, like intolerable job pressures or getting fired.

For all three of those sources, Odom had tried to set the motivation levels at their maximums. Obviously, this man knew a lot about motivation theory. But the practical question remained: Would it work?

"Our motivation system," Odom assured me, "is what keeps our costs low and our profits high."

In the construction business, the biggest variable cost is labor. Subcontractors are paid by the job, and they pay their employees by the hour. So the formula for maximizing profits is to get them into a house as soon as they are needed, make sure they work quickly and correctly, and then get them out so other workers can move right in to handle the next jobs. The trick is to set a tight schedule and keep to it. Whether that actually happened at U.S. Home was up to the superintendents. That's what made their role critical.

I felt the time had come to get to the point. So I said, "Mr. Odom, what can I do for you?"

He smiled again. "I need to know if our motivation system is really as good as we think it is," he said. "I need an appraisal from an expert." Then he walked over to a bookshelf and pulled out a copy of my book. "And you," he said, "are an expert."

At this point, it would help to reiterate that the project that Odom assigned to me was to evaluate motivation in the entire organization, not just the construction superintendents. For example, the sales organization was also analyzed. What follows, therefore, is a small part of a much larger study, selected because of what it reveals about strong-willed people under high pressure.

HIRING TIGERS

Before I left his office, I persuaded Odom that the best way to find out how the motivation system actually worked was to get the perspective of the people to whom it was being applied. I would interview as many U.S. Home employees as I could (including, in the case considered here, construction superintendents) in the cities where they were concentrated, which were mainly in Florida and Texas. Then I would prepare a questionnaire that would be sent to all of them, wherever they were. I would also prepare a separate questionnaire that would be sent to U.S. Home's "alumni": former employees who had left the company, for whatever reason.

First I wanted to learn more about the way in which construction managers were recruited. U.S. Home had division personnel managers in various parts of the country who tested and hired job candidates, so I had a long talk with one of them.

Neither she nor any of her colleagues was a psychologist. Odom did not consider that a serious handicap, and by the time I finished talking with her, neither did I. All the personnel managers really did with tests was to match the scores against the patterns that Odom wanted.

She was very busy, but she answered all of my questions. "We're constantly looking for new managers," she explained, "because the demand is so high now and the supply is always low."

Three factors combined to set U.S. Home's requirements for new management trainees. One was promotion. Whenever one of them was promoted to lead superintendent, he or she left behind a vacancy that had to be filled. The second factor was attrition. When someone left, whether voluntarily or otherwise, another vacancy was created. The third factor was the company's growth. When a new housing development was started, new superintendents were needed to get it going.

"What about the supply?" I asked her.

"We're looking for people with a really intense determination to win," she said. "You just don't come across that kind of person every day."

So she ran ads in the newspapers and asked existing managers for recommendations. Someone who looked interesting was invited in and asked to take the G–Z. If he had the right profile, he was also given the Wechsler, a commonly used intelligence test for adults.

"And if they're OK on all of that," she told me, "I tell them what this job is really like. Managing the construction of a house is very, *very* tough."

I like to recapitulate what people tell me in interviews, partly to be sure I've gotten it right, but also because that encourages them to add more details. So I said, "OK. If you like them when they come in, you screen them with these two tests, and those who survive your interview and the tests are hired. Is that it?"

"That's it," she said. "But you've got to look at a lot of people to find the few that can meet our standards."

I asked for her impressions of the people who did well on the tests.

"They are the kind of people," she said, "who are just dying to take charge. They are determined to get their own way. They know enough to be polite, but they don't just sit there and let you lead the conversation, either."

"Like caged tigers?" I asked.

"Something like that," she agreed.

I asked whether she knew how to interpret the Guilford–Zimmerman. She told me that she didn't actually try to read anything into the test results. She just laid the template over the answer sheet and counted the answers that fit Odom's desired pattern. So I asked her what happened when candidates' test responses showed that pattern.

"That's when we give them the Wechsler," she said, "just to make sure they're as smart as we think they are. We want a manager who is ascendant and smart. If they can get past the personality survey and the IQ test, I'll probably offer them a job."

I asked whether she looked for people with previous experience in construction.

She said it was considered a plus, but it wouldn't help them if they didn't get a high ascendancy score. It wasn't really necessary for them to know how to build a house, because company experts would teach them what they needed to know. "That's why we make them take the IQ test," she said. "We want people who can learn fast."

I asked how she managed to attract a large enough pool of candidates.

"To put it bluntly," she said, "if you're good enough, you can get rich. We're frank about that. You'd be surprised how that pulls them in."

HIGH RISK, HIGH REWARD

I asked one of the division managers to tell me what he told the new hires. These management trainees would actually work under a lead superintendent, so the division manager would be his or her boss's boss.

"I just tell them the truth," he said. "I've been through it myself. I tell them that if they want to make big bucks in this company, they can forget about their private life. They won't have one."

A superintendent had to make sure that dozens of subcontractors, most of them highly individualistic, were all doing exactly what they were supposed to do, exactly when they were supposed to do it, even if other

builders were screaming for their time and attention. When a superintendent wasn't chasing down a plasterer who had taken on more work than
he could handle, he might be calling the brick company to make sure the
bricks were not delivered to the wrong place.

If a superintendent wasn't punching out the checklist on a half-finished
house, she might be on the phone, answering her division manager's
questions. And after a long, hard day, a superintendent would probably
settle down with a new management book, because he'd be expected to
speak knowledgeably about it in the management development meeting,
a few nights later.

"So you get up at five in the morning," the division manager told me,
"to be on the job at six, and if you get home before midnight, you're lucky.
And it just goes on like that, relentlessly, month after month. Even on
Sundays, you're out crawling around the building site, catching up on
details that got away from you during the week."

"Lots of time pressure," I said.

"Yes, but that's only part of it," he replied.

The real pressure on the trainees, he explained, is from their immediate
boss.

"That lead superintendent," he said, "is all over you, all of the time,
making sure you don't fall behind. A few months ago, he was probably at
your level, hustling the tradesmen. But his own boss, who is a division
manager like me, is all over him, too. My lead superintendents are merciless, because I make them merciless. If one of them has to choose between
giving you a break and saving his own ass, you're going to get a written
warning. You get three of them, and you're out."

"What's the attrition rate for superintendents?" I asked.

He said that it varied, that he didn't keep track of it because he didn't
have the time, and that frankly he didn't care.

"Let's just say," he said, "that it's the survival of the fittest. We promise
a house by a certain date, and it's going to be ready by that date. Period.
No excuses accepted. That's all there is to it. But most of them don't
complain about the work load. Instead, they ask about what you have to
do to get promoted, and how much they can make. To me, that's a good
sign. It means they're hungry."

"It sounds like you can get rich, or you can quit, or get fired," I said, "with
nothing in between."

He told me that the system filters out people who are not as tough as
they thought they were. Possibly some good people were lost in the process,
but that couldn't be helped. It was the price of getting all of those houses

built on time. What's more, he assured me, those who survived were *very* effective.

"They're the ones who drive this company," he said. "And you can see the results for yourself. We're number one, and this is why."

THREE SUPERINTENDENTS

I met with superintendents where they worked, usually during their lunch break or a coffee break at a construction site. Most were dressed in jeans, plaid shirts, and leather boots. All wore hard hats and had pagers clipped to their belts. I judged most of them to be in their late twenties or early thirties.

At one such meeting with three young management trainees, I asked them to talk about their jobs.

"It's Murphy's law, every day," said one. "Anything that can go wrong, will."

He had learned quickly not to take anything for granted. If a particular project was on schedule, that was no guarantee that nothing would go wrong. If a subcontractor or a supplier promised to do something for you, that didn't mean he would. He found that he had to follow up on everything, again and again, until he could see for himself that it had been done right.

"A house goes through different phases," said the second superintendent. "One day you're pouring concrete, and as soon as it dries, your frame goes up, and right after that the roofers go up on top. The whole trick is to squeeze down the delays between the phases."

Once construction had begun, the superintendent wanted each phase to run like clockwork, smoothly and predictably. The schedule was always very tight.

"That means," he said, "that you can't let anybody screw up, or not show up, or take off before he's finished. So you're in there all the time, checking up, making sure they know that you're right on top of them."

The third superintendent said, "I have literally gone to a subcontractor's house at six o'clock in the morning, and banged on the door to get him out of bed, and dragged him over to our construction site."

He was quick to point out that most subcontractors and their tradesmen were not lazy. The problem was that most houses were built at the peak of construction booms. At such times, subcontractors try to get as much work as they can, knowing that lean times probably lie ahead. So they tend to take on more work than they can handle.

"With them," he said, "it's either feast or famine. But that's their problem, not mine. I can't let them decide when they're going to get around to working on my house. I tell them I'm going to be their number one priority, and they damn well better know it."

I asked them to tell me what they liked best, and least, about their job.

"That's easy," said the first. "I've had jobs before where it could get boring, but you'll never get bored on this job."

He told me that he enjoyed having to keep up with a constant flow of unexpected changes, which forced him to improvise continually. Doing this successfully, day after day, was an ongoing affirmation of his growing skill. Here was a man who thrived on challenge. "No matter what comes at me," he said, "I can handle it. I love it."

"Now, what do I like least?" he continued. "That's easy too. It's my boss. If I didn't have to spend so much time answering all of his questions, I'd get more work done, and faster. I know he's got a job to do, but he just gets in the way."

The second superintendent agreed. "This company is like a college fraternity. The sophomores make the freshmen miserable."

He explained that his boss had been a trainee, just like him, a few months earlier. Having survived that, he'd been promoted to lead superintendent and now supervised five or six of his former peers.

"When he's not here, breathing down my neck," he continued, "he's on the phone, following up on me. I don't know who taught him how to manage, but he's all threats. He keeps saying he has zero tolerance for a missed schedule or a failed inspection. I don't mind the pressure, but I don't need him to motivate me. I motivate myself."

The third superintendent said that he'd seen some good managers quit after receiving two warnings, because the risk of being fired had become too great. This had made him fatalistic.

"You can bust your butt," he said, "but if something slips, your lead superintendent has to prove to his boss that he did something to fix it. The easiest way for him to look like he's got the problem solved is to sock you with a warning. Simple as that."

The first superintendent interjected, "But tell the truth. If you become my boss, and I fall behind on a house, wouldn't you do the same thing to me?"

"Absolutely," said the third. "I'm in this for the big bucks, just like you and everyone else. The only way to get there is to survive. If I have to sock it to you to survive, you'll get another warning. I wouldn't give it a second thought."

DIVISION PRESIDENTS

I interviewed several division presidents, one at a time. This one was fairly typical:

In any big outfit, including this one, you're going to get some bitchers and some moaners. You've probably run into a few. If I were you, I wouldn't pay any attention to them. The truth is, we set high standards. Everybody knows that. I wouldn't want to work for an outfit that didn't have high standards. That's what makes it fun.

To illustrate his point, he cited a contest that had been held several months earlier. It was a competition between the different divisions to see which one could put up a properly built house in the shortest time. Each division had started with a raw lot and built a house from the same set of blueprints. Subcontractors were lined up in the street, shouting at the ones who were still in the house to hurry up and get out so they could get in. Floodlights were brought in so they could continue working after dark. As each stage was completed, a regular inspection had to be passed. Impressively, the winning division finished its house in just over twenty-four hours.

"That's a little more than two days of ordinary work time," the division manager explained. "Nowadays, the industry standard, nationwide, is around a hundred or a hundred and twenty days. That shows you what can be done, if everyone makes a maximum effort."

I was a bit skeptical, so I asked, "And what about the house?"

"It's been sold," he said. "Somebody's living in it. As far as I know, they haven't had any more warranty claims than the average house."

"It sounds like a party," I said. "Everyone joined in the fun."

"That's what I mean," he said. "Some people call it pressure. I call it a chance to show how good you are. In this job, you put your ego on the line every day, and you prove yourself every day. It's definitely a high-adrenaline job. I love the excitement. And how many people can say that about what they do for a living?"

"What about the bitchers and moaners?" I asked.

"Somebody made a mistake when they were hired," he said. "You can't tell for sure how good someone is until they try to put up a house for you."

After a few weeks, he explained, some superintendent trainees just gave up. Others were fired after falling behind repeatedly and being unable to catch up. The pressure served two functions: It kept the houses on schedule, and it weeded out those management trainees who couldn't stand the pace.

"I tell my managers right up front," he said, "that if you're behind schedule, you just do whatever it takes to catch up, even if you have to stay up all night. You're not paid to sleep. You're paid to put up houses."

"And what do you get out of this, yourself?" I asked.

"I'm having a ball," he said. "My job is great fun, I'm making good money, and I'm going to make even more. I admit I'm not very tolerant. But I can't afford to be. We're the best in the business, and that's *because* we don't tolerate mediocrity."

MEETING THE ALUMNI

It was not easy to arrange interviews with former U.S. Home superintendents. Many could not be located, and those we did find were sometimes disinclined to cooperate. But I managed to contact enough of them, either in person or by telephone, to get a sense of their perspective on what it had been like to work for U.S. Home.

Some had resigned, and a few had been fired. Understandably, their views of U.S. Home differed from those of the superintendents who were still employed.

"It was quite a revelation," said one. "I thought I knew myself pretty well, but I guess I didn't. I thought it was exactly what I wanted. I knew about the stress, but I figured I could take it."

What finally got to him, he told me, was the relentlessness of the pressure. He handled one crisis only to face another, and then another, and so on, seemingly ad infinitum. Eventually, it had worn him down, and he found himself asking why he was enduring this. He began thinking that life was too short to spend so much of it on a seemingly accelerating treadmill. The big payoff he had dreamed of seemed to recede, always further away, like a mirage.

"Maybe I could have made it," he said. "We'll never know. It would have been suicide to tell my boss, 'Hey, let's go get a beer and let me get some things off my chest.' So what I discovered in U.S. Home, I guess, is that I'm mortal, and there's a limit to what I can take, and maybe that I need somebody to tell me once in a while, 'Hey, you're OK, you're doing fine.' "

On another occasion I spoke to a former superintendent who had been fired. This is what he said:

"It was more than a year ago, but to tell you the truth, I'm still bitter about it. I never had a failure in my entire life, until this happened. And I didn't really fail. That's the part that really galls me."

He had run into some problems involving sloppy workmanship but felt he was getting them under control. The problems themselves were not unusual. His attitude had been "Hey, I can fix it. No problem!" But his lead superintendent, he said, was afraid he'd be blamed if something weren't done about the problem right away.

"He knew damned well," he told me, "that I was getting it all straightened out. But that wasn't the point. Your work record didn't really matter. All that mattered to him was keeping his district manager from getting upset."

He felt that his boss was grandstanding, trying to impress everyone by making dire threats and then carrying them out. He seemed obsessed with proving how tough he was, at whatever cost. The ex-trainee I was interviewing was convinced that he'd been fired mainly because he'd had the misfortune to be in the wrong place at the wrong time.

When you talk to someone whose pride has been wounded, as this man's had, you have to allow for a certain amount of defensiveness. Had I also spoken to the lead superintendent who had fired him, I would probably have heard an altogether different story. Each would have told the truth selectively, omitting or dismissing parts that the other considered vital and blaming the other for what happened. Each would behave, in other words, as humans always behave when they find themselves caught in a conflict, from which they all struggle to emerge with their egos intact.

THE COMPANY CULTURE

The central issue here was not which party to the conflict was right and which was wrong. Rather, it was the conflict itself, which was more than just the clash of two feisty personalities. You could have substituted other pairs of U.S. Home managers, almost at random, and probably seen similar results, because a trap had been laid for them all by the company culture.

A group's culture broadly defines what its members accept from, and expect of, each other. The best analogy I can think of to illustrate how a culture affects behavior is a script. When you enter an unfamiliar group, it is rather like stepping onto a stage where you will try out for a role in a new play. You are handed a script and you proceed to read from it.

You can deliver your lines as you wish, but the lines themselves are already written. As long as you are part of that group, your freedom of action (and everyone else's in that group) is limited by the script. The odds that you will act the way you think the group expects you to are overwhelming. To do otherwise is to risk being thought a fool.

The "script" written for U.S. Home managers by its culture was Darwinian. It virtually prescribed conflict between them, to force each individual to extremes of effort. Casualties were the price of superior performance by the survivors. As long as the personnel managers could keep pumping enough capable people into the system, the houses would get built, and many of those capable people would be absorbed into division management. But other people, possibly equally capable, would be discarded.

Which fate awaited which manager? The former employees felt that this was the luck of the draw. If you happened to be in the wrong place at the wrong time, or, worst of all, under the wrong boss, you were doomed. Some of the still-employed superintendents felt the same way. But they managed to view their predicament in a positive light: While they still eluded the ax, they found it bracing to continue eluding it. Their attitude reminded me of a remark of Winston Churchill's, about his experiences in the Boer War: "Nothing in life is so exhilarating as to be shot at without result."

But other superintendents were being slowly ground down by the seeming inevitability of being fired, if not for one offense, then for another. It was a culture in which strong egos fed upon each other, making profligate use of human talent but still, undeniably, getting the job done. Guy Odom had contrived a money-making machine that was fueled by ambition and ruthless internal competition.

Still, as long as enough highly motivated people kept entering the system, U.S. Home kept its managerial pipeline full, and its revenues and profits remained high. From a managerial point of view, the system did what it was supposed to do. But at what cost? And could it work better if the culture were changed?

As I mulled over what I heard in the interviews, and what I subsequently read in the questionnaires, I recalled the old debate about efficiency versus effectiveness. Odom's motivation system was certainly effective, as far as reaching the company's goals was concerned. Homes were going up, on schedule, all over the country. But a closer look showed little teamwork or loyalty, a wholesale waste of talent, and a widespread attitude of "every man for himself." The company's most precious resource was used inefficiently. Talent was being squandered.

This was no way to build a company that had staying power, I decided. There was a dark underside to U.S. Home's marketing and financial success. I sensed that this was not what Odom wanted to hear, and I approached my final meeting with him, at which I would present my report, with some trepidation.

CLOSING ARGUMENTS

Guy Odom had asked me two questions: Was U.S. Home's motivation system as effective as he thought it was? And could it be improved?

I told him when he retained me that if he was looking for a psychologist who would bless and endorse his system, I wasn't interested. If he wanted an objective evaluation that pulled no punches, I could provide one. "I wouldn't have it any other way," he answered. "I'm giving you access to anyone you want to talk to. Come back and tell me what you find."

So on the appointed day I went back to Houston, where Odom had convened most of his division presidents and top executives in the ballroom of a suburban hotel. The meeting was supposed to be a free-for-all, in which everyone could ask questions, and for a while it was. There were questions about the sales organization and various other matters. But when I turned to the question of the construction superintendents, the conversation turned into a dialogue, or rather, a debate, between Odom and me.

"You already know," I said, "that as far as superintendents are concerned, your motivation system is doing what you want it to do. You see that every day in your construction status reports. So I'll concentrate instead on whether the system could work better. Yes, it could."

Some of the lieutenants glanced quickly at each other, and a few shifted uncomfortably in their chairs. Odom just smiled. He was a man who enjoyed a good fight but didn't find many people who would take him on.

"The system you have developed," I continued, "uses good people wastefully. You don't develop talent; you consume it. U.S. Home could raise the average experience level of its superintendents, which would probably improve its productivity, just by giving them more of a chance to learn from their mistakes, instead of getting shot down for them.

"You think you understand these people," I said, "because their psychological test profiles resemble yours. But I think you misunderstand both them and the test. They are not inherently ruthless, and they are not driven by fear. They quickly learn that to survive in this business, they have to become callous. So they adopt a veneer of toughness.

"All of you have done that," I told the assembled executives, "so you know what I'm talking about. What really motivates them, and you too, is the desire to win. The most important thing for them is to get whatever they set out to get, and they'll do whatever they have to do to get it. If that means they have to become hard-hearted in order to survive and get ahead, so be it. But they're not innately hard-hearted. They're simply dealing as pragmatically as they can with the environment that you've created for them.

"If they behave ruthlessly with each other," I continued, "that's because you've created a culture in which ruthlessness pays. If you think they try harder because they're afraid of being fired, you're wrong. These people are already working as hard as they can, because that's the only way they know how to work. Threats are just a nuisance to them, not a motivator.

"What attracts them?" I asked. "Why do they put up with the long hours, the constant pressure, the ever-present possibility of being fired? Is it the lure of making a lot of money, if they can win enough promotions? The money certainly gets their attention. That's what pulls them in to the personnel manager's office.

"But is it the pot of gold that also makes them endure all the hardships and risks?" I asked. "With this kind of person, big money would be nice to have. But it's not something they must have. It's dessert, not the main course. The main course is doing better than everyone else at whatever they do. In this case, it's mastering a trade they may have known nothing about a few months ago and then surpassing everyone else at it."

Then Guy Odom spoke up. "This is all very interesting," he said. "I may even agree with you about some things. But I'd like to ask a few questions. First of all, you said we don't understand the test. What did you mean?"

"When people have the same results on a test," I said, "that doesn't mean that they will react the same way in the same situation. All it means is that they are somewhat similar, close enough to be lumped together if you insist on classifying people. But classifying people, by sticking labels on them like 'ascendant' or 'aggressive,' is simply a convenience. It doesn't make them identical, or any less unique as individuals."

"Do you mean," said Odom, "that if I know someone's test scores on the G–Z and the Wechsler, and it fits the profile I'm looking for, that I still don't know how he'll work out on the job?"

"If you have enough people like that," I said, "say, fifteen or twenty, then you can probably predict how at least half of them will work out. But you won't know in advance which ones will be in that half and which won't. Everything in that test is based on statistical probability. That's how Guilford and Zimmerman built it, and that's how you have to interpret it."

"Then how do you account for this?" he asked. "In literally hundreds of cases, the closer someone comes to matching our profile, the better are his chances of not only surviving, but of being promoted, and even winding up in this room this morning."

"I'd love to see your data," I said. "I presume you have all that recorded somewhere. If you can prove your case, I'd gladly write it up for one of the professional journals. It would surprise a lot of psychologists."

"I don't need records," said Odom. "I've got something much better than records." He tapped his head. "A *very* retentive memory."

"I'm sure you do," I replied. "But memory can also be selective. We remember what we want to remember. That's why documents are better than anyone's memory. Documents don't have egos."

A lesser man would have bristled at that. Guy Odom merely smiled again. He was enjoying what I gathered was one of the better arguments he'd gotten into for quite some time.

"I think we'll just have to agree to disagree on this," he said. "Obviously, I have access to information that you won't accept, because you don't have access to it. So let it go at that. But I need to know whether you think we could improve our selection process for management trainees."

"You could probably improve it a little bit," I said, "but what you really need to improve is not selection, but job performance. Selection is one way to do that, but you are probably already pushing that one pretty close to its limits. Beyond a certain point, there are better ways to improve job performance than just being choosy about whom you hire."

"Tell me about the better ways," said Odom.

"You could teach your division managers to be coaches," I said. "You could reward them for holding down turnover, for getting houses built with the smallest number of superintendents coming and going."

"I wouldn't want to tinker with a system that's working," said Odom. "I wouldn't want to dilute the incentive for peak performance."

"If your selection system works as well as you claim," I said, "you wouldn't weaken the incentive, because the people you are selecting aren't motivated by mere survival. Their incentive is to win, to excel. That's already built into them. Now, if you could teach them to help each other, instead of hounding each other, they'd all become more effective."

Odom looked around the room. "Any further questions, gentlemen?" he asked. There were none.

REENCOUNTER

After that last meeting in Houston, Odom and I went our separate ways. He left the company in 1984. Today's U.S. Home Corporation is, of course, under entirely new management, with its own ideas about how to motivate its managers.

A few years afterward, I learned that Odom had written a book in which he explained his ideas about leadership. (Guy R. Odom. *Mothers, Leadership and Success*. Houston: Polybius Press, 1990.) Reading it was almost like meeting this commanding, powerful personality all over again.

Guy Odom dominated U.S. Home so completely when he was its CEO that it became, at least during those years, very much a projection of his own core beliefs. And those beliefs are in his book.

This man knows more about leadership at first hand than I ever will, and has read more widely than most other people, including me. So his views deserve respectful attention. Nevertheless, in certain respects, I did not find them persuasive. Once again, Guy Odom and I will have to agree to disagree.

I'll comment here on only those sections of Odom's book that pertain to the "debate" we had in Houston: specifically, on the nature and origins of leadership. As for the rest of his book, I'll only say that it is serious but somewhat oversimplified, and that Odom himself would probably agree with that assessment.

In his book, Odom expressed his belief that "dominance and leadership are synonymous, and that every leader of consequence was or is dominant, and that anyone lacking high dominance never has been or will become a great leader." I interpret that to mean that for Odom, "leadership" is the art of getting people who are disinclined to do what you want done to do it anyway, and that the best way to do that is by dominating them.

Of course, you could be dominant in an adroit way or a harsh way, as the occasion demanded. But Odom's central point is that one way or another, leaders have to *make* their followers do what the leaders want them to do. And that's where I disagree.

Leadership is much more than just a quality that some people have and others lack. It is better understood as a *relationship*, in this case, between those who would influence others and those whom they might influence. Any attempt at doing that has to rest on certain assumptions about the particular people whom you want to do your bidding.

If those people were really disinclined to work, a leader would somehow have to counteract that attitude. In that case, Odom would be right: The job would call for a leader who would either subtly undermine or unsubtly overwhelm the workers' lack of interest in work. It would take an insistent, uncompromising leader to do that.

But what if they weren't disinclined at all? What if all they really wanted were tools to do the job and permission to use them? In that case, an altogether different kind of leadership would be called for. You would provide them with the tools, make sure they knew how to use them properly, and then stand back and stay out of their way. Coercion and guile would both be counterproductive.

Alas, some people who are entrusted with power come to think of it as an end in itself, rather than as only one of several means to larger ends: hence all of the jokes about egotistical tyrants in the executive suite. Unless a manager has outgrown the idea that the right to command is more important than the effects of those commands, he or she is not qualified to lead anyone.

Such managers are using their jobs, rather than doing them, and that's an important distinction. You use a managerial job when it serves to inflate your ego. You do it when you accomplish the organization's goals at the least cost, which includes minimizing any damage to other people's egos.

Since there are all kinds of people out there, in all kinds of situations, having only one style of leadership simply won't do. The best leaders don't dominate unless they absolutely have to. Instead, they seek to understand what the people whom they are supposed to lead may lack to be as effective as possible. Then they provide whatever that is. If they lack nothing, then that's exactly what effective leaders have the good sense to provide.

Effective leaders don't lead unnecessarily. Neither are they obsessed with power. For them, dominating others is merely one of several ways of getting work done, and not necessarily the best way. It is neither an end in itself nor a psychological necessity for feeling good about themselves.

An effective leader dominates only selectively, not habitually. Therefore, Mr. Odom to the contrary notwithstanding, the trait of dominance is not synonymous with leadership. Instead, it is only a part of leadership, and a readily misused part, at that.

Next, where does leadership, and for that matter, dominance, come from?

Odom asserts in his book that leaders are made, not born, and that in fact they are very largely made by the time they emerge from childhood. He proposes that the children of dominant mothers will learn to be dominant themselves, precisely to protect themselves from maternal domination.

To a psychologist, that's an interesting theory, but it isn't central to the questions we're analyzing here. What is central is that if Odom is right, and if you knew enough about the circumstances in which kids had been raised, you could identify the potential leaders among them even before they were grown up.

I doubt that, for three reasons. First, whether you could ever get that kind of information reliably is dubious at best. (We're talking here about youngsters who won't come onto the job market for a decade or longer.) Second, even if Odom is right (and that remains unproven), you'd be selecting young people because they habitually insist on getting their way. They'd probably be bossy, but (as already argued) that doesn't equate with effective leadership.

Third, and most important: For most people, leadership potential is not really fixed by the time they leave grade school. In fact, it is only beginning to take shape, and what it eventually becomes is to a large extent up to the kids themselves.

What really determines the kinds of adults children become is whether (to use the biblical phrase) they are able to put childish things behind them as they grow up. It is a question of whether they can at some point in their lives finally *outgrow* the circumstances into which they were born and take charge of their own lives.

I wish we understood more about that "growing up" process than we do. But I can say this: Whether you acquire the restraint and flexibility that effective leadership demands depends more on how grown-up you are than on how dominant you are. Nothing qualifies you to be in command of others so much as being in command of yourself.

Two final points:

It is a rare executive who can articulate his core beliefs. Ordinarily, the consultant is left to figure them out, and that can be a tedious and uncertain process. Rarer still is the executive who publishes those beliefs in a thoughtful, carefully researched book. Entirely apart from whether I agreed or disagreed with Odom (and I did some of both), his candor made it intellectual fun to work with him. I never had to guess at what he really meant.

Guy Odom read a prepublication draft of this chapter and helped me to correct certain inaccuracies. He also pointed out, proudly, that many of his former management trainees now head their own successful construction firms. That certainly suggests that he did a good job of selecting them and grooming them. But on the other issues that we debated in Houston, especially the role of selection and the nature of leadership, we have once again agreed to disagree.

Chapter Ten

The Bad Boss Problem

To my knowledge, no one has ever attempted to determine the percentage of managers in a given organization who were insensitive, or even brutal, to the people who reported to them. Most companies are still very much in denial about the extent of the bad boss problem among their managers, just as they were, until a few years ago, about the frequency of alcoholism and drug-related problems among their employees. So no "bad boss" surveys are likely to be authorized any time soon. Nevertheless, it is common knowledge in many companies that certain managers tend to have, shall we say, very unfortunate relationships with the people whom they supervise.

Later in this chapter I'll present a "bad boss" case that I handled for a corporate client. But in order to understand what happened there, and why I did what I did, we'll first have to answer five questions: (1) What, exactly, defines a truly "bad" boss? (2) How much damage do bad bosses do, not merely to morale, but also to the bottom line? (3) How many bad bosses are there? (4) Why do companies tolerate them? (5) What can be done about them?

HOW BAD CAN A BOSS BE?

When you take two adults and give one power over the other, you create an inherently tense and potentially explosive situation. The unasked question lurking behind all such relationships is whether the supervisor is qualified to wield such power. The supervisor is likely to read that word to mean training and experience, and the subordinate is likely to read it to mean wisdom and fairness. So the relationship is likely to begin with at least an implicitly critical attitude on the part of the subordinate and an implicitly defensive one on the part of the supervisor.

That's why managers are inevitably criticized, and not always fairly. To be a manager is to be, at least potentially, the butt of someone's ridicule and someone else's contempt. These handicaps come with the territory. The odds are overwhelming that every boss, at some time in his or her career, will be considered incompetent, unjust, or uncaring by at least one subordinate, and probably many more. So unpopularity is close to inevitable for most supervisors, at least some of the time, with at least some subordinates.

Whether managers are liked or disliked is not a serious issue. That's why unlovable bosses usually keep their jobs and may even be promoted. But whether managers are *effective*—that is, whether the work of their unit gets done properly—is a very serious issue. And if a boss's relationships with the people under his or her supervision are bad enough, the effect on the unit's efficiency can be devastating.

We have to distinguish, in other words, between bosses who are merely difficult to deal with and bosses who actually make their subordinates *less* productive. The former are certainly abundant, but at worst are merely a nuisance. The latter, although not so common, pose a real economic threat to their companies. They are the true "bad bosses."

THE ECONOMIC EFFECTS OF BAD BOSSES

How much damage do bad bosses do? That depends on the number of people whose performance is impaired, and on how critical their work is to the organization that employs them. A bad boss usually demoralizes nearly everyone in the chain of command below him. So does a lower-level boss who's been demoralized by his own bad boss. The negative effects cascade downward.

In general, the number of employees whose work would be negatively impacted by a bad boss is a direct function of his or her organizational level. Although bad bosses can be found at all levels, the ones that management brings to the attention of psychologists are usually vice presidents or higher. That's for two reasons: First, there are so many people in the chain of command below a vice presidential bad boss that the negative effects on the company's performance can be very serious; second, people who reach that level are usually difficult to replace, because of their specialized experience. (As we'll see, both conditions applied in the case of the "bad boss" I'll present later in this chapter.)

Therefore, management is more likely to tolerate, or try to save, a vice presidential bad boss than to resort to its traditional remedy for poor performance at lower levels. That, of course, is simply to fire the offending manager and be done with it.

HOW MANY BAD BOSSES ARE THERE?

Using the strict definition of a bad boss that I've suggested here, I'd say that the frequency of this problem in most companies is at least large enough to be noticeable, and sometimes much more than that. But I can cite no hard numbers, only anecdotes and impressions based on many contacts in many companies. Anecdotally, what is striking is that in virtually every company where I've raised the subject, the response has been similar. It runs something like this:

Yes, I think I know what you're talking about, and yes, we may have a few people in management who more or less fit that description. But it's not a serious problem, and therefore we'd rather not meddle with it.

What matters here is that management is usually aware of the problem and could even name some perpetrators, if it chose to. That's an admittedly slender thread on which to base an estimate, but since it leads to a conclusion similar to one I've reached independently, I'll just stick my neck out and say that on average (and no doubt with wide variations around that average), perhaps 5 percent of the managers in major American companies are bad bosses, as I've defined that term here. Since I've tried to be conservative in arriving at my estimate, the true figure (at least in some companies) could be higher.

Is that 5 percent figure sizable enough to worry about? That would depend on exactly *who* is in that 5 percent and (because of those cascade effects) on *how high up* in the hierarchy he or she has already risen or is earmarked to rise in the future.

WHY ARE BAD BOSSES TOLERATED?

Management usually reacts to the bad boss problem in one of three ways. In most cases, the problem is simply ignored. Sometimes, the manager in question is fired. And in by far the smallest number of cases, management attempts to fix the problem, usually by calling in a psychologist.

First, why is the bad boss problem ignored?

Sometimes, of course, there are sound reasons for deciding to leave well enough alone. But too often, management simply doesn't want to deal with the problem. If pressed for an explanation, they'll present some plausible reasons for doing nothing. Here are a few of the more common "good" reasons for ignoring or tolerating the difficulties created by a bad boss:

The "problem" has been exaggerated; it really isn't *that* bad.

Nobody is perfect. So he has a few faults. So what?

You can't make an omelet without breaking a few eggs. No boss can keep everybody happy.

And so on. The underlying theme is that there would be little to gain, and possibly much to lose, by trying to resolve the problems that the bad boss creates for his subordinates. And indeed, in some cases, that might be a realistic conclusion. In too many other cases, however, they are probably just rationalizations—that is, partial truths that conveniently ignore the rest of the truth.

But beneath those good reasons there probably lurks another set of reasons, of which the decision makers may be only dimly aware. These may very well be self-serving, or unheroic, or otherwise unpresentable. (Self-deception of this kind is by no means peculiar to managers. We all resort to it at one time or another, and managers are no less human than the rest of us.)

The most common underlying reason (the "real" reason, if you will) why managements often prefer to overlook the bad boss problem has a lot to do with corporate culture. Specifically, the bad boss problem is most likely to occur in companies that exalt managerial independence, where top executive oversight of lower managerial levels is reluctant and halfhearted, and where revising a manager's decision, once it has been made, is seldom even considered.

Petty tyrannies can spring up like weeds wherever management is too permissive with itself. Executive permissiveness is especially likely with bad bosses, because they are often rather formidable characters themselves. Even their own bosses may be reluctant to confront them with what may seem like an intensely personal issue: whether the bad boss's own conduct may contribute to operational difficulties in his department. The result, paradoxically, is that a bad boss—who *needs* to be supervised closely—is likely to be more loosely controlled than a good boss, simply because the good one is more approachable.

The bad boss's own supervisor is too likely to deal with him subtly, hoping that he will respond to indirect hints about his management style. But the bad boss is usually too focused on results to give much attention to what will probably seem, to him, like mere trivialities. As a result, when he's finally called in for a serious review of his shortcomings, the bad boss often reacts with genuine bewilderment.

That's why, to get the attention of a bad boss, muted subtleties won't do. Instead, you have to hit him with the verbal equivalent of a two-by-four. And even though most management teams consist mainly of strong-minded people, many managers are reluctant to address one of their colleagues that bluntly.

WHY BAD BOSSES ARE FIRED

The decision to fire a bad boss is usually based on the belief that he is incorrigible, and for that matter that the behavior of *all* adults is unchangeable. But that isn't necessarily so. An adult personality is best understood as a bundle of potentialities, only some of which have been fully developed. But the rest of those potentialities are still there, albeit latent and undeveloped, like unsprouted seeds. Under the right conditions, some of them can be made to grow.

We can't remake an adult personality altogether, in the same sense that you can install a completely new engine in an old car. But we can teach that person to make more use, selectively, of potentialities that are already embedded within his or her personality and to make less use of others. The result can be a more effective version of someone who is still, in all other respects, recognizably the same person. In the case of a bad boss, the result can be a not-so-bad boss—even a reasonably effective one.

Some managements—admittedly, not many—have decided that although the bad boss's effect on his department is intolerable, the prospect of losing him is also intolerable. That makes the third option, uncomfortable as it may be for all concerned, more tolerable. The president of the company to be described shortly was able to grasp that harsh reality. Once he had made that breakthrough in his own mind, he knew that the time had come to call in a psychologist.

FIXING THE PROBLEM

Since the objective here is to change overt behavior, rather than to restructure the individual's inner life, the usual methods of psychotherapy have little to offer. We don't need to plumb the depths of the bad boss's psyche or to dredge up deeply buried information. Instead, we can achieve our limited goals by working with information that is already available to him. We want to increase his control over his own behavior by focusing his attention on aspects of his relationships that he has previously ignored.

The method I'll describe is usually called "behavior modification." We aim to make a number of relatively small but strategic changes in the way the bad boss conducts himself with subordinates. *Small* changes in almost anyone's behavior are quite possible: All you have to do is focus the person's attention on what must be done, explain why it must be done, and provide a strong incentive for doing it. On the other hand, for psychologists to induce behavioral changes in a bad boss that would startle people who knew him well is the province of fiction.

Still, enough small changes can add up to a major change if they are carefully selected. The objective is to make the bad boss *tolerable*—not lovable, or even likable, but just tolerable. We want to change his behavior only by degrees, so that it no longer interferes with the ability of his subordinates to get on with their work. If we can do that and make those changes last for a long time, we will have solved the bad boss problem *for all practical purposes*.

So the trick is to identify those particular acts that do the most damage to the bad boss's relationships and work on getting them under his conscious, deliberate control. How much difference can small changes make? A lot, if they're the *right* small differences. To illustrate the point, here's a brief (and I'm afraid, somewhat embarrassing) anecdote:

A former boss once accused me of not paying attention to what other people said at meetings. Of course I denied that, but he brushed aside my objection. "You have a habit," he said, "of sliding forward to the edge of your chair. Whenever you do that, you're about to jump up and tell people what you think. But you've stopped listening to anyone else, and the proof is that quite often, the points you make after jumping up are the same as those being made by the speaker while you were poised at the edge of your chair."

Sad to say, I was signaling my inattention to any astute observer. And I must admit that I still can't claim a perfect record for focusing on everything that is said at a meeting. But you will *never* catch me sliding forward to the edge of my chair.

And that matters. Now, even astute observers get one less clue that I may be indulging in my bad old habit. And to that extent, I am now more welcome in meetings, and more likely to be listened to, than I used to be. One small behavioral change has made a useful difference.

That's the sort of thing we try to do with the bad boss. We try to find out what he does, *specifically*, that makes him hard for others to tolerate. Then we set out to change those particular bad habits. We aim for a small number of narrowly defined changes, partly because that's all we can usually do within the time available, but also because that's all we really *need* to do to save him.

SAVING A BAD BOSS

In the case I am about to describe, the "bad boss" has asked that neither he nor his company be identified in this chapter. Therefore I will call him "Mac," although that is not his real name. He is still a high-level executive with a major company. As for the company itself, I will only say that it is well known and well respected, and let it go at that.

The company's vice president for human resources called me in and asked, "Have you ever seen an executive who was a technical genius, but a human relations dummy?"

I said I had, fairly often, in fact.

He then proceeded to tell me about Mac, who was a vice president in charge of one of the company's divisions.

"This man is a detail junkie and a classical workaholic," he told me. "There are thousands of details involved in running his division, and he wants to be in on all of them. He has an unbelievable capacity for work, but by now even he is stretched too thin. The result is that decisions get made too slowly, and opportunities are lost, and the division's profits are starting to slip."

"And that," he continued, "is what finally got the attention of our president. I've been trying to get him to intervene with Mac for some time, because Mac's division has the lowest morale in the company, and Mac just ignored me when I told him that something had to be done. But the president is prepared to order Mac to cooperate with you, if you can convince him that you've got a way to straighten him out."

I had made several previous attempts to deal with similar problems, and through trial and error I had learned that there were two prerequisites to a successful outcome. First, the bad boss had to be highly motivated to change. Otherwise he would probably just say that he didn't need a shrink to tell him how to do his job. Second, the "chemistry" between the bad boss and the consultant had to be right. Both had to feel that they could work together effectively.

"If the president decides to go with you," said the vice president, "I can guarantee that Mac will be highly motivated. As you will see, our president has a very unambiguous way of expressing himself. And as to whether you and Mac are compatible, we'll see."

Then I met the president, a no-nonsense person who got right to the point. "Can you teach this guy to delegate?" he asked.

I told him that I didn't think that would solve the problem. Mac had probably learned all there was to know about delegation at the various seminars he had attended. The problem was to motivate him to use what he already knew.

"Then what *are* you going to do about it?" asked the president.

I told him that I would work not only with Mac, but also with his direct reports, because they were probably part of the problem, too. I would meet with them all at least weekly for the first few months, and then, if all went well, I would begin making my visits less frequent. The whole process, I said, would take about a year.

"A year?" he asked. "Why so long?"

I explained that simply changing behavior was the easy part. We could probably do that in a few months. The more difficult part was making those changes permanent. If you don't keep reinforcing the process for at least a year, I told him, the danger of reversion is very high.

"What are you going to do during your visits?" he wanted to know.

I said I would meet with each of them individually for perhaps half an hour. With Mac himself it might be an hour or more. In each case I'd ask them to tell me about their contacts with each of the others during the preceding week. Then we'd all get together to review their effectiveness as a team and to set behavior-change goals for each of them during the coming week.

"And how about Mac?" asked the president. "How does all of this help him?"

It would help Mac in two ways, I told him. First, his division can't improve unless his management team improves, so he'll have a strong incentive to help make that happen. Second, by defining the problem as the team's, rather than as Mac's, we make the process easier for him to accept. He'd be more likely to change if he saw other people making the same effort.

The president gave me his assessment of Mac. "He is very valuable to this company," he said. "That's why I've been willing to overlook some of the problems that my human resources people have been telling me about. But now he seems to be creating *business* problems, and that used to be his greatest strength. I want you to save this guy, if you can, because I really don't like the alternative. I'll talk to him and tell him to cooperate with you. Good luck."

MEETING MAC

I met Mac for the first time in his office, which looked like a walk-in filing cabinet. The desk, the chairs, and even the coffee table and sofa were all piled high with folders, most of them bulging with papers. "What's all this?" I asked. He explained that these files were all awaiting his review. It was his practice to review all documents created by the three executives who reported directly to him, as well as the middle managers who reported to them.

I wanted to bring the compatibility issue up to the surface fairly quickly, because if Mac felt uncomfortable with me I would have to recommend that the company find another psychologist to work with him. So I said, "Why do you burden yourself with so many other people's work? Why do you act as your own assistant? Why do you try to run a big division all by yourself?"

To my surprise, he pulled a pencil from his pocket and began to jot down everything I said. He had immediately slipped into the role of a student and had thrust me into the role of his tutor. Those were all good questions, he said, and he would think about them. To me, this was a favorable sign that Mac and I could work together.

Next he called in his three key lieutenants and explained that I had been retained as a consultant to the division and that my mission was to help improve working relationships and teamwork. He asked them all to cooperate with me and then invited me to speak to them.

I began by saying that I wanted to talk about the difference between an adult and a grown-up. To be an adult meant only that you had reached a certain age, could sign a contract, and could drink beer legally. The world was full of adults, but not all of them were grown-ups. Grown-ups were people who could do well, if necessary, things they would greatly prefer not to have to do at all. That was an important distinction, I told them, because during the coming year we would all have to work together on some uncomfortable issues, and we would deal with them responsibly, as grown-ups.

They all knew that the division had not done well lately. I told them there was nothing to be gained by trying to assign blame for that. The important thing was to do better. We knew that they were all highly competent at their own jobs, but the question I wanted to address was the effect each of them had on the job performance of the other three.

Of course, this would not only involve Mac's impact on each of his lieutenants, but it would also involve their impact on him and on each other. If all of them could become experts at helping the others on the team to do well, the chances of improved divisional performance would be greatly enhanced.

Each of the three executives who reported directly to Mac was quite different from the other two. One, whom I'll call Ken, was serious and reserved. Another, whom I'll call Marty, was intense, brooding, and given to sudden outbursts. The third, whom I'll call Roger, was jovial and witty. Roger opened the group discussion by saying, "It all sounds just dandy, but exactly what are you going to do with us?"

I explained that I'd meet each of them privately a few days later and that on that occasion I'd ask three questions about each of their colleagues: What does he do now that helps you to do your job better? What does he do that actually makes it more difficult for you to do your job well? And what is he not doing that you wish he would do, because it would be helpful to you?

That way, I'd get three inputs on the way in which each of them impacted the performance of their colleagues. Then I'd sit down with each of them and tell him what his colleagues had to say about him. I'd give him time to digest that, and then we'd all meet together to discuss what needed to be done to make the team more effective.

Then, I said, we'd come to the critical part of the whole process. Each of them would set for himself a short list of specific, narrowly defined targets for dealing with each other more helpfully than they had been. And they'd commit themselves, to each other, to trying to achieve those behavior-change goals during the week immediately after that meeting. I'd be back a week later, to find out from each of them how well his three colleagues had actually met his commitment during that week. Then I'd give each a "report card," as given to me by his colleagues.

After that, we'd meet again as a group, to discuss the lessons that could be learned from their own experiences and to set new goals for the following week. And that follow-up would continue, week after week, for as long as it took to produce some worthwhile improvements; and it would continue after that on a less frequent schedule, in order to cement the changes and try to make them permanent.

THE BASELINE

The initial round of interviews helped to define the dynamics within the group at that time and gave me a baseline from which to measure any

subsequent changes. Actually, Ken, Marty, and Roger all had minor problems with each other, most of which were largely alleviated by the time the
project ended. But the major problem for all three of them was Mac, and
since the attempt to modify his behavior is the main focus of this chapter,
I will concentrate here solely on that aspect of the project.

Ken portrayed himself as an obedient, reliable "good soldier." He said it
had never occurred to him to question any of Mac's decisions. He had seen
what happened when either of his colleagues suggested alternative solutions to those Mac had proposed. Mac would launch a lengthy, point-by-
point rebuttal, refuting every aspect of the opposing argument in
exhaustive detail. Although Ken sometimes saw flaws in Mac's ideas, he
did not consider it his proper place to point them out.

I told Ken that by keeping his criticisms to himself, he was actually being
disloyal to his boss. "You're letting him fly blind," I told him. Whether Mac
agreed or disagreed with him was not the issue. Mac needed the input of
everyone on his staff so he could assess the realism of his plans. What he
did with that input was his responsibility, but if Ken did not provide it, the
division might stumble into otherwise preventable failure. I asked him
whether he felt able to speak up when he saw potential problems in Mac's
plans, and he agreed to try.

Marty resented the intervention of the corporate human resources
department. He felt that they had overreacted to some minor problems that
were actually no worse than those of other divisions in the company. Mac,
he said, was irreplaceable, and for that reason Marty would oppose any
attempt to undermine him.

I told him that the vice president had shown me the statistics from the
attitude surveys of the past few years, and that the differences between
divisions were indisputable. Morale in Mac's division *was* the lowest in the
company. But comparing divisions, or even companies, I told him, was not
nearly as important as figuring out why this division's profits had begun to
slide. The president thought it had something to do with the way the
division was managed, and our job was to find any such problems and fix
them.

I also praised Marty for his loyalty to his boss and assured him that I was
here to reinforce Mac, not to undermine him. I needed Marty's help to do
that, and I bluntly asked him for it. Marty eyed me cautiously for a moment
and then said that I could count on him. I had the impression, as I left his
office, that if I played my cards right, Marty could be won over.

Roger regaled me with a few jokes when we met. But when we got down
to business, he voiced some serious concerns. He told me that he had given

up on trying to submit completed staff work to Mac, because Mac would find fault with anything. Besides, he said, many of the changes Mac would insist on were arbitrary and impossible to anticipate. So Roger had found that the simplest way to get his job done was to submit "finished" reports to his boss that were really just rough drafts, then wait to see what changes he would demand.

Remembering those piles of papers in Mac's office, I said, "Doesn't that just create a lot of extra work for Mac?"

"Not really," said Roger. "He creates a lot of extra work for himself, and for everyone else, too. I know it must look ridiculous, but doing things this way actually takes less *total* time than if I tried to do it right the first time. Mac always finds a reason to buck my reports back to me. So I might as well let him edit the whole thing, because that's what he wants."

I was beginning to understand why the division's reaction time had slowed.

Finally, I met with Mac himself. He told me he'd been thinking about the questions I'd put to him when we met. He said he'd always had a horror of sloppy work, or errors of any kind, as if they were some kind of permanent stain on his honor. Besides, he had a talent for organizing masses of details, and it made him feel good to exercise it. So the reasons why he ran the division the way he did were that he had to, for his own peace of mind, and also that he simply *liked* doing it that way.

There is nothing abnormal about enjoying an activity that one does well. But being haunted by the fear of mistakes is not normal. It suggested that Mac was in the grip of unconscious needs he could barely articulate, let alone control. Obviously, there were more efficient ways to deal with his managerial problem, such as having all key documents proofread by someone who hadn't written them, and if necessary proofread again by another independent reader, all *before* they reached Mac's desk.

What's more, Mac fully understood that such procedures would actually save time and allow him to concentrate solely on critical issues, while he decided whether or not to approve a report. But he had never actually tried such methods, because he felt too uncomfortable letting anyone else screen the directives and reports that flowed across his desk. In effect, he functioned as his own staff, thus vastly increasing his work load.

People who can't, and won't, do things that they know make sense are probably under the control of unconscious forces. Trying to reverse that situation, by digging out and exposing those forces and enabling the individual to control his own behavior with conscious choices, is what psychoanalysts do. It is also an extremely difficult, time-consuming, and—

in the end—uncertain process. In Mac's case, with the company paying for my work, and providing Mac's only real incentive for cooperating, that approach wouldn't have been practical.

Instead, I would use a narrower and more superficial approach, which had a greater chance of success within the constraints I had to work under. It might not be a permanent solution, but it would probably last at least several years—and in the context of a dynamic, constantly changing company, several years was certainly good enough. I would concentrate on Mac's overt behavior and leave his unconscious forces pretty much alone. And by now I had reasons to feel pretty sure that this approach would work.

My initial decision to involve Mac's staff in the corrective process was based on two assumptions, and it was now clear that both were correct. The first was that defining the issue to be dealt with as a *shared* problem, rather than as a problem that was uniquely Mac's, had made it much easier for Mac to accept having a psychologist assigned to his division. The second was that it really *was* a shared problem. The staff contributed to it, in no small way. Therefore I couldn't hope to change Mac's behavior without also changing theirs.

BREAKING VICIOUS CIRCLES

I asked Mac to let me attend a few of his staff meetings, to see for myself how they interacted with each other. Of course, these sessions were somewhat strained at first. But I just sat silently in the corner, and as they had business to conduct they presently became engrossed in it. Ken busily took notes. Marty tried to offer refinements of Mac's ideas, which drew lengthy, and astonishingly well-informed, rebuttals from Mac. Roger provided comic relief, making wisecracks about the competitors. Significantly, the administrative bottleneck in Mac's office, which all three of the lieutenants had told me about privately, was never discussed.

The time had come to set some goals for changing behavior. I set four or five for each of them, all based on what I had heard in the interviews and on what I had seen in the staff meetings. However, to keep the focus primarily on Mac, I'll only present one that I set for each of his subordinates, and three of the goals set for Mac himself.

I told Ken that contributing ideas was more important than taking notes and that he should present at least one suggestion at each meeting. Actually, he began presenting two or even three. He was perhaps the most thoughtful member of the team but had suffered from an excess of humility. It was almost as though he had needed someone's permission to say what

was on his mind, and I had granted him that. The other three members of
the team all told me how pleased they were that Ken's vast experience was
now more available to them.

I had reckoned Marty to be the most ambitious and best organized of
Mac's three lieutenants, and Mac agreed with that estimate. But Marty had
been concentrating on relatively minor adjustments to Mac's ideas and had
so far considered it ill advised to raise any major issues in the staff meetings.
So I urged Mac to direct Marty to draw up a plan for expediting the flow
of paperwork through the division, with emphasis on getting quicker
approval. It took Mac a while to become comfortable with that idea, but
presently he gave the order. In the meantime, I suggested to Marty that he
might propose at least one new opportunity for the division at each weekly
staff meeting, instead of concentrating exclusively on ways to reach existing goals.

Roger's personality was less similar to Mac's than those of his two
colleagues, and the result was a certain amount of friction between them.
Mac considered Roger's work sloppy but evidently hadn't discerned that it
was, in a sense, deliberately sloppy. I told Roger that although his tactic
might accelerate decisions in the short run, in the long run it only
perpetuated the problem. So I challenged him not only to submit flawless
reports to Mac, but to document them with as many footnotes as it took to
convince Mac that nothing had been overlooked.

The three most important goals I gave to Mac were (1) liberating
himself, eventually, from at least 90 percent of his current paperwork, by
appointing a "chief of staff" to screen all documents that required his
approval, and by drastically culling his review list, to eliminate any documents that did not have major strategic importance; (2) spending at least
one day each week visiting customers and just letting the division "run
itself" on those days; (3) limiting the length of his monologues during staff
meetings to five minutes.

All of these proposals made Mac very uncomfortable at first, since they
amounted to a wholesale revision of his management style. I told him he
could go about it gradually, but that it was important to make a commitment and begin. I would be his "conscience," showing up weekly and asking
questions of everyone that they all knew I would ask.

EARLY RESULTS

Actually, Mac made all of these changes within three months. Marty
became his very capable chief of staff, seeing to it that all documents

reaching Mac required only a crisp yes-or-no decision. Nearly half of the documents he had been reviewing were now assigned to Ken, Marty, or Roger for a final decision. Weekly staff meetings, which had been mostly line-by-line reviews of the documents Mac had edited, now consisted mainly of information swapping: Mac would report on his field visits, and the others would tell him what they had done, and why they had done it, during the preceding week. And one memorable day, Ken, Marty, Roger, and I made a great show of presenting Mac with a five-minute egg timer so he (and everyone else) could see how much time he had left for his monologues.

By the end of the first three months, Mac's average comment in staff meetings was down to two minutes, and the clutter in his office had largely disappeared. The atmosphere in the division's headquarters was clearly more relaxed, and profitability had begun to improve. Mac was ecstatic. The time had come, he said, to declare victory and say good-bye to the division's psychological consultant.

TEMPORARY SETBACKS

I had made that mistake before and was not about to make it again. The changes I had sought had been easily attained, simply by keeping everyone's attention focused on them. My weekly visits were, by design, just a bit too frequent for any of them to postpone or forget what he had promised to do. And since the behavior-change commitments were known to all four of them, each of them had the other three looking over his shoulder, so to speak. A bit awkwardly at first, but later with increasing ease, they had slipped into their newer, more effective roles. But I knew that all of those gains would be endangered if I ended my visits prematurely.

So I told Mac it would be best if we stayed the course. Actually, he had come to regard me as his private professor and enjoyed using me as a sounding board for his ideas on the various management problems that he faced. It turned out that his main reason for wanting to terminate the consultations then was his continuing embarrassment over having a psychologist imposed on his division.

He told me, for example, of vice presidential colleagues who poked fun at him with remarks like "Mac, I hear you are now so screwed up that your division has its own private shrink." I asked him how he had replied. "I just told him," he said, "that as soon as I was through with you, I would send you over to him." I laughed and said that was a good answer.

But a few weeks later there was a setback. Mac had become upset during a staff meeting and delivered a lengthy denunciation of decisions made by all three of his subordinates. Ken was crushed, Marty was hurt, and Roger was alarmed. "The personality transplant didn't take!" he told me. "The old Mac is back!"

But when I went in to see Mac, he was apologetic and worried that he had disappointed me. "I was having a bad day," he said, "and I just blew it, right in front of my own staff." He wanted to know whether he should apologize for his outburst or just act as if it had never happened. "Whichever way makes you more comfortable," I said. "You can't erase the damage. You can just try to live it down."

Mac was shaken. He now agreed that for the present, it would be best for me to continue visiting the division. I first had to explain what had happened, so he would not lose confidence in himself. Then I had to warn him about the opposite danger.

Mac was forty-four years old. I told him that what he had learned during the past four months had to compete with what he had learned in the preceding forty-four years. His new-found willingness to let go—to trust other people to do their work competently—had to contend with his age-old fear of mistakes. That fear was in his bones, and probably always would be. He could throw up his defenses against it, but the fear would always be probing those defenses, looking for a weak spot through which it could burst out and reassert itself.

"The question is, who is in command?" I said. "Is it you, or your past? You can never afford to be complacent about this, any more than a recovered alcoholic can afford to take just one little drink. You're going to have to fight this battle on a daily basis for the rest of your life. And every once in a while you may lose one of those daily battles, just as you did the other day. But you haven't lost the war. The important thing is to forgive yourself for being human. Learn your lesson, pick yourself up, and get ready to fight the good fight again tomorrow."

After we had discussed that for a while, I turned to the next problem. There were two dangers in a counseling relationship, I told him. One was that it would end before the gains had become self-sustaining. The other was that it would last so long that the individual became dependent on the counselor. "There's a fine line," I told him, "between being a coach and being a crutch, and we don't want to cross it."

ENDGAME

My visits during the next few months were more like check-ups. I had become part of the expected routine. There were very few regressions, by Mac or anyone else, and these were quickly corrected. Still, there was a lingering concern among Mac's subordinates that he was going to revert to his old ways the minute I walked out the door for the last time. When I asked why they felt that way, they all cited his outburst during the staff meeting. That was the "real" Mac, they said, not the friendlier, more relaxed Mac of the past few months.

I told them to give the man credit for a tremendous effort. But to the extent that Mac *had* changed, I said, it was mainly because *they* had made it possible for him to loosen his grip on the reins. They did that by proving that they could be just as fastidious with details as he needed them to be. The best way to prevent a reversion to the old Mac, I told them, was to continue treating him as they had been treating the new Mac.

By now, Mac had begun to understand some of the psychology of interpersonal behavior. He realized that Ken, Marty, and Roger were all making conscious efforts to avoid arousing the "beast" in him: his intolerance for errors. And he also realized that by delegating much of the division's decision making to the three of them, he had not only improved the division's efficiency, but also reassured the president, who had called me in precisely because of doubts that Mac had a future in the company.

Mac had a lot riding on whether his three lieutenants would continue their effort to keep his "beast" in its cage. And he also knew that the best way for him to sustain their efforts was to do all he could to prove that the "new Mac" was here to stay. In that sense, all four of them had a stake in preserving the new relationships they had worked out with each other.

As the last months approached, I began scheduling my visits to be less frequent. Mac began taking me out for long, chatty lunches in which we discussed virtually everything *but* the division. In part that was because the division was doing fine, but he was also intent on "picking my brain." After all, he had a free psychologist, and that benefit was about to disappear.

I anticipated that the president would call me in for a final assessment. To prepare for it, I consulted the notes of my earliest visits and drew up a list of things Mac had done at that time that his subordinates had found particularly difficult to endure. Examples were interrupting them in mid-sentence and countermanding their directives after they had already been sent to the field. In all, there were nine items on what Roger promptly dubbed my "Bad Mac" list.

I then had a long private chat with Mac's subordinates, going through the list item by item and asking them to recall whether any of these things had happened during the preceding three months. The best possible outcome would have been twenty-seven "no's," and Mac got twenty-one. "Not bad at all," I told him, "but you can do better."

After I said good-bye to the four of them for the last time, I had occasional informal contacts with one or another of them over a five-year period. Mac evidently had some rare relapses in those years but always recovered quickly. He was variously described as a more effective manager, a happier man, and someone who was relatively easy to work with. Even allowing for the probability that my sources wanted to please me, this was about as good a result as could be hoped for.

In retrospect, the two key players in achieving this outcome were the president and Mac himself. The president's decision to try to save Mac was gutsy. There was no guarantee that the process would work, and in the meantime he risked being seen by other executives as reluctant to make a tough decision. Probably no one would have criticized him for firing Mac, but he knew that on balance, doing so would almost certainly have weakened the company.

As for Mac, he found himself thrust into a situation in which he had to grow beyond his accustomed psychological limits or lose his job. I doubt that many people could have responded as splendidly to such a challenge as he did.

Chapter Eleven

Lessons Learned by Listening

The time has come to draw the main conclusions suggested by these cases, and to comment briefly on their meaning. Although the cases permit many inferences, to me the most important ones are these:

SPOOK PSYCHOLOGY

An uncomfortable fact of life for psychologists is that most of the world is either unaware of, or unimpressed by, their science. They are in a position not unlike that of well-intentioned missionaries who have come to enlighten the ignorant, only to find that the "ignorant" are often quite satisfied with their own beliefs. The customers, in other words, are not convinced.

The result is that the findings of psychologists are accepted mainly when they do not challenge existing beliefs and are often resisted or rejected when they do. The managers at Caterpillar-Joliet were an example: They were perfectly willing to buy an ambulance that did not challenge their beliefs, but balked at changing methods that were embedded in them.

So it should not be surprising that many people are content to explain human behavior with what amounts to a "spook psychology": that is, commonly accepted explanations of behavior that do not withstand investigation. Spook psychology is mostly just folklore, masquerading as common sense. It is much more widely believed than scientific (that is to say, evidence-based) psychology and can even have a major influence on managerial decisions and public policy, for example, Cyanamid's belief that it had to overpay its highest-ranked scientists, and the belief of Senator Long and other legislators that ESOPs would transform the behavior of employees.

Nevertheless, evidence-based psychology can more than hold its own against spook psychology, provided one essential element is present. The *sine qua non* for the application of scientific psychology to management problems is an enlightened executive. For example, had the president in the "bad boss" case been less willing to risk the use of a psychologist, the episode would not have occurred, Mac would have been fired, the company would have lost an irreplaceable asset, and everyone from the president on down would have lost something of value.

So the key to bringing the skills and insights of psychology to bear on more management problems is to have more enlightened executives. The best way to create them is for the institutions that train potential executives (business schools, law schools, and corporate management development programs) to include more psychology in their curricula. In particular, these programs should teach the difference between an attractive oversimplification and an inference based on relevant, repeatable evidence.

The reader will note that I take it for granted that having more psychologists analyzing more management problems would be a good thing for all concerned. Of course, that is why I undertook to write this book in the first place.

OVERESTIMATING THE EFFECTS OF MONEY

Perhaps the most attractive of all the oversimplifications emanating from spook psychology is the notion that if you had enough money, you could motivate just about anyone to do just about anything. Hence there is no end of merit pay, profit-sharing, gain-sharing, deferred compensation, and stock option plans, not to mention so-called golden parachutes, sign-up bonuses, commission plans, and so on, ad infinitum.

What makes the idea attractive is that there is some truth to it. Most people earn their living by selling their labor, and like all sellers they have an interest in getting the best possible price. But whether they will work harder and longer for the best available price than they will for a marginally acceptable price is a question that has no easy answer. That would depend on many other factors.

The human mind manages to integrate a great many of those factors when it is deciding what to do. That's why there is no universal, or even majority answer to the question, How would people react if we offered them *x* dollars in exchange for satisfying *y* conditions? The answer is indeterminate, because a great deal more than just *x* and *y* would be involved.

To mention just a few: Exactly *who* would be involved? (Some people are more susceptible to money than others.) How does *x* dollars compare to the income these people could receive *without* expending extra effort? And would *y* (the conditions that have to be satisfied to earn *x*) seem reasonable and attainable to the individuals involved? And so on. The point is that the human mind is subtler by far than most incentive planners assume it to be. That's why their plans usually have the desired effects only with some people, some of the time.

But it is precisely their deceptive simplicity that makes most compensation plans so attractive to those who contrive them. That's why Louis Kelso was convinced that he could put an end to inflation and unemployment simply by letting employees benefit from the price appreciation of their company's shares. His reasoning went straight from "it ought to work" to "it does work," with no intermediate stops along the way. But it was precisely at those intermediate stops—in the differing ways in which individuals perceive their circumstances—that ESOPs failed to achieve their promised effects.

Caterpillar-Joliet provides another example of how complicated money actually is. The strikers would have been better off financially if they hadn't struck at all or if they had settled for management's first "sweetened" offer. The strike not only denied them three months of income but depleted their savings and pushed many of them deeper into debt. If money had really been the key issue, the strike would not have lasted as long as it did.

The point is that monetary considerations are inseparable from a host of nonmonetary considerations that have motivational effects of their own. Therefore, the alleged "simplicity" of money motivation is deceptive to the point of being treacherous. Money may or may not be a powerful motivator, depending on circumstances; but it is certainly the most complicated motivator, by far.

THE LIMITS OF SELECTION AND THE PAYOFF FROM TRAINING

When management relies too much on selection, and too little on training, it becomes a mere spectator sport. It simply bets on certain individuals, sits back, and waits to see whether they will sink or swim. The results of that strategy are nearly always high turnover and low productivity. That was the mistake that too many wholesalers made in the beverage company case. It is the mistake that was corrected at Würth Fastener. To a lesser degree, and with a very different caliber of individuals, that was the mistake made at U.S. Home. And it remains a very common mistake, even today, in entirely too many otherwise well-managed firms.

But when management becomes, instead, a participant sport—in which managers actively try to *make* their subordinates successful—the results are likely to be the reverse: lower turnover and higher overall productivity. That's why it's a false economy to spend freely on selection, in the hope of being able to spend next to nothing on training.

Today, employee selection—especially sales, managerial, and executive selection—has become an industry in its own right, providing gainful employment for many of my fellow psychologists. The demand for their services comes straight from our natural uncertainty about strangers. Eventually, of course, we will learn all that we need to know, and perhaps more than we want to know, about the strangers whom we decide to hire. But by then we will have spent huge sums on salaries, benefits, and training, not to mention having had to endure heaven only knows what disappointments.

Anything that promises to reduce those risks will be welcome. So the selection industry rests on a firm bedrock of customer demand. There is really only one question that could cloud its future: Can it actually reduce those risks enough to matter? My answer is that when it is done right, selection probably pays for itself. But that still leaves us a long way from the real goal of the companies that employ psychologists, which is to get optimal organizational performance. And there are contributions that psychologists can make to achieve that goal that are more valuable than merely sizing up job candidates.

Selection, like money motivation, poses a deceptively simple question. Can a good psychologist, equipped with the proper instruments, give you a reliable yes-or-no forecast of a given person's chances of success in a given job? Unfortunately, the question itself rests on faulty assumptions, so it has no clear-cut answer for two reasons.

First, the performance rating that the psychologist is asked to predict will depend not only on qualities *in* that person, which we can only measure imperfectly, but also on qualities *outside* that person, which we can't really "measure" at all (such as the people with whom they'll be working and the particular challenges that they'll encounter together). So the psychologist is reduced to making a performance forecast based on imperfect measurements of only some of the factors that will determine the outcome. If you ever wonder why psychological evaluations tend to be hedged with disclaimers, that's why.

Next, there's the question of what is a "good" psychologist. To the executives who authorize payment of their invoices, a good psychologist is intelligible, reassuring, and convincing. To his or her colleagues, a good psychologist doesn't stray very far from the data and produces forecasts that correlate decently with outcomes. My own definition of a good psychologist is all of the above.

But psychologists—even good ones—quickly run into the limits of what selection can do to improve job performance. Barring unforeseen breakthroughs, we are probably already as good at the inexact art of evaluating job candidates as we will ever be. To increase their usefulness, psychologists will have to shift their emphasis from merely *predicting* performance to *enhancing* it. That would involve more coaching, team building, and behavior modification, and less assessment and testing. The frontier of industrial psychology is now in the classroom, not the testing room.

This is an appropriate point to mention the strategy of using the best performers as models for the rest of a group, as at IBM, Würth, and the "Shop Floor Strategists" case. The result of this kind of training is to push the bulk of the group closer to the performance standards of the leaders. The performance distribution itself narrows, and the median shifts upward, so the overall average is raised. This does much more for group performance than just allowing most of a group to maintain its comfort level, while searching (usually in vain) for heroic achievers who can thrive without managerial support.

THE RECIPROCAL NATURE OF BEHAVIOR

Why do people act as they do? The commonsense answer is that each person's behavior is internally generated, expressing who he is and what he wants. But that is only part of the story. Our behavior is also, to a large extent, *reciprocal*—that is, we each respond to the way that others around us are behaving, and they then respond to our response, and so on, ad infinitum.

The best analogy I can think of to describe the reciprocal nature of behavior is a tennis game. Each player is obliged to run to where the opposing player has hit the ball. You return that ball, and the situation is now reversed: Your opponent must now run to where you have hit it. The game is a constant back-and-forth interaction. So is life.

What we do at any given moment is to a large extent a function of whom we are with and how he is trying to deal with us. Therefore, you can't predict behavior (except in the most general way) merely by knowing what someone is like. You also have to know who that person is with, at any given moment, and what that person is like.

In other words, we do not behave as we do simply because that's the way we are. Instead, much of what we do is a reaction to what other people do, or what we think they will do. (That deceptively simple formula also defines markets, courtship, teaching, politics, team sports, and most other human activities.) That's why it grossly oversimplifies the complexity of an adult's behavior to study him in isolation, as psychologists usually do, because he doesn't live in isolation. In order to predict behavior, you also have to study the social context in which it occurs.

Most people's waking lives consist almost entirely of involvements, or anticipated involvements, with each other. That rather mundane observation has some major consequences for both the management of organizations and the practice of industrial psychology.

For management, it means that *mentoring* is required to ensure a company's future managerial strength. That's because few managers can reach their full potential on their own, without the guidance and encouragement of other managers. For example, mentoring might have made a big difference at U.S. Home.

That same observation means that *performance appraisals* have to be taken with yet another grain of salt. That's because there is no way (short of impractically elaborate record keeping) to filter out the subjective aspect of any manager's evaluation of any subordinate. An appraisal tells us as much about the appraiser as it does about the appraisee, and it's often difficult to tease the two apart. (Incidentally, the same point could be made about most interviews.)

And that "mundane" observation also means that sales managers have to consider the compatibility factor when assigning sellers to customers. That's why Jim, the marketing manager in the beverage company, urged his wholesalers to stake out sales territories on the basis of relationships, not geography. It's also why the best salesmen at Würth Fastener were not the pushiest or the most persistent, but the ones who best read their customers' moods.

For psychologists, that same observation means that the accuracy of *performance predictions* can't improve very much until, and unless, a practical way is found to factor in the compatibility effect. That's because the people with whom you work affect your job performance, as we saw in the "Bad Boss" case.

BEHAVIORAL BREAKTHROUGHS

Some remarkable events are recounted in these cases. Certain managers were able to rise above their habitual ways of dealing with some of their most vexing problems. They recognized that those problems were partially of their own creation, and made a conscious decision to undo at least their contribution to those problems. To recall the language I used with Mac's subordinates, these managers decided to be grown-ups.

Thus the managers on the Chicago & Northwestern decided that some of their costly labor relations problems were due to supporting, or at least condoning, a confrontational attitude among their first-level supervisors. And they decided that they had to undo that, if only to protect the investment that all of them had made when they bought the railroad.

Similarly, the middle managers at Caterpillar's Joliet plant realized that the disastrous strike might possibly have been prevented, or at least shortened, if they had been more actively engaged in supervising their foremen. To acknowledge that was uncomfortable enough, but the prospect of having to go through yet another horrendous strike was even more uncomfortable.

And Mac, who had been a quintessential bad boss, decided that his preferred way of running his division wasn't working and that to preserve his job he'd have to learn to run it in a way that he found awkward and even frightening.

We could even cite the human resources executives at American Cy-anamid who decided that although the forced distribution system of appraising employee performance had made their jobs easier, it was no longer worth defending, given the opposition to it that had developed among line managers. What was at stake in that case was their own credibility.

In each of these instances, we saw managers do things they would have preferred *not to do*. But they did them anyway, because they realized, however grudgingly, that something larger than their own feelings was involved. Also, they had a strong stake in ending a problem they had helped to create. These managers decided, in other words, to grow beyond their previous limits. They moved out of denial and into active coping.

That kind of breakthrough, to a more responsible level of behavior, is all too rare. We have to admire those who summoned the courage to do it. But the point is that it can be done, at least when the stakes are high enough and when the individuals involved are willing to consider the awful possibility that their previous attitudes just *might* have contributed to an intolerable result.

What these cases demonstrate, I think, is that given high enough stakes and sufficiently open minds, ordinary people are capable of rising to extraordinary heights. Sometimes they need help to do that, but at other times they can do it by themselves.

I must admit that I approach this conclusion with some trepidation. It smacks suspiciously of the kind of miracle-promising nonsense that one finds in countless "inspirational" books. But having said that, I still have to contemplate what these executives did, some with my help and some without it. Like Galileo, I profess aloud my belief that adult personalities are highly resistant to all but the smallest change. But under my breath I hear myself muttering, "But still, *they changed.*"

From which it follows that there just may be potentialities in all of us that few of us have plumbed.

LEARNING BY LISTENING

The method I used in many of these cases involved listening to what as many knowledgeable people as I could reach had to say about the topics that interested my clients. It is in one sense a rather naive approach, because you start without assumptions and simply let your hypotheses build themselves up from your information, as it accumulates. But in another sense it is quite sophisticated, because it exposes you to most of what is known about a topic and enables you to integrate it in a concise, intelligible summary.

That's what I did, for example, in the Schering and Caterpillar cases. The various points of view that I heard had been debated for years, but no one had listened to all of them, or weighed them against each other from the perspective of a detached outsider. The point is that there are advantages to knowing relatively little about a problem, because that enables you to listen to the various perspectives on it with a comparatively open mind.

In the Würth Fastener and "Shop Floor Strategists" cases, the method I used was direct observation. I was focused on what people did, more than on what they said. But except for that, the method had the same features, and the same advantages, as the interview method I used in other cases. That is, I accumulated a mass of relevant data, which I was able to analyze with a fairly open mind, since I knew little about the topics beforehand.

I recommend these methods to anyone who needs to develop an informed, yet reasonably objective, insight into issues about which the people involved disagree.

Recommended Readings

Most of the available literature on industrial psychology deals with its conventional applications to employee selection, performance appraisal, and counseling. For a good overview of what these psychologists are up to these days, see:

Cascio, Wayne F. "Whither Industrial and Organizational Psychology in a Changing World of Work?" *American Psychologist.* November 1995, vol. 50, no. 11, pages 928–939.

Cascio reviews the implications for psychologists of revolutionary changes now sweeping the business world, such as globalization, downsizing, and the effects of technology on jobs. With regard to psychological interventions into working relationships (such as, for example, the "Bad Boss" case) Cascio says that the greatest need is for "methodologically sound evaluations of (their) relative impact." In other words, we need to know more about what works, and what doesn't work, under various conditions. Acknowledging that tightly controlled research methods are simply non-starters in the busy world of industry, he endorses "quasi-experimental designs (and) qualitative research methods." I couldn't agree more: that's what this book was all about.

Another good review of current concerns in the field is:

International Review of Industrial and Organizational Psychology. Vols. 10 (1995) and 11 (1996), both published by Wiley (Chichester, NY).

These volumes include reviews of current developments in various sub-specialties within industrial psychology, such as managing diversity, the psychological costs of unemployment, self-esteem and work, and employee involvement. Each article summarizes the recent literature, thereby saving an enormous amount of time for busy practitioners by enabling them to decide which articles should be read in their entirety, and which need only be skimmed.

One of my favorite reviews is:

The Applied Psychology of Work Behavior. Edited by Dennis W. Organ. Homewood, IL: Irwin, 1991.

This book of readings includes a good cross section of articles from various academic journals covering such topics as work behavior, employee attitudes, job satisfaction, motivation, stress, and leadership. Too much of this type of literature has a well-deserved reputation for being impenetrably dense, but in this case, the editor has a fine eye for works that are not only pertinent, but readable.

Leadership, the topic which I debated with Guy Odom in the U.S. Home case, is well reviewed in:

An Integrative Theory of Leadership. Martin Chemers. Mahwah, NJ: Lawrence Erlbaum & Associates, 1997.

Chemers presents an up-to-date analysis of what we know about this complex subject, including new findings on male-female differences in leadership styles.

Most of the works cited here are fairly recent. However, the material in the older books and articles is for the most part still relevant. That is because scientific psychology advances at a majestic, if glacial, pace, while its subject (which is human nature itself) changes even more slowly.

Psychologically speaking, the principal difference between our ancestors and ourselves is that we have more information than they did, especially about psychology. But there is no reason to believe that we are using that information any more wisely than they would have, had it been given to them. We are all chips off a centuries-old block, at least in the way our minds process the information to which we have access.

That very slow rate of change in human nature is why I give more weight to what a book or article has to say than to its publication date. Anything about psychology that was published during your lifetime, and possibly your parents' lifetime, too, that was sound to begin with is probably still sound today.

Turning from psychology to its practical application in management, I would recommend:

Managing People and Organizations. Edited by John Gabarro. Boston: Harvard Business School, 1992.

This is a selection of management-related articles, mostly from the *Harvard Business Review*, many of which are considered classics in their field. Most of them are more "how to" oriented than theoretical. This is a good book for psychologists who are interested in learning about what will be, for many of them, a fascinating new setting in which to ply their trade.

Another good source for the same purpose would be:

The Craft of General Management. Edited by Joseph L. Bower. Boston: Harvard Business School, 1991.

Index

Absenteeism, 149
Acquisitive instincts, 68–69
Alienation, 69
"Alumni" (former employees), 172
American Cyanamid Company (now
    American Home Products Corpo-
    ration), 1, 4, 7, 17, 199–200, 205
American Management Association,
    85
American Psychologist, 207
*The Applied Psychology of Work Behav-
    ior*, 208
Ascendancy, 163, 167, 176
Attrition, 164, 166, 168, 174
Avis Rent-A-Car System, Inc., 82

Bad boss, definition of, 181–82
Bad boss problem, 181–87, 205
Behavior, reciprocal nature of, 203–4
Behavior modification, 186, 203
Bell curve, 19
Bias (by researchers), 152
Blame, 139, 189
"Bloody-minded" syndrome, 125–26
Bower, Joseph L., 209
Business Week, 161

Cascio, Wayne F., 207
Cash flow, 61
Caterpillar, Inc., 69, 121, 123–24,
    139, 199, 201, 205–6
Centralization, 47, 53, 62
Chemers, Martin, 208
"Chemistry" (interpersonal compati-
    bility), 95–96, 187, 204
Chicago & Northwestern Railroad,
    72, 74–75, 80, 83–84, 205
Churchill, Winston S., 174
Collective bargaining, 121–22
Company politics, 2, 7, 20, 43, 58–
    59, 81
Competition (between shifts), 132,
    136–37, 157
Congress, United States, 71–72
Congressional Record, 81
Congressional Research Service, 80
Conrail, 72, 81, 83
Consultants, 59, 65, 160
Control, 45, 55, 107; financial, 57,
    64; of subsidiaries, 56, 59
Conversation focus, 97–99
The Craft of General Management, 209
Critical incident technique, 25–26

Culture, company, 173–74, 176, 184
Currency exchange rates, 46, 52–53

Daydreaming, 148
Decentralization, 50, 52, 62–64
Decision-making, 26–41; irrational, 111, 114, 119
Delegating (contrasted with abdicating), 137
Distribution system, 103–5, 110, 116
Dominance, 178–80
Durocher, Leo, 115

E. F. Hutton & Company, 72, 78–79
Entrepreneurs, 104, 116–17
ESOPs (Employee Stock Ownership Plans), 67–83, 200–201
Expatriate managers, 57, 64

Flanagan, Dr. John C., 25
Focus groups, 105, 107, 114
Forced distributions (of performance ratings), 4–6, 9, 12–13, 16, 20
Ford, Henry, 31, 33
Ford Motor Company, 31
Foremen, 127–28, 131–32, 133–34, 135–37, 141–46, 151, 153–54, 157–60
Freud, Sigmund, 92, 106

Gabarro, John, 209
Galilei, Galileo, 206
Global strategy, 62
Growing up, 180
"Grown-ups" (contrasted with adults), 189, 205
Guilford-Zimmerman Temperament Survey, 163, 165–67, 177

Hawthorne effect, 9
Hierarchies, psychology of, 129
High risk/high reward motivation system, 164–65, 167–68
Hodgson, Dr. William G., 1–5, 17–18
Human error, 151

Human Resources Departments, 2–4, 7–10, 12, 15–17, 19–20, 74, 191, 205
Humphrey, Senator Hubert H., 79–80

IBM Corporation, 21–41, 144–45, 203
Inflation, 68–69
An Integrative Theory of Leadership, 208
Internal Revenue Service, 70
International Review of Industrial and Organizational Psychology, 207
Interpersonal behavior, psychology of, 197

Javits, Senator Jacob, 80
Joint Economic Committee, 67, 79
Joliet, Illinois (Caterpillar plant site), 121–23, 125–28, 131, 135, 137–39, 199, 201, 205

Kelso, Louis R., 67–70, 75, 77–82, 201

Labor costs, 69, 71, 75, 143, 165
Labor unions, 34–35, 69, 74, 77, 80, 121–22, 124, 130, 138
Leadership, 138, 178–80
Lederle Laboratories, 1, 4
Locus of control, 117–18
Long, Senator Russell B., 67–68, 70–72, 74–75, 78–79, 81–82, 200
Luck, 153

Management by Motivation, 162
"Management by not getting involved," 135
Management development, 161, 164, 168
Managing People and Organizations, 209
Market research, 104, 111, 114
Markets, free, 109, 113–14
Mentors, 29, 34, 204

Middle managers, 126–27, 129, 132, 134, 135, 137–38, 141–42, 144, 205

Money, motivational effects of, 19, 109–11, 113, 116, 163–65, 167–68, 170, 174, 176, 200–201

Morale, 13, 18, 187, 191

Mothers, Leadership and Success, 178

Motivation, 4, 7, 20, 75–76, 78–79, 81, 87, 116–128, 161–65, 170, 175

Murphy's Law, 169

Mythology, American, 116–17

New York Times, 70

Nonfinancial goals, 69

"Not invented here" problem, 159

Odom, Guy R., 161–65, 174–80

Organ, Dennis W., 208

Organization structure, 43–46, 52, 57, 60, 101

Penn Central Railroad, 71, 83–84

Peoria, Illinois (Caterpillar headquarters site), 122, 126–27, 129, 137

Performance appraisal, 2–5, 14, 18, 25, 204

Performance prediction, 23–41

Personality, adult, 185

"Preventive detachment," 135

Prices, 114

Price controls, 53

Priorities, supervisory, 156

Product launches, 103–4, 119

Production pressure, 128, 133, 135, 167–70, 172–74

Productivity, 68, 75, 81, 87, 141, 143–44, 149, 165, 201–2

Profitability, 107–8, 115

Profit sharing plans, 73

Promotion, 18, 130–31, 137, 166, 168

Psychoanalysis, instant, 106–7

Psychoanalysts, 192

Psychological breakthroughs, 84, 185, 198, 204–6

Psychological tests, 87, 92, 163, 203

Psychologists, armchair, 25

Psychologists, research, 25, 105–7, 139, 202–3, 208

Psychology, evidence-based, 200

Quality, product, 133, 159–60

Railroads, eastern, bankruptcy of, 71, 78–79

Recessions, 13–14

Reinforcement, 160

Resistance to technological change, 151

Retailers, 104–6, 107–10, 112; chain, 104–5, 114; "hardheaded," 109–11, 113–16, 118–19; independent, 104, 109, 115, 119; "soft-hearted," 107–9, 111–18

Safety, 128, 131–32, 136, 151

St. Paul, 139

Salary increases, 5, 13–14

Sales representatives, 107–10, 119–20

Sales tactics, 99, 101

Schering-Plough Corporation, 43–65, 206

Scientific method, 9

Self-fulfilling prophecy, 58

Self-deception, 184

Short interval scheduling, 147, 149, 153–54, 169

Spook psychology, 199–200

Start-up, psychological reactions to, 96–97, 99, 146–47, 154–56

Statistical analysis (by computer), 123, 129

Stock purchase plans, 73–74

Strikes, 121–22, 126, 132, 134–36, 139, 205

Subcontractors, 162, 165, 167, 169, 171

Succession planning, 22, 51, 56–57

Sullivan, Louis, 65

Superintendents, construction, 162–71, 174–75

Supervisors, selection of, 134–35, 144–45, 163, 171, 177, 180, 201–2. *See also* Foremen

Supervisory style, 156–59

Swaak, Reyer A. ("Rick"), 43–44, 47, 51, 57–60, 64–65

Tax preferences, 70, 83

Third country nationals, 49–51

Towers, Perrin, Forster & Crosby, Inc., 73, 78–79

Trade-off decisions, 60

Transportation, U.S. Department of, 71

"Truth": differing perspectives on, 132; pragmatic definition of, 105–6

Turnover, 101, 149, 177, 201–2

Two-factor theory, 67–70

Uncertainty, tolerance for, 56, 58–59

Unconscious needs, 192–93

Unemployment, 68–69

United Air Lines, 82

U.S. Home Corporation, 161–66, 172–75, 177–78, 202, 204

USRA (United States Railway Association), 67, 71–72, 78–79, 81–82

"Veto factor" (inhibits use of abilities), 92, 97

Waste, 143

Wechsler Adult Intelligence Scale, 166–67, 177

Wholesalers, 103–5, 107–8, 110–15, 118–19, 201–2

Workers, shop floor, 128, 133–34, 136, 138, 142

Würth, Adolf GmbH & Co. KG, 85–86

Würth, Reinhold, 85–88, 100–101

Würth-USA, 86–88, 90–91, 95, 97–98, 100–101, 202–4, 206

About the Author

SAUL W. GELLERMAN is a Management Consultant and Professor of Management at the University of Dallas. His long, distinguished career as a consulting industrial psychologist has taken him into corporations and management associations in 35 countries and provided him with material for nine previous books and numerous articles. He holds a doctorate in clinical and industrial psychology from the University of Pennsylvania and is a Diplomate in Industrial and Organizational Psychology from the American Board of Professional Psychology. An earlier book, *Motivation and Productivity* (1963) was awarded the McKinsey Foundation Prize by the Academy of Management. He is also the producer of 29 management training films.